The Nation, Europe, and the World

The Nation, Europe, and the World

Textbooks and Curricula in Transition

Edited by

Hanna Schissler and Yasemin Nuhoğlu Soysal

Berghahn Books
New York • Oxford

First published in 2005 by
Berghahn Books
www.berghahnbooks.com

Library of Congress Cataloging-in-Publication Data

The nation, Europe, and the world: textbooks and curricula in transition / edited by Hanna
   Schissler and Yasemin Nuhogul Soysal.
      p. cm.
   Includes bibliographical references.
   ISBN 1-57181-549-X -- ISBN 1-57181-550-3 (pbk.)
      1. History--Study and teaching. 2. History--Textbooks. 3. International
education--Curricula. 4. Place-based education--Curricula. I. Schissler, Hanna. II. Soysal,
Yasemin Nuhoglu.

D16.2.N29 2004
907`.1--dc22

                                                                        2004049098

British Library Cataloguing in Publication Data
A catalogue record for this book is available from the British Library
Printed in the United States on acid-free paper

ISBN 1-57181-549-X hardback

Contents

❖────────

Part III: Global Frameworks and Approaches to World History

List of Figures and Tables

❖────────────────────────

Figures

Tables

Preface

❖

This book presents the work of historians, sociologists, and anthropologists on recent developments in curricula and textbooks in the United States, Germany, France, the Netherlands, Greece, Turkey, Bulgaria, Spain, and the Russian Federation. In the face of the ongoing process of transnationalization, the expansion of the European Union, immediacy of globalization, and worldwide migration, it addresses the need for history to be taught differently, rather than the traditional "container model" of national history. It emerged from a project, which the editors have been pursuing for some time. In order to promote transatlantic collaboration, in 1999 the National Endowment for the Humanities and the German Historical Institute in Washington D.C. together with the American Institute for Contemporary German Studies looked for researchers in the United States and in Germany, who worked on similar projects and gave them parallel grants. We were thus given the chance to engage in an interdisciplinary and transnational exchange of ideas and in a collaborative research project. We not only presented our initial findings at the German Studies Association in Atlanta in 1999, but also went on to organize a number of conferences in New York, London, and Florence in the following years. At these conferences, we brought together a number of scholars to engage in a lively exchange of ideas on textbooks and curricula at a time, when national narratives were no longer sufficient to educate students. We explored ways to make sense of current transnational contexts and global development. With this book we present the outcome of our research. We wish to thank a number of institutions: the National Endowment for the Humanities, the German Historical Institute in Washington, D.C., particularly its current director, Christof Mauch, as well as the American Institute for Contemporary German Studies and its then director of research, Carl Lankowski, for bringing us together in the first place. We also thank New York University, the German Academic Exchange Service, the European Commission Office in London, and the History Department as well as the Schuman Center of the European University Institute in Florence, which sponsored and hosted our conferences. Our work was also supported by the Economic and Social Research Council in Britain 'One Europe or Several? programme', the University of Essex, and the Georg Eckert Institute for International Textbook Research in Braunschweig. What started as a transnational and interdisciplinary research project, unexpectedly developed further and turned into a personal friendship. That then might be our ultimate reward.

Hanna Schissler and Yasemin Nuhoğlu Soysal
Braunschweig and London, June 2004

Introduction

❖────────

Teaching beyond the National Narrative

Yasemin Nuhoğlu Soysal and Hanna Schissler

Education has been one of the most important tools in the short but deter-mined career of the nation-state as the organizer of collectives (Anderson 1992; Assmann 1993; Gellner 1983). Historically, subjects were transformed into citi-zens through the teaching of history, geography, and the language of the nation. People were anchored in illustrious pasts, in particular territories, and in the grammar of (national) self-recognition and the logic of collective reassurance. Thus, peasants were turned into Frenchmen (Weber 1977); Bavarians, Hessians, or Westphalians were turned into Germans; English, Scotts, and Welsh into British; and Irish, Germans, Mexicans, and Chinese into Americans.

Creating Citizens: Education and National Narratives

The nation-state and historiography traditionally have an intimate relationship. This is true for historiography in general, but school historiography in partic-ular. In the eighteenth and nineteenth centuries, schooling for the general public and state control of curricula and textbooks were part of the process of nation-building and the creation of social cohesion in the interest of the emerg-ing industrial society (Assmann 1993). Academic historians everywhere enthusiastically entered the service of the nation-state, thus creating and legit-imizing national narratives. The education of their citizens is something that states take very seriously. School textbooks in history and in the social sciences convey a knowledge that has been subordinated to particular control mecha-nisms by the state and/or dominant elites in the process of nation building and the creation of loyal citizens. Indeed, in schools, the production of knowledge was from the outset closely connected to national objectives. No nation-state can afford not to dedicate resources to the general education of its citizens and to authorize the provision of teaching materials. The steady expansion of insti-tutions of mass education throughout the twentieth century, even in the regions of the world where ideological and material sources pose a severe hindrance to its implementation, is yet another indicator of nation-states' dedication to the idea of forging collective meaning and establishing common values through education (Meyer et al. 1992).

Attributing to education the role of "the forum through which citizenship is shaped" naturally invites struggle over its content (Hein and Selden 2000; see also Graves 2001). Creating citizens requires attention to the scientific and moral content of education. No aspect of education is immune to these struggles and quarrels. In particular the teaching of the collective past, the shaping of spatial and temporal memory, has been loaded with meaning. The subtext of historical instruction most often conveyed the importance of the nation. Struggles over these issues have been especially fierce in nations where the past has been difficult and where memory is disrupted, in other words, where the past cannot easily be made amenable to linear and uplifting narratives.[1]

Teaching history has thus been a priority for modern nation-states. It carried and continues to carry the burden of identity-building of citizens. Crafting an account of the nation's origin, its past, and its evolvement has been of the utmost importance for the nation and the state-building process (Anderson 1992; Hobsbawm 1990). Such an account would justify the nation-state's claim to authenticity and legitimacy as well as to its boundaries. It would provide a rationale for the national parameters of society. It is no coincidence that the rise of academic history is concomitant with the institutionalization of the nation-state as the dominant model of political organization (Frank et al. 2000; Novick 1988). In the course of the twentieth century, however, the very model of the nation-state itself has changed and with it the modes of nation-states' narration of their origins. What is taught as a nation's history in schools is no longer simply bound to a preordained national narrative as it used to be the case in the nineteenth century and (in most countries) up to the 1970s. Although national history continues to be "history by default" practically everywhere, historical accounts nowadays go beyond the national narrative.[2]

National Narratives under Siege: Pressures on Textbooks and Curricula

As far as textbooks continue to be national narratives, they provide a key through which national and citizenship identities are projected and constructed vis-à-vis a wider world. Thus, it should not come as a surprise that what textbooks teach is always political (Stein 1976). What is true for textbooks also pertains to curricula: the era after the Second World War witnessed major curricular changes in Europe, in the United States, and in other parts of the world, through which canonized understandings and representations of the nation and national history have been transformed. David J. Frank et al. (2000)

have identified major trends in curriculum development. Curricula have tended to become similar all over the world in the last one-hundred years, as well as becoming more strictly focused on contemporary history. National history has lost in importance practically everywhere (not just in Western Europe and in the United States). The histories of social groups below the national level on the one hand, and transnational entities on the other, have gained in importance. Finally, curricula seem to stick to social-scientific approaches rather than promoting ethnoculturalist interpretations. It has to be stressed that Frank and his coauthors mainly examined higher education and curricula in colleges and universities. Nevertheless, we think that some of the trends that this study identifies also hold true for school curricula and textbooks.

In the period after the Second World War, the pressure for change in school textbooks and curricula has come from a variety of sources. A series of interlocking changes in the post-war era that complicated the national order of things (Malkki 1995) underlie these changes.

1. There is what we would like to call individuals' increasingly authoritative actorhood and rights, which are conceived as independent of and going beyond the national collective (Meyer and Jepperson 2000; Soysal 1994, 2000). This trend correlates with the broadening of the human rights discourse and the creation of instruments to enforce individual rights within a transnational framework. As human rights ascribe a universal status to the individual that is not associated with belonging to a particular national collective, it thus de facto limits the importance of national narratives. This trend is not only legitimized by legal and scientific discourses, but also adheres to popular conventions.

2. The process of mass decolonization after 1945, which led to the creation of a multitude of newly independent states that now play a significant role at the international level, also contributed to an awareness and an assertion of the rights of formerly colonized people. With decolonization, peoples of Africa and Asia learned to employ European universals, such as "the abstract figure of the human or that of Reason," and to make European principles work for them in claiming their rights and identities (Bright and Geyer forthcoming; Chakrabarty 2002: 5). Like feminism, postcolonial thought has engaged those very principles that were instrumental in suppression (of women, of indigenous peoples, of colonized populations), in order to overcome the suppressors' ideologies. The Enlightenment idea of humanity has now become part of the global heritage.

3. Not only did all nation-states receive an equal standing on a formal level, but the era after the Second World War also witnessed the celebration and codification of cultural standards that adhered to the principle of "different but equal"—the right to one's own identity and "otherhood." Transnational agencies such as the United Nations and UNESCO were major promoters of

this trend. Codified as "rights," identities have become important organizational and symbolic tools for creating new group solidarities and for mobilizing resources. This can be observed in the cases of civil rights, women's, and gay and lesbian movements, in the surge of ethnic and regional identities and interests, and in the collective articulations of indigenous groups and immigrants (Castells 1997). These groups, which were previously excluded from the various aspects of the national collective and citizenry, have raised their voices in demanding that their group narratives and identities become part of national education, among other things. The mobilization of social groups around principles of identity—new or old, progressive or regressive—challenged the master narratives of the Western world on all fronts.

4. Democratization and liberal ideologies have been increasingly codified as "globalization." The collapse of the dichotomous structure of world politics at the end of what Hobsbawm has called "the short twentieth century," and the incorporation of the formerly "socialist" countries into the fold of Europe and the West in general, have played a major role in accelerating the globalization of these ideas and expanding their realm. The transformations in Southern and Eastern Europe, but also in Latin America and other parts of the world, while challenging the notions of development, modernization, liberalism, and democratization, at the same time strongly reaffirmed these notions and strengthened their grasp, frequently using Enlightenment principles such as human rights and universalism. In Western Europe, the unfolding of the European Union as a transnational political entity has equally put pressure on the national narratives of collectives and reified the globalization of the same ideals.

To summarize: the process of decolonization, the increasing dominance of the rights discourse, the social movements from the 1970s on, and the end of the Cold War have challenged political configurations on national as well as transnational levels. They have redefined national prerogatives, altered conceptual and real boundaries, and created tensions for existing national narratives that no longer can claim sole validity.

All these developments have laid the ground for important changes in the organization of societies. While the nation-state was affirmed as the universal mode of polity formation, the closure of societies and their definition as purely national collectives has become increasingly difficult to sustain, ideologically as well as institutionally. With these changes, "what counts as history" has also changed (Berghahn and Schissler 1987; Frank et al. 2000). Accompanied by epistemological crises, major changes in the historical and social sciences took place. These changes had to do with two main issues. First, the question of agency: who has subject status and who acts in history? Second, the question of direction: where are we going, is history moving us into a certain direction?

A new cultural relativism became pervasive: nondominant groups such as workers, women, or minorities now also claiming agency, replaced conventional notions of political and military history with their underlying assumption: "Great men make history." History stopped being only what conventionally had counted as *national* history. Hand in hand with these reconstructive endeavors came the critique of the notion of continuous progress in history as Eurocentric. The idea of a clear upward motion of historical development was discarded. The dominant Western narrative has given way to narratives of different histories with equal value. More of what constituted the world became incorporated either in world history (as is the case in the United States) or was recognized as "valid" civilizational background (as in many European countries). Even though the focus of most curricula and textbooks in Europe and the U.S. continues to be on the West as the widely accepted model of development, other cultures and traditions (e.g., Islam and China, never mind the incongruous juxtaposition of a religion and an empire) and their contributions to world civilization in science, technology, and economic advancement have come to receive greater acknowledgement. Consequently, as the chapters in this volume assert, the expansion and recognition of other civilizational and cultural narratives have necessarily relativized national history as the unquestioned locus of history education.

Patterns, Trends, Paradoxes

In Europe as well as in the United States we observe trends toward a taming of national history. This taming of national history and the contextualization of history in frameworks below and above the national level reflect the pervasiveness of processes that lead to increased world-wide interaction and communication, to rapid diffusion and standardization of norms at the world level, and to intensified differentiation of identities and belongings. However, when these processes translate onto the national level, we see different trajectories at work. Nation-states continue to follow their own patterns in responding to the particularities of the problems they encounter in various settings.

In Western European textbooks, the nation is being tendentiously recast in a European framework, although the teaching of history continues mainly to be framed in national settings. This means that we simultaneously observe the Europeanization of the nation, and see how the nation is being resituated within a variety of European frameworks. The French Revolution, for example, regains new importance not simply as a national (French) event, but as an important turning point in European history with implications for the self-understanding of all of Europe. This trend towards Europeanization is less pronounced in Eastern and Southern Europe. Particularly in the newly created nation-states following the break-up of the Soviet Bloc, we see the reemergence of outright nation-centered narratives.

In the United States we see somewhat different trends. On the one hand, the teaching of world history is much more apparent than in Europe. On the other hand, the national American narrative remains largely intact, since American History and World History constitute separate curricula, and the world history approach hardly affects American history at all. The juxtaposition of the two amplifies the impression that there is "us," and there is "the rest of the world." Despite the fact that the introduction of World History curricula was meant to generate a better understanding of the world at large and an incorporation of the national into global developments, this division privileges the specificity of the American national narrative.

It is in the role that "Europe" and European traditions play, where teaching, curricula, and textbooks face a paradox. In European countries, the teaching of Europe would require that we go through a thorough process of reassessing not only national but also European narratives. It would require what Dipesh Chakrabarty (2002) has called "provincializing Europe," by which he means that Europe should be treated as *one* world region among others. This does not imply that Europe's historical impact and significance for the world is being minimized, but it requires narratives that no longer deem progress and humanity as purely and exclusively European, setting the standard for the rest of the world. "Provincializing Europe" would also mean acknowledging Europe's uniqueness—acknowledging the European roots of universalism, human rights, and progress. However, at the end of the twentieth century, these principles are adhered to by much of the world. They are everyone's, every nation's modernity. This is what makes it difficult to provincialize Europe and its uniqueness. At the same time, the universalizing tendencies of Western thought, their continuing claim to objectivity and progress are at odds with a Europe that no longer casts itself as unique and dominating. These dilemmas need to be understood and worked through.

When we look at the United States, we face a dilemma of a different kind. By relativizing the claims of universality and validity of Western thought through the teaching of world history, in contrast, the United States tends to "provincialize" the universal and firmly place it into its original European context. However, a typical American paradox arises when the struggles of minorities are narrated and when postcolonial thought enters the story, as there is "no easy way of dispensing with universals in the condition of political modernity" (Chakrabarty 2002: 5). Particularistic assertions and histories then become universalizing claims to difference—which pose a whole new set of problems and paradoxes that also need to be understood.

These paradoxes point to the fact that canonized knowledge is indeed in flux. Teaching European or teaching world history requires an understanding of the past, the present, and the future beyond national narratives. In this process, teaching European or world history can only refer to conflict-ridden traditions and challenging futures.

In addressing these challenges, this book pursues various tasks and confronts a number of issues. It investigates some of the ways in which national narratives have been transformed in selected countries. In particular, the book seeks to determine the ways in which concepts of space and time have affected changes in the narration of "our country" and the wider world in which it is located. It explores the ways in which the nation is being resituated within a European or a world context, and within that process how it is being reinterpreted and recast. "Europe" has lost its dominant place to "world history," at least in the case of the United States, where the effort to offset the Eurocentric perspectives of traditional historical narratives is much more pronounced than in West European countries. The margins of Europe, countries in the Balkans and East Europe, and in some Mediterranean edges of the European Union, have their own issues with the nation. Whether they are prospective candidates for membership of or just ancillary players in the European Union, these countries need to readjust their narratives to the unfolding "Europe" and to conform to European standards, not only in their policies and economies but also in their education. Finally, the book looks at the ways in which contemporary conceptions of "the other," personified as racial, ethnic, and religious minorities, and as foreigners (immigrants), are either integrated into the dominant narrative or function as a "disturbance" to national self-perceptions.

Recent developments in the field of textbooks and curricula open fascinating perspectives on the changing foci in positioning societies in the West as well as in the East.[3] The chapters in this book cover both the core and the margins of Europe (France, Germany, the Netherlands, Spain, Greece, Turkey, Bulgaria, and Russia). Occasionally, we take a glimpse at developments in Japan and in the United States, bringing into focus European and global comparisons and perspectives.

Textbooks do not just convey knowledge; they represent what generations of pupils will learn about their own pasts and futures as well as the histories of others. In textbooks, we find what a society wishes to convey to the next generation. Thus, a careful analysis of school textbooks, of school and university curricula, reveals the notions of time, space, and agency that a society aims to instill in its students. The chronologies and narratives of "us" and "them" underscore the moments, events, and developments that are to be celebrated. This is one reason why the analysis of textbooks is an excellent means to capture the social and political parameters of a given society, its social and cultural preoccupations, its anxieties and trepidations (Berghahn and Schissler 1987; Jakobmeyer 1998; Schissler 1989/90).

More importantly, though, textbooks are excellent conduits to explicate and compare classification schemes at work and to locate the shifts in the ways of mapping out the world over time. History, geography, and civic textbooks, though simplified, lay out for us the basic temporal, spatial, and discursive organization of regions, nations, and the world. Our cognitive maps of understanding and engaging with the world surely correlate with the schemas the textbooks provide for the pupils who read them and for academics like us who study them. They are products of our collective debates and labor. Their effortless rendering of classificatory systems carries the potential for crafting productive analytical inquiries and exposés.

Notes

1. See Hein and Selden (2000) for the attempts to reform educational content in Japan, Korea, China, and Germany after the Second World War.
2. See the chapters by Schissler and Soysal, Bertilotti and Mannitz in this volume.
3. Although there are numerous studies of textbooks and curricula, systematic empirical research on the topic of textbooks and curricula is rare. For exceptions see Berghahn and Schissler (1987), which is now outdated, and Hein and Seldon (2000). Hein and Seldon's *Censoring History* limits itself to wars and the nation in Asia, and primarily addresses the question of how educational systems come to terms with traumatic pasts.

References

Anderson, Benedict. 1992. *Imagined Communities. Reflections on the Origin and Spread of Nationalism*. London: Verso.

Assmann, Alaida. 1993. *Arbeit am nationalen Gedächtnis. Eine kurze Geschichte der deutschen Bildungsidee*. Frankfurt: Campus.

Berghahn, Volker and Hanna Schissler, eds. 1987. *National Perceptions of the Past. International Textbook Research in Britain, the United States and West Germany*. Oxford: Berg.

Bright, Charles and Michael Geyer. Forthcoming. "Global Integration and the Production of Difference in 20th Century World History." In *Interactions: Regional Histories and Global Processes*, eds. Renate Bridenthal and Jeremy Bentley.

Castells, Manuel. 1997. *The Information Age: Economy, Society and Culture, vol. II. The Power of Identity*. New York: Blackwell.

Chakrabarty, Dipesh. 2002. *Provincializing Europe. Postcolonial Thought and Historical Difference*. Princeton: Princeton University Press.

Frank, David John, Suk-Ying Wong, John W. Meyer, and Francisco O. Ramirez. 2000. "What Counts as History: A Cross-National and Longitudinal Study of University Curricula," *Comparative Education Review*, vol. 44, no. 1, 29–53.

Gellner, Ernest. 1983. *Nations and Nationalism*. Ithaca: Cornell University Press.

Graves, Norma. 2001. *School Textbook Research. The Case of Geography 1800–2000*. London: Institute of Education Publications.

Hein, Laura, and Mark Seldon, eds. 2000. *Censoring History. Citizenship and Memory in Japan, Germany, and the United States*. New York: Sharpe.

Hobsbawm, Eric J. 1992. *Nations and Nationalism Since 1780: Programme, Myth, Reality*. Cambridge: Cambridge University Press.

Jakobmeyer, Wolfgang. 1998. "Das Schulgeschichtsbuch – Gedächtnis der Gesellschaft oder Autobiographie der Nation," *Geschichte, Politik und ihre Didaktik*, vol. 26, issues 1 and 2, 26–35.

Malkki, Liisa H. 1995. *Purity and Exile: Violence, Memory, and National Cosmology among Hutu Refugees in Tanzania*. Chicago: University of Chicago Press.

Meyer, John W., Francisco O. Ramirez, and Yasemin Nuhoğlu Soysal. 1992. "World Expansion of Mass Education, 1870–1980," *Sociology of Education*, vol. 65, no. 2, 128–49.

Meyer, John W., and Ronald Jepperson. 2000. "The 'Actors' of Modern Society: The Cultural Construction of Social Agency," *Sociological Theory*, vol.18, no. 1, 100–120.

Novick, Peter. 1988. *That Noble Dream. The "Objectivity Question" and the American Historical Profession*. Cambridge: Cambridge University Press.

Schissler, Hanna. 1989/90. "Limitations and Priorities for International Social Studies Textbook Research," *International Journal of Social Education*, vol. 4, 81–89.

Soysal, Yasemin Nuhoğlu. 1994. *Limits of Citizenship: Migrants and Postnational Membership in Europe*. Chicago: University of Chicago Press.

——— 2000. "Postnational Citizenship". In *The Blackwell Companion to Political Sociology*, eds. K. Nash and A. Scott. Oxford: Blackwell Publishers.

Stein, Gerd. 1976. *Das Schulbuch als Politikum: Sozialwissenschaftliche Beiträge zur Medien- u. Unterrichtsforschung*. Duisburg: Verlag der Sozialwissenschaftlichen Kooperative.

Weber, Eugen. 1977. *Peasants into Frenchmen: The Modernization of Rural France, 1870–1914*. London: Chatto and Windus.

Part I

Europe Contested

Chapter 1

❖

Projections of Identity in French and German History and Civics Textbooks

Yasemin Nuhoğlu Soysal, Teresa Bertilotti and Sabine Mannitz

The European Union (EU) aims to achieve a transnational political entity in the form of a union of nations, regions, and localities. Yet the possibility of such a transformation poses important questions regarding nation-state identities and collective affiliations. What happens to collective identities and affiliations (historically shaped by the boundaries of the nation-state) when centrifugal forces undermine the premise of national collectivities and the national closure of cultures? This is the starting point of this chapter: the transformations in nation-state and citizenship in relation to the ongoing consolidation of Europe as a transnational entity. Our goal is to capture the shifts in nation-state identities as represented in school curricula and textbooks. Our comparison expands on two core European countries: France and Germany. Both countries have been major players in European policy making, but they hold different positions regarding Europe and the European Union.

The approach of Germany's textbooks to the study of nation-state identities seems, at first glance, somewhat puzzling, and provides an interesting puzzle from a comparative perspective to the study of nation-state identities in textbooks. More so than in other European countries, in Germany, social science textbooks display remarkable prudence in representations of national identity. Rather than asserting national myths and irredentist narratives as the core components of nationhood, the textbooks focus on the representation of a more globalized and diversified world and the place of a relativized German identity in it. This departure from the traditional notions of national identity should, no doubt, be understood vis-à-vis the critical juncture of the National Socialist Rule, the Holocaust, and the Second World War. Given this harrowing nationalist and militarist past, the Federal Republic of Germany—which is our point of reference for the period before the 1990 unification—had no choice but to scrutinize the stock of national traditions and anchor its identity within the prospect of an integrated Europe and thus a transnational context.

By contrast, the depiction of nation-state identities in French textbooks is less puzzling. Traditional "French values" such as citizenship and secularism still figure prominently in the definition of the nation. However, the newer emphasis on Europeanism in curricula and textbooks restructures these national properties within a framework that lends more interpretive weight to Europe and its history. Thus, as we shall see, certain periods of twentieth-century French history appear to be given more attention (for example, the *Résistance*—a historical moment for Europe), whereas other periods lose their symbolic significance and specificities (for example, the birth of the French Kingdom).

Several institutional factors need to be taken into account to understand differing identity trends that are emerging in European countries. The disposition of member-states vis-à-vis the European Union, the unification process itself, the institutional structure of the school system and textbook production, and the nature of the actors involved in textbook reformation efforts all play a role in shaping the projection of identities (see Soysal 2000). In this chapter we set ourselves a limited goal, however. Rather than focusing on the specific variables that underlie the different trajectories of identity definitions in France and Germany, we explicate the very definitions themselves. Our concern is to bring out the patterns, however tentative, in the presentation of nation-state identities in French and German textbooks and curricula.

National textbooks are representative of officially selected, organized, and transmitted knowledge (Goodson 1987a, 1987b; Meyer et al. 1992; Young 1971). They are products of contestation and consensus. Thus they are indispensable to the explication of public representations of national collectivities and identities. Our discussion of the changing nation-state identities draws upon an analysis of history and civics textbooks for lower secondary schools, because they reflect more standardized, mass aspects of education. History textbooks have an amplified significance, for history is not only a definition of the past and present but also an attempt at continuity in national memory, upon which a collective identity is founded and the future is predicated (Levy 1996; Maier 1988). Civics textbooks on the other hand are deliberately written with the future in mind: they aim to construct responsible individuals in their anticipated collectives.

Our analysis of curricula and textbooks scrutinizes the presentations of the nation, from within and without. We specify three dimensions that delineate the boundaries of the nation-state identity:

1. *Valorization of the nation*: the nature of values, ideals, loyalties, and civic duties celebrated.
2. *Celebration of Europe*: the coverage and emphasis given to values attributed to Europe, such as progress, environment, and human rights.
3. *Recognition of diversity*: the degree to which cultures and histories of ethnic, religious, and regional minorities are incorporated into the representation and definition of the nation.

Valorization of the Nation

The first thing that strikes one about the teaching of history in Germany is the relatively small amount of curricular time devoted to explicitly national history. European and world history share relatively equal curricular time with national history. In Lower Saxony, for instance, the history program for the first year of secondary school allocates 39.9 percent of teaching time to national history compared to 49.8 percent for European themes and 10.5 percent for non-European civilizations (Jeismann and Schönemann 1989: 75).

Expectedly, German history books have the customary narratives of the origins, historical progress, and consolidation of the nation—from the times of ancient Greeks and Romans and the Christian Middle Ages to the coming of age of the nation-state. However, when compared with textbooks from other European countries, German textbooks give contemporary history a much more prominent place. Ancient and medieval history is relatively marginalized in favor of coverage of the Weimar Republic, the Nazi period, and the Cold War. For example, *Die Reise in die Vergangenheit*, one of the popular secondary school history textbooks, reserves three volumes out of six for the history of the nineteenth and twentieth centuries, with separate volumes devoted to the Weimar and Nazi periods and to post-war world history. In another popular textbook series, *Zeiten und Menschen*, out of a total of 237 pages covering twentieth-century history, one-hundred pages are devoted to the study of the Weimar Republic, the National Socialist Dictatorship and the Second World War. This heavy emphasis is not coincidental: in all *Länder* [states] of the Federal Republic, the teaching guidelines require extensive coverage of twentieth-century German history, starting with the Weimar period.

The extensive attention to this disastrous phase in German history, which is characterized as an "erroneous path" in one of the textbooks (*Die Reise in die Vergangenheit*, vol. 5, 2000: 185), obviates celebration of the German nation through narratives of unbroken continuity. The tone is hence rather skeptical, and stress is put on 1945 as a historical break that separates the present from the past. The political reorganization as it proceeded in the western part of Germany, and particularly the constitutional and federal structure of the new republic, are described as responses to the experience of totalitarianism and as means to prevent any such radical development again. Thus *Zeiten und Menschen* reads: "In many of its details, the Basic Law. ...takes up regulations from the constitution of Weimar, but the Parliamentary Council took the experiences into consideration, of how the Weimar Republic declined and what happened during the NS-dictatorship" (*Zeiten und Menschen* vol. 4, 1997: 180).[1] On the same issue, *Die Reise in die Vergangenheit* quotes the former president, Walter Scheel: "The Basic Law which we created is born out of the suffering and errors of German history. ...As long as the people and the state respect the values which are laid down as fundamental rights there, as long as we are willing to defend these values within and outside, we—the citizens of this state—rise up to our responsibility ... to leave the next generation a constitutional state that is among the most liberal and social ones of our world" (vol. 6, 2001: 90). Instead of invoking nation and its enduring legacy, German history textbooks articulate an affirmative discourse on responsibility and the legitimacy of the federal and constitutional order as a way to validate the present-day Germany.

In many of the German history book series we analyzed, the nation is valorized negatively, if not disavowed, for its dangerous inclination toward nationalism. This tendency can be found even in books that cater to Bavaria and have to meet a relatively conservative agenda to be approved there. The textbook series *Erinnern und Urteilen* is such an example and is used for the teaching of history in the state of Bavaria. In this text, whether the first German National Assembly of 1848 or the phase of Imperialism at the end of the nineteenth century is at issue, the idea of the nation appears to be countered by perils of nationalism: "Pride in one's own nation was mostly connected to liberal and social claims in 1848, e.g., freedom of press, wealth and education for all. In the second half of the 19th century, the national is often separated from the liberal movements and developed into nationalism. It no longer meant just pride in one's own nation but also arrogance as well as hatred and devaluation of other peoples" (vol. 8, 1999: 116). According to current German history books, it is under these ideological circumstances that the world has become a stage for destructive national rivalries from the nineteenth century on, with the two world wars being the tragic culmination points. As the narrative goes, the Weimar period is marked by rather promising endeavors to overcome national competition and to make the world a better place. Among them, the foundation of the Nations' League and Gustav Stresemann's policy of reconciliation as "pioneer of Europe" are counted as the most significant (vol. 9, 1993: 88 ff., 91). However, the textbook amends, the global economic crisis of the 1920s and the success of dictatorships in Europe (Mussolini, Stalin, Hitler) led to the disastrous backlash of the Second World War.

The picture that is drawn of the post-1945 period is none too optimistic, either. It depicts a world shaken by crises, civil wars, East-West confrontations and economic inequalities. On the whole, the textbooks leave no room for doubt about Europe's complicity in this unfortunate state of affairs. This becomes very clear in chapters that treat global politics, decolonization, and the Third World. In particular, the difficulties that decolonized countries have experienced after independence are related in much detail to the wrongdoings of the European nations, their imperialist rivalry, and colonial rule. The message is clear: "we" are responsible for the current state of the world and cannot close our eyes to the global problems. The North-South division between developed and underdeveloped countries needs to be overcome, for the world we live in is one of mutual dependency. Agency for enabling such a process toward "global peace and international cooperation" is seen to lie with the United Nations (*Erinnern und Urteilen* vol. 10, 1992: 152).

The mutual dependence and oneness of the world also frames the narration of German unification. Although "nation" is present in unification narratives (as expressed in the then popular slogan *Wir sind ein Volk* [We are One Nation]), the explanation of unification is sought not in the inevitable unity of the nation but in an international context. In *Erinnern und Urteilen*, it is asserted that Germans necessarily considered the post-war separation of Germany as "unnatural," but that it was ultimately the international security concerns and dangers to other states emanating from "the existence of two German states [that] solved the 'German issue' " (vol. 10, 1992: 94). In *Zeiten und Menschen*, the breakdown of the GDR is explicitly located in the larger transnational context of revolutionary changes in the Eastern Bloc and the "completely changed attitude of the Soviet leadership toward their satellites" (vol 4, 1997: 200ff.). In brief, under the burden of the Nazi period and in a globalizing world, nation ceases to constitute a suitable frame of reference. The nation is principally to be seen in an internationalized setting.

The tendency to distance the present from the nation is so strong that even the unification of the two Germanies under the roof of the Federal Republic is greeted without much emotional enthusiasm. *Die Reise in die Vergangenheit* devotes a chapter of one-hundred pages to the "history of the German separation" and its eventual solution (vol. 6, 2001). In those pages, the unification process is rationally and very briefly related by an unsentimental account of the course of events. In this account, the fact that the unification celebrations of 1990 were not effusive but rather reserved is considered to be "certainly quite good" (vol. 6, 2001: 112). Again, although there are references to the former existence of two German states as an "unnatural separation," thus confirming one nation-state as a natural condition or even necessity, it is nonetheless made explicitly clear that the German nation has been divided effectively by living in two different states. The phenomenon of mutual indifference, disapproval, and alienation between East and West Germans takes up several pages (vol. 6, 2001: 152–57) and this internal division is seen as posing a historical challenge to the new Germany. Despite this concern, the same chapter places strong emphasis on post-war efforts for international reconciliation with the French, the Poles, and the Jews. Hence, the issues concerning nation are counterbalanced by a normative international perspective and by insisting that one should not make the national concerns too big an issue.[2]

Similarly to the German textbooks, French textbooks also deploy an increasingly less nation-oriented approach, and a certain openness to world history. This shift away from particularism and toward more world-openness can be seen especially in the textbooks based on the 1990 curricular program. *Le Monde d'aujourd'hui* (1999), a text for final-year college students, begins with introductory remarks and questions aimed at providing students with a working frame of reference for comprehending the history of the twentieth century. In this introduction, history proceeds from an encompassing view of the world, from a consciousness of the world at large. The first question reads: "What is the political map of the world today?" The question accompanies two maps that outline the organization of world space at the end of the nineteenth and twentieth centuries. The first map highlights the strategic zones of the most important colonial powers (France and Great Britain, in particular) and the second map identifies the major power centers of the twentieth century. The text makes it clear that the world we live in is connected, albeit with differential power relations: "Today the main world powers have wealth and play a central role in decision-making, operating as a central pole of attraction which the other nations have to converge to and depend on." Other questions further the emphasis on world consciousness and direct students to identify and think about the issues in a larger context of the world: "What are the most important imbalances concerning the process of development? What are the most significant tensions in the present world?" (Bouvet and Lambin 1999: 8–15).

This move to establish "world" as the proper framework for understanding history becomes more apparent in the way textbooks deal with world wars. World wars are presented first and foremost as tragedies of humanity, not as instances of calamities inflicted upon the national body. At center stage is not French, but human suffering. In a section appropriately entitled "Human Suffering," the text reads: "In this war the twentieth century has experienced the first genocide in history," referring to the Armenian genocide (Bouvet and Lambin 1999: 32–33). In another volume, the dossier section, entitled "The Unnameable Barbarity," states: "The violence and barbarity of the Great War, exemplified by not only the trench wars but also the Armenian genocide, announced the coming of the 20th Century and its massacres" (Marseille and Scheigling 1999: 34–35). Placing the accent on Armenian genocide and the massacres to come, along with "trench wars," which were the epitome of French suffering, sets the stage for a broader perspective, away from a singular focus on national events and memory, and highlights a methodological shift from French-centered history teaching to taking "world" as the reference point for the narration of history.

The tendency toward a world view, one less oriented to France, goes back to the 1985 curricular program, which also explicitly introduced the idea of "Europe-building" to French education (Ministère de l'Éducation Nationale 1985). However, while national history now receives less emphasis, the notion of nation still permeates the program. Compared to German textbooks, French books are much more forthcoming in presenting the nation. Even so, the nation here is an abstract notion, interwoven with the notions of nationality, citizenship, and laicism, all of which are also defined and elaborated as universalistic principles.

In French history textbooks, students are offered a wide range of definitions for "nation." Citing formulations of historians, sociologists, philosophers, and political scientists, and translated into accessible terms for students, the nation is variously defined as a "human community with a specific language, history, and common culture" (Klein and Hugonie 1998: 52); a "group of people speaking the same language or sharing a common culture and a common history, and living within the borders of a same country" (Klein and Hugonie 1998: 140); or as "people sharing the same language and origin, having consciousness of a certain unity" (Stern and Hugonie 1997: 50). The nation is also defined in terms of voluntary political effort as a "group of people willing to make a political community" and a "group of people who have common traditions and intend to live together" (Klein and Hugonie 1998: 62, 198). Despite the diversity and the highly prosaic nature of the definitions, the nation in French textbooks is, in the first place, the "Grand Nation", the "name given to the revolutionary France, the first free nation" (Klein and Hugonie 1998: 94). As such, the concept of nation carries the revolutionary, universalistic values of freedom and citizenship, and national feeling means simply "to love France"—nothing more, nothing less, a platonic abstraction (Stern and Hugonie 1997: 114).

The way gender history is treated in textbooks further illustrates how a nation's historical analysis and the way it relates to universalistic principles is an expression of the nation and its values. Women in French textbooks are almost exclusively mentioned in relation to citizenship issues and civic concerns: in ancient Athens, the bedrock of democracy, women are not citizens and excluded from the public sphere. The schoolmistresses of the Third Republic bear the responsibility and honor of educating citizens; and female suffrage is singularly the most important accomplishment toward the emancipation of women. By coupling gender and citizenship in this manner, French textbooks exalt the nation as the engine for both emancipation and gender equality, both of which are considered to be universalistic achievements of revolutionary France.

While teaching French history invokes loosely elaborated abstractions, French civic education accents human rights, citizenship, democracy, and the Republic. The 1999 curriculum states the goals of civic education as follows: "to teach human rights and citizenship, through the acquisition of the principles and values that organize the democracy and the republic, through the knowledge of institutions and laws, and rules of the social and political life; to train to have a sense of individual and collective responsibility; and, to educate to acquire faculties of critical analysis especially through the practice of discussion." These three goals are to prepare the students to participate in the public sphere at large, not only to serve France: "Civic education forms the citizen in the French Republic, in Europe and in the international world" (Ministère de l'Education Nationale, de la Recherche et de la Technologie, Direction de l'enseignement scolaire 1999: 37). What emerges from this curricular design is a universal citizen equipped with civic qualities and ready to participate in a multitude of public spaces—local, national, European, and global. And, as the citizen, qualifications and duties become universalized, the nation—and that which is claimed as Frenchness—loses its national particularity.

In today's German and French textbooks national ancestors and heroes, like the nation itself, lose their uniqueness and particularity. Ancestral tribes, such as the Germanic and Gallic tribes—the Normans, Franks, and Celts increasingly are depicted not in heroic but in cultural terms; through the images of quaint village life, hospitality, food, and artistic achievements. Rather than being introduced as establishing a national genealogy, ancestors are placed in a framework of everyday culture and intercultural encounter. In a German civics textbook this is evident in a chapter entitled "People of Different Cultures Live Together," where a potpourri of peoples from different times and geographies is described. Here the "culture" and "everyday life" of Turkish immigrants and native Germans simply follow sections on ancient Romans, Germanic tribes, North American Indians and "the Whites" of past and present (*Welt- und Umweltkunde 5/6, Niedersachsen* 1993: 154–85). Categories of time and space are thus expressly suspended in favor of the cultural perspective (we come back to this discursive shift later when discussing the incorporation of diversity). Such a violation of historical linearity is a very common trend in all the newer textbooks—and also has to do with changes in pedagogical approaches to history.

In German history textbooks that are currently in use, representations of national heroes are deeply ambivalent. This clearly reflects the discontinuity represented by the year 1945. In the treatments of twentieth-century history, one does not find any "national heroes" in the proper sense at all. Instead, on display are model figures of upright democrats of the 1920s and the anti-Nazi resistance, the founding fathers of the democratic constitution of 1949, and the architects of the post-war economic success story [*Wirtschaftswunder*] in the Federal Republic. Some textbooks prefer to introduce some of the pre-twentieth-century figures, Friedrich the Great, for instance, as representatives of a glorious national past. However, this rehabilitation of the concept of national heroism is not without its difficulties and is immediately designated as matter for discussion. *Die Reise in die Vergangenheit*, for instance, refers to the controversies raging among historians since 1945 as to the deeds and personality of Friedrich the Great and confront students with competing points of view (vol. 3, 2001: 118ff.). In another history textbook series, the assessment of the Prussian king is more explicitly ambivalent, accentuating a mixed record of achievements and failures: inspired by the ideas of Enlightenment, the textbook asserts, Friedrich transformed despotic absolutism to a more liberal form of rule while neglecting to address the traditional class structure in Prussia. This negligence is said to have limited the impact of all state reforms of his reign (*Geschichtsbuch* vol. 3, 1995: 28–32).

Bismarck presents a similar case in point. Praised for having founded the German Empire in 1871, the "Blacksmith of the German Empire" nevertheless appears as a double-edged character. On the one hand, it is acknowledged that Bismarck installed a foresighted social insurance system, and that, as foreign minister, he managed to avert the latent danger of war in Europe. On the other hand, these positive aspects are countered by his decided, antidemocratic tendencies and by the fact that even the social insurance legislation was introduced for political reasons to diffuse the power of Social Democrats (see, for example, the respective parts in *Die Reise in die Vergangenheit* vol. 4, 1995: 74, 164; *Geschichtsbuch* vol. 3, 1995: 140; *Zeiten und Menschen* vol. 3, 1995: 146). This negative, authoritarian side of Bismarck's policies rendered "bad consequences" or even "fatal" effects later on, the textbooks explain. The conclusion that students are expected to draw is that one should not simply admire the hero, but take a critical approach to historic context and the hero's efforts. This surely contrasts with the tenor of earlier textbooks, in which the founding of the German empire is characterized as the "fulfillment of the national longing of many Germans" and Bismarck is presented as the bright and politically artistic hero of his time, without any mention of his militaristic tendencies.

The same critical and distanced approach to national heroes and events also applies to the French case. In French textbooks we observe that the "national myths" and critical moments of the national history, utilized in the past not only to build national identity but to evoke nationalistic passion, have assumed a different dimension. A good example of this is the treatment of the birth of the French kingdom, the Carolingean Empire, and the national symbol Jeanne d'Arc. The unsentimental rendition of the deeds of the preeminent French heroine Jeanne d'Arc, is representative of the general move away from charisma and myth in textbooks. She is presented with utmost detachment: "After her death, she is seen as a national heroine; she becomes one of the great historical figures of France," and there is emphasis on post facto canonization rather than inherent heroism (Stern and Hugonie 1997: 116–17). She is invoked not as a personification of a glorious French moment but as a device to teach a methodological lesson on "how to study a historical figure"—in terms of understanding the life and role of heroes in their own times and explicating their symbolic image and significance thereafter.

Equally telling, the textbooks we have analyzed (based on the latest national curriculum) narrate the origin of the French kingdom and of the Carolingean Empire without much reverence to special sentiments of national pride. The textbooks begin as expected, by paying tribute to the growth of national feelings, but continue by significantly relativizing the birth of France. The relativization, the undoing of French particularity, occurs as the French empire is equated with the birth of the German kingdom, and put into the context of a particular historical era which gave rise to other European kingdoms: "With the Verdun treaty in 843, the Franc Empire is divided into three independent kingdoms. Two of them are at the origin of France and Germany" (Stern and Hugonie 1997: 50). In this narrative, the Carolingean Empire comes into being not out of any French exceptionalism or peculiarity, but as a consequence of ordinary historical circumstances. It is the common regional past that is stressed here and not the particular status of the event as a source of French identity. Hence, the French nation becomes like others, nondescript and ordinary.

Celebration of Europe

In both of our cases we observe the penetration of a pronounced European dimension into national education (see also Pingel 1995). In practice this means the incorporation of "Europe" as a formal subject of study, and an increasing emphasis in school curricula on wider European ideals and civic traditions (broadly defined as democratic principles, social justice, and human rights) that replaces nationalist content and the nationalizing mission of education. Our analysis, however, also testifies to divergence in identity projections and formulations. While the *idea* of Europe is accepted and incorporated in school curricula and textbooks in expansive ways, its appropriation varies in form. In German history books, contingent upon the history and institutional trajectory of Germany's education system and federal state structure, both Europe and local regions figure prominently in the narration of history and identity, while the nation steps back. In French textbooks, on the other hand, the French nation, historically conceptualized as an abstract and universalistic entity, is equated with Europe. In other words, Europe becomes French, or "European" is transfigured into "Frenchness."

School guidelines in several German states specifically include four dimensions to be dealt with across all subjects: environment, gender equality, intercultural education and the European dimension. Since the German education system is organized in accordance with the principles of federalism and subsidiarity, such issues are usually first taken up in the form of advice or resolution that is taken by the Standing Conference of the Education Ministries of all German *Länder*.[3] It is then within the area of responsibility of each federal state to translate the conclusions into its own guidelines. Yet despite the regional variation that is favored by this system, even in Bavaria, a typically conservative state, topics that deal with Europe, democracy, and human rights have been assigned a higher priority—along with themes that emphasize regional affiliations in terms of the *Heimat* [homeland], as in "my homeland Bavaria."[4]

The tendency toward assigning a more prominent place to the European dimension in teaching programs came forward in many interviews Soysal conducted among ministry officials, educators, and the heads of teachers' associations. One ministry official from Lower Saxony reported that the changes in their guidelines were made "in response to the technical, economic, political developments in Germany, Europe, and the whole world." For him the direction was clear: "You cannot preach a European Union and at the same time continue to produce textbooks with all the national prejudices of the nineteenth century. …We must lose our national prejudices, we must change our point of view." Accordingly, the ministry produces supplementary teaching material specifically designed to help the teaching of a European perspective in history and civic subjects (Soysal 2000: 132).

Similarly, in an interview, the head of the German History Teachers' Association stressed a shift in their approach to teaching history:

> The aim is more and more to cover what is important for Europe. For example, in teaching about the towns and cities in the Middle Ages, the former textbooks spoke about the German old towns. And we saw in these towns the typical German character. And now, we do not cover the German character of these towns, but their European character. For example, we have buildings in Poland like buildings in Germany. And in the former times, a teacher would have said, 'You see in Poland there are the same buildings as in Germany, and therefore these buildings are built by Germans.' Now we say, 'In both countries, in this period, people built similar buildings.' This is a question of perspective. You can teach the same material from a national perspective or from a European perspective. And now, we have, we want to have a European perspective. (Soysal 2000: 132)

Again, the European approach is often conceptualized in textbooks as a lesson to be learned from the destructive nationalism of the German past. Not surprisingly, *Die Reise in die Vergangenheit* connects the idea of a unified Europe to the transnational resistance against Nazi Germany: "During the Second World War, the resistance movements all over Europe saw their fight against the Hitler-Reich as a fight for Europe" (vol. 6, 2001: 160). In the same vein, *Zeiten und Menschen* explains that "in all countries there were fascists, communists and democrats, and they felt connected across borders. In a concentration camp, members of the different nations shared their fates; for the French resistance fighter, the German opponent of Hitler was closer than his own 'collaborating' compatriot; fascist volunteers from many European countries fought in the German army" (vol. 4, 1997: 124). National Socialism, according to these books, effectively fractured national identification patterns and underscored broader political connections and alliances.

Post-war European integration and unification is thus presented as a common project of pacification and reconciliation, not yet translated into reality to a satisfying extent but proceeding nonetheless. Holding on to "national interests" is cited as the main obstacle impeding political unification, which should proceed in step with economic unification. Critical voices regarding the prospects of the European Union or particular problems of cooperation do not question the project as such. The textbooks admit that the process of "growing together" in Europe, as it is referred to in *Die Reise in die Vergangenheit* (vol. 6, 2001: 162), will take time and entails serious difficulties and frictions. Even so, the integration process is seen as natural and without alternative. Throughout the German textbooks, European integration is dealt with in a highly affirmative fashion: a united Europe is taken for granted for the present as concerns the economy, and equally it is taken for granted that Europe will and should be the future framework for political agency. In view of the nationalist German past, the necessity to give up previous national certainties appears to be relatively effortless: it was "easier for Germans than for other people to consent to the establishment of supranational organizations after 1945" (*Zeiten und Menschen* vol. 4, 1997: 209).

In the French textbooks we also encounter examples of increased emphasis on Europe. As we have mentioned before, a good example of this can be seen in the rearrangement of the teaching of such historical topics as the world wars to make them less French and more European. The foreword in one history textbook fittingly states: "To become a citizen of France and Europe at the dawn of the Third Millennium demands, more than ever, a good knowledge of the historical evolution" (Klein and Hugonie 1998: 3). In civic education, topics such as human rights and citizenship are increasingly viewed as European: we find extensive sections on "Human rights and Europe" as well as "European Citizenship." In geography we read that "European integration has modified the organization of the French space" (Brogini et al. 1999: 149). With this European theme come supplementary themes that emphasize regional specificities as sources of identity.

The redefinition of "French space" in the teaching of civic education and geography is particularly interesting. The move follows the administrative reforms of the 1980s. In the 1959 Civic Education Program (*Horaires et programmes de l'enseignement du second degré* 1959) the focus is on municipal institutions (sixth grade), department institutions (seventh grade), the state (eighth grade), and the nation, state, and citizenship (ninth grade). Ten years later, a new program, within the framework of studying the administrative organization of the Nation, opens to discussion the territorial organization of France, with a view to matters of centralization and decentralization. In 1985, as civic education again becomes a separate subject (from 1976 to 1985 it was integrated into history and geography lessons), the teaching of national administrative structure explicitly focuses on regional governance and decentralization, and places more emphasis on the responsibilities of local administrations (Ministère de l'Éducation Nationale 1985). In the case of geography teaching, the effect of the reforms is twofold: on the one hand, the cultural specificity of French regions is brought to the fore and amplified; on the other, this "new" French space is overtly linked to the European context.

The 1985 program broaches the new approach affirmatively but with caution, recognizing the residual opposition to the EU. One of the textbooks reads: "Similar to inhabitants of the USA in 1919 searching for a 'return to normality', a number of French people regard the building of Europe with suspicion and prefer to maintain more traditional links to France. Some dream of a magic potion, which could resolve all problems and, with humor, they recognize themselves in *Asterix*. But they know very well that the small *Gallic* village cannot escape the flux of change" (Drouillon and Flonneau 1994: 154). Here, the invocation of the comic book *Asterix*, the quintessential illustration of French particularity against the universalistic sweep of Roman Empire, is telling. In *Asterix*, with "magic potions" and "humor" the Gallic heroes stand up to the "serious" and "brutish" Romans and protect their village and preserve their way of life. But the textbook implies there is no sense in and possibility of averting the "flux of change." Europe is simply not the invading armies of Rome, and France is not the Gallic village of *Asterix*. Accordingly, the accompanying visuals juxtapose a map of a Gallic village with a twentieth century photo of peasants "from all over Europe" demonstrating in Strasbourg. In another chapter, the same book asserts "Europe-building entails a dynamic and international approach. The European Community helps regions with difficulties. With the realization of an ambitious program of transports (Euro tunnel, TGV, highways) the French territory is going to be integrated into the large European space" (ibid: 212). Consequently, the French region becomes a Euro region, "a region that promotes the implementation of economic policies open to the European context and encourages solidarity among different countries" (ibid: 258).

Complementing the discussion of the connection of France to European space, the textbooks devote special attention to regions and regional culture. In the above quoted textbook, in a section entitled "Regional Cultural Diversity," it is explained that "although the nineteenth century historians invented the 'nation-state' and proclaimed the Republic as 'one and indivisible,' regional diversity still exists, especially in the cultural field" (Drouillon and Flonneau 1994: 230). This section is supplemented by a map showing linguistic diversity in France, the European Charter of regional and minority languages, and a text about regional languages which states: "Linguistic differences are arranged in a rich national harmony … French regional languages are similar to some European languages and for this reason they constitute a precious bridge towards the languages of neighboring countries, thus enhancing important political and economic links with Germany, Italy, Spain and the Netherlands" (ibid: 231). More pictures and documents are included to bring home the merits of regional diversity: a road sign written in two languages, a bank advertisement from the "d'oc" region, a text on "To be Breton" praising pride in ethnic origins, a table summarizing the legal shifts in language policy in France (for example, *Villers-Cotterets* ordinance that substituted the king's language with Latin; *Thermidor An II* that annulled regional languages; the 1951 *Deixonne*'s law that officially recognized Basque, Breton, Catalan, Corsican, Flemish, Occitan), another table reminding the pupils of the dates of regional reforms in France, and a text about France and European regional development policy. This emphasis on regional and linguistic diversity is quite remarkable for France, where regionalism has always given way in favor of the center, as opposed to Germany where regional autonomy is rather taken for granted.

The 1995 French Curricular Program constitutes a further step in introducing Europe by taking as its task to define a European culture and society: "Although EU States differ from each other in many respects—as to their demographics and nature and geography—and exhibit strong national sentiments, they share a common cultural background," (Brogini et al. 1999: 115). This "common cultural background" is tied in particular to the long-running and world-wide cultural and artistic influence exercised and enjoyed by Europe:

> From the XV to the XIX century, Europe dominated and populated large sections of the world. European ways of living and thinking penetrated extensively to many places and continents. Today, the European presence continues to be evident throughout the world: through press, books, radio and television European states keep and expand their influence. European languages are spoken and studied by large populations: English is dominant in the field of international trade, whereas French, Spanish and Portuguese are broadly spoken in Africa and in the Americas. Through its universities, museums, libraries, artists, researchers, and writers, the EU comprises the oldest and most important cultural pole among the industrialized countries. (Klein and Hugonie 1999: 280)

In other words, French textbooks place the French/France under the prominent umbrella of Europe, the French influence gives way to European influence, and French values converge into Europeanness.

Furthermore, under this European umbrella, Euro-regions undermine the nation and the state, and bridge the nations to European space: "The EU is a supranational construction, which, with certain difficulties, aims to build a unity 'above and over the nations.' Euro-regions tend to erase the state boundaries at local level. Especially, in accordance with the principle of subsidiarity, Euro-regions become more powerful and their interventions prove to be more efficient than that of the states acting separately by themselves (for example, in the fields of European environment preservation, international solidarity, and so on)" (Brogini et al. 1999: 115).

The overall picture is a European society characterized by "strongly rooted cultures," "a heterogeneous human ensemble," and a "strong element of diversity." "The EU does not accept less than 11 official languages!" the textbook claims, but adds a cautionary note to its celebratory account: "The abolition of internal frontiers and the growth of exchanges, however, may result in a standardization of the European society" (Brogini et al. 1999: 119). The same cautionary tone surfaces as regards the regions. Along with stressing regional specificities, attention is drawn to their possible dangers: "Regional feeling comes back: the manifestation of regional cultures increases. More and more regions ask for independence (Northern Italy, Belgium), at times in violent ways (Northern Ireland, Corsica, the Basque country)" (ibid: 119). On the same page, the following questions accompany a picture of a Belgian carnival: "Do you know a similar manifestation in your region?" and "Could defense of regional identity produce more violent manifestations?" Regional emphasis and

European unity certainly have their limits, as made apparent by these advisory warnings against separatism and standardization.

What is remarkable in this shift in French textbooks and educational goals is its objective, namely promotion of the European identity. The lesson to be drawn is that Europe is incontestable, inevitable and affirmative. This is a gesture away from nation: French universalism becomes one with universal Europeanness. The gesture also brings regions to the fore at the expense of the nation—albeit with caution. Like national identities, however, regional identities also undergo a change under the umbrella of supranational Europeanness and become Euro-regions, altering French space. The particularity of Frenchness and the unity of French space are no longer intact. As we indicated before, for France, this process of reassessing regions marks a greater change than for Germany, where regional diversity and federalism have a rather long tradition and have been given more emphasis as institutional principles since the Second World War.

Recognition of Diversity

In textbooks, the nation is not only appropriated by Europe and by regions, but also by the increasing incorporation of linguistic and cultural diversity. The support by the EU for "lesser-used" languages, such as Cornish, Sardinian, and Occitan, and the accommodation of regional languages in schools even in France, which has long resisted any such recognition of diversity, are indicators of this movement.[5]

In Germany, following the advice of the 1996 Standing Conference of Education Ministers, many local states have integrated "intercultural education" in their programmatic guidelines as an aspect that should be reflected in teaching. Topical reference works and manuals for teachers assert that "information about life in different cultures is an essential element of learning," and this would imply taking "the emotional and living conditions of migrants and refugees into account as well as investigating the relations between indigenous people and their fellow citizens from other cultures of origin" (Hölscher 1994: 9).

This approach is demonstrated in the way Islam is presented in textbooks. Whereas in books from the 1950s Islam appears only as a brief subplot to the history of the Crusades, in current textbooks the chronological accounts are supplemented by narratives that depict Islam as a "culture" or a "way of life" (*Menschen, Zeiten, Räume,* vol. 2, 1999: 210), and recount "cultural encounters between Islam and Europe" (*Gesellschaft Bewusst* vol.2, 2001:172ff.; and *Menschen, Zeiten, Räume* vol. 2, 1999: 197). Unlike the coverage of Christianity, with which German students are supposed to be more familiar, the chapters on Islam include extensive information about the rites, practices and foundations (that is, the five pillars) of Islam, as well as contemporary, everyday-life pictures of bazaars, mosques and Muslims at prayer. More often than not, gender issues relating to Islam draw particular attention as topics that requires classroom discussion. Even in a history textbook that otherwise manages to avoid controversy, pupils are asked to discuss gender-related passages from the Quran: "What does the text say about the position of women in Islam? What do you like, what do you maybe dislike about the rules prescribed in the 4th Sure?" (*Die Reise in die Vergangenheit* vol. 2, 2001: 34).[6] Other series commonly attempt to generate comparative discussions on Islam and Christianity by setting quotations from the Quran next to similar quotations from the Bible, without targeting Islam for controversy. What the current books have in common, irrespective of their different emphases, is that gender roles are put up for debate when Islam is at issue—this was not the case in the corresponding editions from the 1970s.

In line with prominence given to intercultural topics, German civics and social studies textbooks of the last decade exhibit a remarkable semantic shift when discussing immigrant cultures. The heightened interest in culture clearly follows from a general shift in education, from a negatively defined target-group pedagogy (the German *Ausländerpädagogik*) to "Intercultural Education," which anticipates a less hierarchical approach between cultures. In current textbooks, the immigrants are depicted as "foreigners" [*Ausländer*] with their own culture and lifeways, commonly under the thematic title of "Living with Each Other" [*miteinander leben*]. This new representation contrasts greatly with earlier textbooks (from the 1970s or early 1980s) where immigrants either did not appear at all or, if they did, only did so as generic "guestworkers"—that is, not in cultural but in economic terms, as an industrial workforce to strengthen the economies of their host countries but that would return once their task was completed. The labor immigrants of then are now people whose "cultural and religious needs" should be reckoned (*Gesellschaft Bewusst* vol. 2, 2001: 175). Their problems arise no longer from lack of economic means but from being "between two cultures" (*Gesellschaft Bewusst* vol. 2, 2001: 186, 191), being "between two worlds" or being in a situation where they, particularly young girls and women, must cope with "both cultural circles," theirs and that of their host country (*Menschen, Zeiten, Räume*, vol. 2, 1999: 198, 206). Their culture nevertheless contributes to the enrichment of the host societies and Europe. As *Menschen, Zeiten, Räume* puts it, "[they] play an important role in the cultural life in Europe" (vol. 2, 1999: 222). This new way of presenting "the others" emphasizes the principle of plurality and at the same time reconfirms the notion of their otherness in terms of a cultural difference.

Civics as well as history textbooks stress the contemporary necessity of recognizing "others" and being in solidarity with them as fellow citizens, mostly through reference to the lessons of the unbefitting German past. In this model, the threat no longer emanates from an "exogenous other" (immigrant, foreigner) but from an "indigenous" one that violates the democratic order and might jeopardize the standing of Germany in international arenas. This "indigenous other" materializes in textbooks as the neo-Nazi youth and invariably appears as the natural, present-day extension of the Nazi past. Comparisons are made with the treatment of Jews in the Nazi period and the current violence against foreigners to discuss the issues of diversity and tolerance. To bring the point home, *Die Reise in die Vergangenheit* for the ninth grade, prominently quotes the former president Richard von Weizsäcker on tolerance from a speech he gave on the fortieth anniversary of the German capitulation in 1945. For the pupils this is their last history lesson of their compulsory education. Thus the book aptly ends with the following appeal to moral responsibility:

> A new generation has taken political responsibility now. The young ones are not responsible for what happened in the past. But they are responsible for what will be made of it in the course of history ... Hitler had always worked by means of exploiting prejudices and inciting hostilities and hatred. Our request to the young people is the following: Don't let yourself be driven into enmity and hatred of other people, be they Russians or Americans, Jews or Turks, the alternatives or conservatives, black or white. Learn to live with each other, not against each other. (*Die Reise in die Vergangenheit*, vol. 5, 2000: 186).

In French civics books, especially the ones written in the 1980s after the socialists came to power, ample space is devoted to substantiate and prescribe plurality and tolerance as correctives to racism and discrimination. The picture and words of the prominent French-Algerian activist Harlem Desire, crowns chapters on "diversity and unity" in French society, as a means to reexamine the notions of nation, patriotism, and chauvinism. The portrayal of the Crusades is also instructive with respect to the depiction of the other—in particular, the Islamic other. The Crusades, once a topic invoked in order to provide narratives of religious wars and victories between the world of Islam and world of Christianity, is now a story of economic advancement. As one history and geography book puts it, "The Crusades gave the Western people and especially the Italian merchants the possibility to control the trade in the Eastern Mediterranean Sea." However, this economic advantage comes at a price: "In addition, the [Crusades] contributed to the development of a hostile image of the West among Muslim people, an image associated with violence and aggressiveness." In summary, according to this French history narration: "The Crusades have dug a ditch between West and East" (Stern and Hugonie 1997: 64). This critical commentary on the Crusades is indicative of the larger trends toward reconciliation of hostilities and reparation with the other.

The instances of historical revision and intercultural elaboration cited here, from Germany and France, are exercises in plurality. In other words, they are requisites for the "world of diversity" that increasingly finds its way into the normative discourses of school textbooks in both countries. As maintained in current textbooks, the world is necessarily plural, and tolerance and acknowledgment of cultural difference is imperative to curtail the past excesses of the nation and to further the prospects of a unified Europe. In the process, the nation noticeably submerges its authoritative singularity, and diversity becomes, and is celebrated as, the future of Europe.

Conclusion: Nation-state Identities in a Unifying Europe

Europe as a unifying project plays an important role in the transformation of national curricula and textbooks. The European integration process itself, and the institutional structure that accompanies this process, facilitates denationalization by creating normative expectations of equal and tamed nation-states. The dichotomy of transnational and national does not appear as natural in the framework of European unification, where member states must prove themselves as fair partners in tightly interlinked transnational political/security arrangements (Soysal 2000).

 Yet another manifestation of this trend toward taming nations and normalizing national canons is evidently the deliberate attempts to reconcile conflicting national histories of European countries by means of bilateral consultation. In Europe, international attempts to reexamine and revise textbooks have a long history, going back to the interwar period. The national and international committees, set up then by the League of Nations in cooperation with teachers' associations in different countries, sought to eliminate national prejudices and stereotypes from textbooks. With the foundation of the Council of Europe after the Second World War, these efforts became more institutionalized. Currently, several joint commissions are at work (among Germany, France, Poland, and the Czech Republic, for example), aiming to harmonize the teaching of historically difficult relations between neighboring countries and create a common vocabulary for the teaching of national histories consistent with today's European ideals.

 Regarding the case in point, French-German consultations on textbooks have a long history and have led to to mutual revisions, a development which needs to be seen as the background for what we have described as the normalization of national canons. The German Society of History Teachers and the French Society of History and Geography Teachers have been meeting intermittently since 1935. At the beginning, their efforts concentrated on identifying areas of conflict between French and German national histories. Since 1981, sponsored by the Georg Eckert Institute for International Textbook Research, a new series of French-German consultations were held to locate the omissions and gaps in respective history textbooks of Germany and France, and to develop an overall framework for interpreting national history. The recommendations of this round of meetings inspired substantial revisions and harmonization in curricula and textbooks in both countries.

The differing ways in which French and German textbooks arrive at a transnational point of view reflect the two countries' differing self-definitions and histories. Germany, for example, with a strong federal consciousness and a clear historical discontinuity concerning the nation concept itself, appears to be more open to situating its own nation and identity within a transnational context. This path has, after all, been followed since the foundation of the Federal Republic of Germany as a means of containing potentially dangerous ramifications of national identification patterns. Although German unification has also modified the discourse on self-definition, the overall trend to anchor German identity within a transnational context has not been abandoned. Thus, Germany does not conform the conventional perspective that poses a conflict between the national and transnational. This appears to be the result of national identity being continuously explicated and recast by the transnational since the end of the Second World War. France, on the other hand, with a stronger tradition of political centralism and a more abstract understanding of nationality, has only recently come to face this challenge. However, because of the universalistic impetus of French self-definition, the distinction between what is national and what is European identity withers away: the principles that constitute Frenchness are also European principles. In the case of France, then, the national identity approximates the transnational.

The post-war evolution of German and French textbooks and curricula display the changing context and meanings of identity in a world where the national is increasingly subjected to reinterpretation by the transnational. European integration provides a unique opportunity to sharpen our analytical and conceptual tools to scrutinize the relationship between textbooks and emerging collective identities.

Notes

The chapter draws upon Yasemin Nuhoğlu Soysal's ESRC project that investigates the changes in nation-state identities through a comparative analysis of history and civic textbooks in post-war Europe. The data for the project come from national textbooks and public school curricula for lower secondary schools in four European countries (Germany, France, Britain, and Turkey). The data set is constructed by sampling the history and civic textbooks and curricula in the case countries at three time points, the 1950s, 1970s, and 1990s, when major educational reforms took place. The project also examines public debates, conflicting claims, and court cases that surround national education systems and national curricula, as well as the incorporation of minority cultural/religious provisions into public education systems. To this end, the project makes use of interviews conducted with officials from state educational boards and ministries, school authorities, teachers' and parents' associations, and the representatives of European and national-level associations and networks on textbook and curricular study. Teresa Bertilotti and Sabine Mannitz are both researchers on the project. Our thanks to Irene Bloemraad and Marion Fourcade-Gourinchas for the initial coding of the textbooks, Hellen Wallace for her support of the project, and Levent Soysal for his extensive comments.

1. The constitution for the three Western Zones, later the Federal Republic of Germany, was called "Basic Law" in 1949, since the final constitution was supposed to be a matter of the unified Germany, including the zone under Soviet occupation that went on to become German Democratic Republic.
2. It should be noted that Germany is not without its controversies when it comes to dealing with the concept of "nation." In one such debate in 2000, Frederick Merz, the leader of the Christian Democrat group in Parliament, suggested that foreigners in Germany must adopt a German "*Leitkultur*" [guiding culture/majority culture]. An immediate difficulty, however, was to define the German *Leitkultur* and everyone seemed to be at a loss for defining what "Germanness" or the "German nation" stands. When asked, Merz himself suggested that the acceptance of a "guiding German culture" merely meant following the constitution and broadly accepting such national values as the emancipation of women. More troubled, Angela Merkel, the party leader, shyly offered the flag, the constitution, and certain landscapes. "When I'm in Russia," she ventured to explain, "I see birch woods and I know what I'm seeing is not German landscape." No one was able to account for how respect for the constitution and the love for the landscape could work to differentiate Germans from foreigners living in Germany, or from French or Polish, for that matter. The failure of Christian Democrats to define Germanness is not surprising in the light of the analysis we present in this paper as regards the recasting of nation within Europe. As we argue later, what is national is increasingly appropriated as European and what counts for national myths, traditions, and landscapes becomes benign cultural artifact to celebrate in an increasingly diverse world.
3. To name just two examples related to our study, the Standing Conference of the Ministers of Education issued a conclusion on "Europe in Teaching" in 1978 [*Beschluss der KMK "Europa im Unterricht,"* 8 June 1978]. In the year 1996 they released the recommendation "Intercultural Education in School" [*KMK Empfehlung "Interkulturelle Bildung und Erziehung in der Schule,"* 25 October 1996].
4. A 1991 circular from the Ministry of Education in Bavaria states that "the European dimension should be introduced into all subjects" and "pupils should become aware of Europe's intellectual and cultural heritage and of common European values such as democracy and human rights" (Council of Europe 1991: 24).
5. In line with this move French historians have argued for a new reading of educational policies of the third Republic, highlighting that such a policy, even though characterized by a centralized power, had not caused a decline of local languages but rather it had contributed to their valorization (see Chanet 1996).
6. The Fourth Sure of the Quran sets the rules governing marriage, kinship, inheritance, and the relationship between men and women. Some of the rules, such as the prescription of "marrying four women," "beating women," and privileging men over women as regards to inheritance, are grounds for controversy as relates to the principle of gender equality, both within and outside Islam.

References

Berger, Stefan. 1995. "Historians and Nation-Building in Germany after Reunification." *Past and Present*, vol. 148, 187–222.

Bouvet, Christian and Jean-Michel Lambin, eds. 1999. *Le Monde d'aujourd'hui, Histoire-Geographie 3ème*. Paris: Hachette.

Brogini, Maurice et al. 1999. *Tout Simplement: Histoire, Geographie, Education Civique 3eme*. Paris: Hachette.

Chanet, Jean François. 1996. *L'école republicaine et les petites patries*. Paris: Aubier.

Council of Europe. 1991. *Education Newsletter*, no. 4. Strasbourg.

Drouillon, Marie-Thérèse and Monique Flonneau, eds. 1994. *Histoire - géographie – initiation économique 3ème*. Paris: Nathan.

Erinnern und Urteilen: Geschichte für Bayern. 1992–1999. Vols: 1–5. Stuttgart, Düsseldorf, Berlin, and Leipzig: Ernst Klett Schulbuchverlag.

Georg-Eckert-Institut. 1988. *La France et l'Allemagne: Espace et Histoire Contemporaine, Recommandations pour l'enseignement de l'histoire et de la géographie dans les deux pays*. Braunschweig and Paris: Georg-Eckert-Institut für Internationale Schulbuchforschung/Association des Professeurs d'Histoire et de Géographie.

Geschichte. 1986. Vol. 4. Munich: Bayerischer Schulbuchverlag.

Geschichte und Geschehen. 1987. Vol. 2. Stuttgart: Klett.

Geschichtsbuch: Die Menschen und ihre Geschichte in Darstellungen und Dokumenten, Neue Ausgabe. 2000 [1992–1996]. Vols. 1–4. Berlin: Cornelsen Verlag.

Gesellschaft Bewusst. 2001. Gesellschaftslehre, vols. 1–2. Braunschweig: Westermann.

Goodson, Ivor. 1987a. *The Making of Curriculum: Essays in the Social History of Schooling*. London: Falmer Press.

——— ed. 1987b. *International Perspectives in Curriculum History*. London: Falmer Press.

Hölscher, Petra, ed. 1994. *Interkulturelles Lernen. Projekte und Materialien für die Sekundarstufe I*. Frankfurt am Main: Cornelsen Verlag Scriptor.

Horaires et programmes de l'enseignement du second degré. 1959. Paris: Vuibert.

Jeismann, Karl-Ernst and Bernd Schönemann. 1989. "Geschichte amtlich: Lehrpläne und Richtlinien der Bundesländer." *Schriftenreihe des Georg-Eckert-Instituts*, vol. 65. Frankfurt am Main: Verlag Moritz Diesterweg.

Klein, Bernard and Gérard Hugonie. 1998. *Histoire et géographie 4ème*. Paris: Bordas.

Leschinsky, Achim. 1996. *Vorleben oder Nachdenken? Bericht der wissenschaftlichen Begleitung über den Modellversuch zum Lernbereich "Lebensgestaltung-Ethik-Religion."* Frankfurt: Verlag Moritz Diesterweg.

Levy, Daniel. 1996. "The Future of the Past: Comparing Historians' Disputes in Germany and Israel." Paper presented at the annual meeting of the Social Science History Association, New Orleans, November.

Maier, Charles. 1988. *The Unmasterable Past: History, Holocaust, and German National Identity*. Cambridge, MA: Harvard University Press.

Marseille, Jacques and Jacques Scheigling. 1999. *Histoire-Geographie 3ème*, Paris: Nathan.

Menschen, Zeiten, Räume. 1999. *Arbeitsbuch fur Gesellschaftslehre. Band 2 (7./8. Schuljahr)*. Berlin: Cornelsen Verlag.

Meyer, John W. et al. 1992. *School Knowledge for the Masses: World Models and National Primary Curricular Categories in the Twentieth Century*. Washington, DC: Falmer Press.

Ministère de l'Éducation Nationale, 1985. *Collèges, Programmes et instructions 1985*. Paris: CNDP.

Ministère de l'Education Nationale, de la Recherche et de la Technologie, Direction de l'enseignement scolaire. 1999. *Enseigner au Collège, Histoire-Géographie Education civique, Programmes et Accompagnement*, Paris: Ministère de l'Education Nationale, de la Recherche et de la Technologie.

Pingel, Falk. 1999. *UNESCO Guidebook on Textbook Research and Textbook Revision.* Braunschweig and Paris: George Eckert Institute for International Textbook Revision/UNESCO.

Pingel, Falk, ed. 1995. "Macht Europa Schule? Die Darstellung Europas in Schulbüchern der Europäischen Gemeinschaft." Schriftenreihe des Georg-Eckert-Instituts, vol. 84. Frankfurt am Main: Verlag Moritz Diesterweg.

Die Reise in die Vergangenheit. 1993–2001 [1991–1995], vols. 1–6. Braunschweig: Westermann.

Soysal, Yasemin Nuhoğlu. 1994. *Limits of Citizenship: Migrants and Postnational Membership in Europe.* University of Chicago Press.

—— 2000. "Identity and Transnationalization in German School Textbooks." In *Censoring History: Citizenship and Memory in Japan, Germany, and the United States,* eds. Laura Hein and Mark Selden, Armonk. New York: Sharpe.

Stern, Marie, and Gérard Hugonie. 1997. *Histoire et géographie 5ème.* Paris: Bordas.

UNESCO. 1953. "Bilateral Consultations for the Improvement of History Textbooks." *Educational Studies and Documents,* no. 4. Paris: UNESCO.

Welt- und Umweltkunde 5/6, Niedersachsen. 1993. Braunschweig: Westermann.

Young, M., ed. 1971. *Knowledge and Control.* London: Collier MacMillan.

Zeiten und Menschen 1995–1998 [1983–1984]. Neue Ausgabe B, vols. 1–4. Paderborn: Ferdinand Schöningh.

Chapter 2

❖

Privileged Migrants in Germany, France, and the Netherlands: Return Migrants, Repatriates, and Expellees after 1945

Rainer Ohliger

The prevailing paradigm of writing European history as a history of nation-states, national communities, and national representation continues to be shaped by the dichotomy of clearly bounded "selves" and excluded "others." Even today, the sense of "self" comes with an open or hidden notion of ethnic, ethno-national, or ethno-cultural difference or even superiority of one's own nation toward other nations. This is due mainly to the ways in which nation-states were formed historically. In the context of nineteenth- and twentieth-century European history national boundaries have been the most important context for belonging, for inclusion or exclusion. However, this rather rigid construction of (national) history was also challenged, as nation-states and their populations always were heterogeneous. Given the rather heterogeneous ethno-demographic patchwork within European nation-states and their populations, ethnic and national identities tended to develop along conflicting and competing lines of belonging. Linear national historical narratives, which often tended to be teleological constructions, did not always provide sufficient space for mirroring the diversity and divergence of national identities.

Immigration into a homogeneous or would-be homogeneous nation-state can challenge identities. It can cause a rift between a nation-state's resident population on the one hand and the nation-state's core ethnic population (titular nation) on the other. Such a rift can also become apparent through the presence of indigenous ethnic, ethno-national or ethno-cultural minorities within a nation-state. Additionally, the homogeneity of a nation-state can be challenged when members of a nation-state's titular nation live outside that nation-state (for example, as a result of voluntary emigration, colonization or border changes). Immigration, the existence of ethnic minorities *within* a nation, which bases its identity on ethnic homogeneity, and the existence of coethnic populations *outside* the nation-state raises the question of how a national narrative can include the perspective of these various groups. How can these (marginal) populations be represented within national history? Popular narratives such as textbooks or representations in mass media have a large impact on society and are, therefore, of particular importance for the inclusion and exclusion of immigrants, minorities, or any kind of "others."

An especially interesting case of dual marginalization in national narratives concerns so-called privileged migrants. These are members or descendents of a nation's ethnic core group who have lived outside the nation-state, usually for generations (due to voluntary emigration or as colonists), but who then voluntarily (re)migrated or were repatriated by force to their countries of origin, or rather the country of their ancestors' origin (due to war or other unfortunate political circumstances). These migrants usually enjoy legal and other forms of protection provided by their "homeland" to which they "return" or, to be more precise, immigrate. As minority groups in other countries they often develop and maintain special political and cultural ties to their "mother country" or even retain their citizenship while abroad. However, return migrants, repatriates, and expellees are often received with considerable hostility and viewed as strangers upon arrival in their "mother country" or "homeland." In spite of their privilege to return to the "mother country", based on citizenship rights or special legal provisions, these privileged migrants can be seen as true immigrants because of their social distance and their considerable problems with integration. Describing repatriates as privileged *immigrants* is thus a more accurate term.[1]

This chapter analyzes the representation of privileged[2] Dutch, French, and German immigrants, who migrated or were expelled to their respective nation-states after 1945.[3] Nearly 250,000 former Dutch colonial settlers returned home between 1945 and 1964, after Indonesian independence had been proclaimed in 1945 and recognized by the Netherlands in 1949. Sixty to seventy percent of these people returned to the Netherlands in the 1950s.[4] In the French case, the emphasis is on return migration of (white) French settlers [*pieds-noirs*] from Algeria. This group of French migrants left Algeria in 1962, after the Algerian war had been ended by the Treaty of Evian, and a referendum for Algerian independence had passed with a large majority in April 1962. After Algeria had gained independence, it revoked European nationals' colonial privileges. Around 900,000 of the one million French settlers, who had rejected and partly violently opposed the decision for Algerian independence, moved to France, primarily to the south of France and to Corsica. In the German case, the focus is on the German and ethnic German population that was expelled from former German territories and neighboring Central Eastern European countries between 1945 and 1949 after the Potsdam Agreement.[5] These (ethnic) Germans constitute the expellees [*Vertriebene*], who were initially transferred to the American, British (about eight million people), and Soviet (about four million people) occupation zones. Also included in the

German case study are the (ethnic) German refugees [*Flüchtlinge*] who fled Central and Eastern Europe and pre-Second World War territories in the east in late 1944 due to the approach of the Red Army.

The National Triad: Nation, National Homogenization, and National Historiography

Starting in the early nineteenth century, European historiography developed parallel to the formation and consolidation of nation-states. These nation-states had the inherent tendency to homogenize European populations, be it as a consequence of modernization and state formation, be it as an effect of (ethno-)nationalism or, finally, as an intricate interrelation of both. One could argue that nation building and homogenization is a continuous process which has not yet ended in Europe, particularly not in its eastern and southeastern parts. (For this same general argument for historical France, see Weber 1976, or for South-Eastern Europe Todorova, 1997.) Nation building, state formation and the writing of history became closely intertwined through this process, producing two important consequences.

First, historical scholarship usually assumed three normative and widely accepted categories of analysis: nation, nation-state, and a homogenous national population, subsequently weaving teleological foundations into historical narratives. Nation-states not only used their power to define national education and national curricula, but also to nationalize historiography, which reinforced the legitimacy of nation building and strengthened the authority of the nation-state. Nation building and the nationalization of historiography can thus only be understood within a hermeneutic circle. As much as national historiography was continuously shaped by national institutions such as schools and universities, historiography contributed and continues to contribute to nation building and to a proliferated yet renewed perception that the nation is longstanding and everlasting.

Second, the ethnic, linguistic and cultural plurality, which was the norm rather than the exception in European societies, was recorded and therefore regarded as a deviant concept in historical narratives. The historiographical focus, thus putting particular emphasis on the history of the nation and the nation-state, was not only restricted by nation-state borders. This focus also marked internal social, linguistic or ethnic minorities as different. Nation-states' constructions of a national "self" set the nation apart from what it did not intend to include. This process of defining the "other" became a pervasive paradigm in nation building and national historiography.

However, migrants and minorities were not always represented in the same manner, as this chapter will argue. Despite similar problems that these groups faced, for instance in terms of social marginalization or problems of integration, they were portrayed differently in numerous respects in national narratives. The line of division among immigrant groups ran between those who were socially, culturally, or politically privileged (either based on their country of origin or on the ability to become permanent residents and citizens) and those without privileged access to social and political resources.

Categories of "self" and "other" have become the prevalent framework to investigate societies when national, ethnic, and social identities are at stake. This framework unites anthropology with history and historiography and owes to constructivist thought. It has become a truism that identities, forms of belonging, and mechanisms of exclusion and inclusion are constructed against an excluded societal group (the "other"), thus drawing boundaries between "us" and "them" and representing these boundaries symbolically, socially, and politically. However, this mode of interpretation, "self" and "other," has some limits when it comes to the border areas of belonging where grey, and not black and white, is the rule. This is particularly true for the inclusion and exclusion of immigrants and minorities. In these cases there is often no clear-cut dichotomy of "self" and "other," inclusion and exclusion.[6] This dichotomy is even less clear for coethnic minorities, that is, privileged migrants prior to repatriation. These groups are potential or would be migrants and long-distance citizens (Münz and Ohliger 1998.) They are usually incorporated in the societies of the receiving countries regulating their legal and social status and do have full access to citizenship and social benefits. Thus, one could label them "privileged" migrants, though the circumstances of their migration often involved force and violence, so that the actual act of migration is not privileged in any sense. This chapter investigates Dutch, French, and German coethnic minorities after they became privileged migrants. This terminology indicates that Dutch, French, and German privileged migrants were perceived by their respective countries of origin as part of the national community even before their repatriation or expulsion. However, privileged migrants' distinctive group identity, their historical fate, and previous spatial separation from their "mother countries" also set them apart from their compatriots in their "homeland."

Merits and Limits of Comparison

Dutch, French and German privileged migrants differed significantly from each other. Not only did they come from a variety of backgrounds, and immigrated at different times, but their legal status in the receiving countries also differed. In France, and partly also in Germany, the respective privileged migrants were citizens of these countries before they returned. In the Netherlands, and to a certain degree also in Germany, citizenship was granted during the process of forced or voluntary return migration.

However, these three groups of privileged migrants have at least four commonalities, thus making them worthwhile cases for comparison. First, they all have or can claim citizenship rights in their country of destination and access to special integration programs upon their immigration. Second, they were usually not viewed as immigrants upon their return to their countries of destination, but as a part of the nation. Third, in all three cases the forced or voluntary repatriation or remigration was the consequence of a lost war (Germany, France) or of a violent process of decolonization (The Netherlands). As a consequence, the image of these repatriates or privileged migrants could be associated with a narrative of (national) suffering and of victimization following (national) defeat. Fourth, the immigrants fell into a dual category of belonging to both the "other" and the "self" while facing the typical challenges of social accommodation after arriving in what they thought of as their "homeland."

Representation of Privileged Migrants in Dutch, French, and German Textbooks

This comparative analysis will be limited to the ways in which Dutch, French, and German textbooks after 1945 represented privileged migrants. It will illustrate and analyze the characteristic approaches these three nations took in representing these groups after forced or voluntary repatriation. I shall not address regional or federal differences (especially in the German case), differences among the various school grades or the textbooks used in different types of schools. The analysis is limited to the representation of these privileged migrants in textbooks of their respective "homelands" or countries of destination. The representation of *pieds-noirs* in Dutch or German textbooks, of (ethnic) German expellees in Dutch or French textbooks, and of Dutch colonial repatriates in French or German textbooks will not be addressed.[7]

In total, I analyzed 152 Dutch, German and French history and geography textbooks published between 1947 and 1997 (see table 2.1), and refer to four Austrian textbooks as cases for comparison.

Table 2.1 *Number of Textbooks Analyzed: References to Privileged Migrants*

	Number of textbooks				Number of textbooks referring to privileged migrants			
	F	GDR	FRG	NL	F	GDR	FRG	NL
1940s/50s	4	2	13	13	0	2	6	1
1960s/70s	20	4	11	16	6	1	9	2
1980s/90s	21	5	26	17	15	4	16	7
Total	45	11	50	46	21	7	31	10

Source: Textbooks analyzed at the Georg-Eckert-Institute for International Textbook Research in Braunschweig

The quantitative analysis shows that privileged migrants figured very differently in the three cases under consideration. German textbooks were quite aware of the issue. References to expellees and refugees were made in more than 60 percent of East and West German textbooks. French textbooks referred to repatriates in less than 46 percent of the books, whereas Dutch textbooks only mentioned colonial repatriates in every fifth book (22 percent). However, the mere quantitative analysis of counting entries does not reveal all that much, because covering the topic and textbooks could range from one sentence to several pages. What matters, though, is that the way in which privileged migrants were portrayed changed significantly over time. Thus, content analysis is important to grasp the issue fully.

Content Analysis of Privileged Migrants

Pieds-noirs in France

The representation of *pieds-noirs* in French textbooks was always embedded in the general history of colonialism and decolonization. The historiography of the French colonial empire and its population as portrayed in textbooks underwent significant changes during the time period under consideration. Three phases can be identified. The first was the immediate post-war period until the end of the 1950s, in which textbooks generally remained in the prewar national tradition of writing colonial history as a success story (that is, the role of France, French colonial administration and French settlers was interpreted within the *mission civilisatrice,* the French Cultural Mission). In this interpretation the French impact on its colonies and the role of colonists, particularly in Algeria, was associated with economic, social, technological, and cultural progress brought about by colonists and through colonization. In this period, *pieds-noirs* did not figure as a distinctive social group in French textbooks (as *pieds-noirs*), but as colonists in general [*colons*] if they were mentioned at all: "France guaranteed peace in all the colonial territories which it administrated. It built streets, ports, cities, hospitals" and "its colonists developed the culture, brought civilization" (David, Ferré and Poitevin 1953: 233; my translation).

The dominant perspective was not a perspective of social groups (or conflicts) in colonial life, but rather of heroic individuals, French colonial policy and colonial conquests. Thus, men like Faidherbe, Lyautey, and Gallieni, nineteenth-century military conquerors, represented the French colonial empire in textbooks. The larger colonial population only appeared on the stage of history as an anonymous and amorphous mass that contributed to the glory of the nation: "*The'Union Française'* [*French Union*] is a greater France, populated by 100 million inhabitants, in which all people—French, Algerians, Senegalese, Indo-Chinese—work together in the same spirit for the *same common task*" (David, Ferré and Poitevin 1953: 233; my translation).

Particularly when the role of soldiers from the colonies in the First or Second World War was mentioned and commemorated, it was this glorious interpretation of French colonial history which dominated textbook narratives (Bernard and Redon 1949: 306). In this first period there was no emphasis on the diversity of colonial populations, cultures, or on the difficulties of colonial life. However, colonial history was not a central issue in textbooks during this first phase. The historical narrative was usually Eurocentric, primarily centered on the European part of the French nation-state (for example, excluding the Algerian *départements*) with only scarce references to developments outside Europe (see indexes of Alba 1947 and Alba 1954).

During the second phase, which lasted from the mid-1960s to the early 1980s, extra- or non-European and colonial history became an important topic. It was in this period (the process of decolonization was mostly over, the colonial war in Algeria had ended with Algerian independence and most of the French and European settlers had been repatriated to France) that *pieds-noirs* became a distinctive immigrant group in textbooks. Within the history of colonialism, which was now predominantly told as the history of decolonization and its problems and/or losses, French-Algerians were turned into a group that was given special representation. The *pieds-noirs* were portrayed in an often exaggerated language as victims of the decolonization process: "The Algerian drama: the *pieds-noirs* arrived in France traumatized, for the most part unable to realize what had happened" (J. François et al. 1981: 83; my translation).

The standard textbook representation from this period as well as from the third period, was a photo showing a large crowd of repatriates with heavy luggage arriving in Marseille. The titles of the photos (as well as the texts) interpreted the process as "The Drama of Repatriation." Thus, the focus was mainly placed on the suffering of this group and on individual pain:[8] "The Algerian drama: Almost all of the *pieds-noirs* suffer from a bitter fate: they have to leave their families' land and property for a French fatherland which most of them do not know" (Froment 1980: 91; my translation). The emphasis was not placed on the diplomatic, political, and military events, which were the reasons for these repatriations. Structural socioeconomic problems in Algeria, which were additional, underlying causes of repatriation, typically were not mentioned. Although the war in Algeria was commented upon widely in textbooks during this second period, only little emphasis was placed on the connection of war, decolonization, and repatriation. Instead, crude demographic arguments could be found in textbooks of this period explaining the basic reasons for the French—Algerian conflict. The increasing quantitative imbalance between Muslims and French Algerians in combination with the lack of interaction and assimilation between the two groups was blamed. The cause was not attributed to the uneven access to power, or to social and economic resources.

The "achievements" of the colonial era and the *mission civilisatrice* no longer figured prominently in textbooks of this second period, though they were still mentioned after the retreat of the French population and administration from the colonies. However, a neocolonial view and a tone of superiority, similar to those associated with the French cultural mission, could now be discovered in French geography textbooks. When it came to providing developmental aid to independent Third World countries, particularly to francophone countries, geography textbooks displayed a condescending tone (Dupaquier and Guiot 1971: 552ff.). What used to be depicted as the colonizer now became described as the economically and technologically superior Western authority in French textbooks.

During the third phase, starting in the late 1970s and early 1980s and lasting until today,[9] the depiction of repatriates in France became more differentiated. It provided explanations that linked the repatriation of *pieds-noirs* with their role in the former colony. Questions of social and political injustice in Algeria under French rule and in the French-Algerian war from 1954 to 1962 were raised. However, despite a more subtle way of representing *pieds-noirs*, they occupied less space in textbooks than in the two previous periods.

A more self-critical stance on French colonialism can be observed in the third phase. The role of French settlers in Algeria was directly linked to forced or voluntary repatriation (D. François et al. 1983: 270). This change of attitude did not only show in a different and more precise terminology. *Pieds-noirs* were often put in quotation marks or just called French settlers [*colons*], French Algerians [*Français d'Algérie*] or a European minority [*minorité européenne*]. This depiction also showed a shift away from a predominantly French perspective to one that gave voice to Algerian viewpoints and critically assessed the role of the *pieds-noirs* within the system of colonial rule.

The narrative of a painful repatriation experience and of victimization—in modified form—now recognized structural inequalities between the colonists/settlers and the rest of the population in Algeria (namely property rights and socioeconomic imbalances), the opposition of the French-Algerians to citizenship reforms and to the extension of voting rights in favor of the Muslim population. Moreover, the political radicalization of the *pieds-noirs* from the late 1950s on was addressed: "The interests at stake: the Europeans of Algeria, more than one million people, were owners of the essential part of the means of production in agriculture, in industry, in transport, but also in large scale trading, banking etc. 22,000 colonists owned 2,800,000 ha of the best soil, which is 40 percent of the cultivated agricultural territory. They owned 5,500 industrial businesses out of 7,000. Thus 80 percent, were in their hands" (Brière 1980: 90; my translation).

The impact of the *pieds-noirs* on the fall of the Fourth Republic in 1958 was also mentioned during this period: "It was a drama for one million Europeans (*the pieds-noirs*) who had been settled in Algeria for a century. They refused independence and did not want to leave their country of birth. (...) The war divided the French population and created a climate of civil war in France which ended in provoking the fall of the Fourth Republic" (Lambin 1989: 124; my translation). Although the status of *pieds-noirs* as victims of the historical process was still reflected in textbooks, it now was considered within a more complex historical narrative. Textbooks of this period mention French and French-Algerian atrocities during the war and thus depict *pieds-noirs* much more ambiguously.[10] The more complex representation of *pieds-noirs* went hand in hand with a more self-critical image of the war in Algeria. For instance, pictures were included in textbooks, which also showed and criticized the violence of French soldiers during the war. Moreover, the texts criticized the euphemisms [*pacification*], which previously had been used to describe cruel military actions (D. François et al. 1983: 272).

However, through all three periods, representation of *pieds-noirs* remained secondary to the narration of colonialism and decolonization and the history of the war in Algeria. Throughout the period which was analyzed they did not play a central role in textbooks. This was partly due to the broadly comparative approach, which French textbooks took toward the history of colonialism and decolonization, thus limiting space for the French case and its peculiarities. History was usually narrated in the comparative context of international political history and international relations, showing the French case as one among others, in particular in comparison to the British and Belgian cases. As a consequence, domestic issues (the decline of the Fourth Republic, the return of de Gaulle to power, and *pieds-noirs'* massive opposition to Algerian independence and French policy) were drastically underrepresented, and often totally absent from the narrative, or only casually referred to.

The role that the *pieds-noirs* played in the French discourse during the war in Algeria was quite controversial and rather ambiguous. As fierce opponents of Algerian independence and partly as protagonists of attacks on French policy in Algeria, the *pieds-noirs* had a reputation of being perpetrators of the colonial era before being repatriated to France in 1962. This older image prevented an easy depiction of *pieds-noirs* as national victims who deserved particular attention and representation. The ambiguity of the past, the controversial role of the *pieds-noirs*, was way too complicated for a straightforward and linear textbook narrative. One could argue that a consensus to disagree would have to be reached in the French public in order to make such an ambiguous depiction possible. However, this would also have implied public consensus to disagree on the historical discourse concerning the war in Algeria. The layers of a complicated colonial past are only now slowly emerging in France through critical and painful scrutiny of its colonial history and colonial crimes. This was not the fact in the immediate decades following decolonization.

Surprisingly one aspect is almost completely missing from the depiction of *pieds-noirs* in French textbooks, namely the social, economic and cultural incorporation of French Algerians into French society. The success of the integration of privileged migrants was almost a non-issue in all the textbooks analyzed for this chapter, except for casual remarks that integration was challenging or problematic (Milza et al. 1975: 241).[11] Unlike the history of nonethnically French migrants in French textbooks, the history of *pieds-noirs* ended with the act of repatriation in 1962. Their fate and history within French society *as an immigrant group* has thus remained invisible and untold.[12]

Refugees and Expellees in Germany

Representation of Privileged Migrants in West Germany and United Germany

A stereotype within German discourse on post-war refugees and expellees [*Flüchtlinge und Vertriebene*] has it that the issue was widely (and adequately) covered in West German textbooks, whereas in East German textbooks it was generally ignored and considered a politically sensitive issue, which was swept under the rug. Its mention was labeled revisionist. When one analyzes German textbook references to refugees and expellees, this broad generalization is partly substantiated. However, there are important nuances that should be recognized. The representation of expellees and refugees in West German textbooks was not linear throughout the Federal Republic's over fifty-year history, but this representation has undergone important changes. As in the French case, three phases can be distinguished: the 1950s, the period from the 1960s to the mid-1970s, and finally the mid-1970s to the late 1990s.

Although integration of refugees and expellees was central to public and political discourses in the first decade of the Federal Republic, textbooks from this period do not contain much information about them. In the first decade of the new West German Republic, history textbooks only casually mentioned this group as part of the—usually brief—Second World War history coverage. However, this was not true for geography textbooks, which gave more space to the representation of expellees, although they did so in a rather traditional way. Geography textbooks from the 1950s tended to emphasize the demographic impact of the expulsion. They drew a picture of expellees as the true victims of the Second World War, people who suffered more than the rest of the German population. The story of suffering and the depiction of expellees as victims was narrated as a backdrop to German colonization, and thus the spread of civilization and development to Central and Eastern Europe since the Middle Ages. Expulsion after 1945—according to geography textbooks of this period—annulled these achievements in Central and Eastern Europe.[13] Geography textbooks during this time still tended to use a rather old-fashioned or even ethnically based [*völkisch*] terminology when referring to Germans in Central and Eastern Europe.[14]

From the 1960s on, the depiction of expellees in West German history and geography textbooks became more nuanced, although some continuity with the previous period still existed as the 1960s history books recorded expellees as a distinctive migrant group. The *völkisch* connotation mostly disappeared. However, the emphasis on expellees as German victims of the Second World War continued to play a role, was even broadened and given more room in both history and geography textbooks. From the 1960s, textbooks often took an individualizing or micro perspective, conveying biographies of individual expellees or select expellee communities in West Germany.[15] During this second period, the history of German expulsion was (still) narrated as an exceptional or unique story of the post-war period. It was not written from a comparative perspective and was not linked to the ethnic and demographic "restructuring" of Central and Eastern Europe during the 1940s by the Third Reich (for example, expulsion, deportation, population transfer and genocide affecting numerous ethnic and national groups).

During the third period, from the mid-1970s (which was also the time of détente and a new German *Ostpolitik*) further changes occurred in West German textbooks. First, narratives, especially in history textbooks, became more comparative, emphasizing the interrelation of German expulsion with forced migration of Poles, Ukrainians, and Czechs. Textbooks thus gave up claiming the exceptional position of German expellees in history, "normalizing" German expellee history within the context of the homogenization of European nation-states and interrelated forced migrations.[16] This shift was particularly visible when it came to visualizing population movements on maps. The topic also became less and less focused on victimization and more on successful expellee integration: "The people who came from the east were not only a burden for the Federal Republic of Germany. Their knowledge and skills proved to aide the task of economic reconstruction" (Schultze et al. 1979: 94; my translation; see also Franze et al. 1994: 63).

As time went on, the topic lost importance in textbooks. Geography textbooks, which were at the forefront of representing expellees in the 1950s, almost completely excluded the topic from the 1980s on. This was partly due to the more international perspective these textbooks assumed after the 1970s. Moreover, shifts within the discipline toward a more sociological approach can explain these changes. Space, borders and population [*Raum, Grenze, Bevölkerung*], the prominent explanatory categories in German geography and in the narration of expulsion until the 1960s, from the 1970s were no longer used. Thus, the previous spatial-demographic emphasis, which had been used to describe expulsions, vanished. Casual references to the "former German Eastern territories" or only to post-war border changes, without mentioning population movements, replaced previous narratives in geography books.[17] As a consequence of these methodological and theoretical shifts within the discipline expulsion increasingly disappeared from geography textbooks. This went as far as having a section on Poland in a geography book without mentioning any forced migration of Germans from these territories, just stating: "Peasants from all over Poland were settled on former German farms" (Brucker 1991: 126).[18]

This sentence remained cryptic and could not be understood by a student who was not familiar with the context of expulsion and resettlement.

To a lesser degree, a decrease in the representation of expellees could also be seen in history textbooks from the mid-1970s to the present. History textbooks did not completely exclude the story of the expellees as did geography text-books of this period. However, in the 1990s, German expellee history was reduced in scope. In one case it was reduced to a single sentence: "Millions of Germans were expelled from their homes, deported into Russian forced labor camps or kept as POWs for years" (Alter et al. 1992: 353; my translation). In contrast, a topic that gained importance within historical research in the 1980s and 1990s was German resistance against the Nazi regime. This topic was exten-sively covered in eight pages of one textbook. Some terminological shifts were evident from the 1980s on. In some cases the term "systematic mass expatria-tion" (Hahn et al. 1984: 6) was used instead of "flight and expulsion," thus creating a more neutral and less emphatic picture of German expulsion, mini-mizing the focus on the victimization of Germans. A new emphasis emerged in history books of the 1980s and 1990s. Expulsion was contexualized in the Nazi past, which also had the effect of weakening German victimization, adding more ambiguity to the picture, and highlighting the role of Germans as perpe-trators in the narrative (Fink et al. 1997: 3).

Integration of expellees remained a topic throughout the 1980s and 1990s. However, integration usually was no longer portrayed as a linear success story, but also told as a story of conflict and achievement: "Tensions originated between old and new citizens, for instance in the process of forced recruitment of housing for expellees or as a consequence of confessional differences"; "In the destroyed West the new arrivals were not always welcome"; and "Through state granted economic compensations [*Lastenausgleich*] and through their industriousness most of them reached their former standard of living or even raised it" (Borth et al. 1988: 167; my translations).

Most of the textbooks have pictures of expellees "on the move." Thus, they have been forming a rather stereotypical image of the expellees, in which the story of the expellees was reduced to the act of flight or expulsion. An example is the stereotypical East Prussian grandmother with a handcart of remaining property on her way to the West in the winter of 1944/45. This holds true for all three periods that I have investigated. Forced migrants were denied any form of agency in this process (Askani et al. 1998: 133; Borth et al. 1988: 166; Böttcher 1998: 182; Feldmeier et al. 1987: 5; Kirchhoff et al. 1992: 16; Grosche et al. 1984: 169; Fink et al. 1997: 11). From the early 1990s on, a different picture arose: Occasional reference was made to the history of ethnic German expellees from Eastern Europe at the end of the Second World War, and to the voluntary migration of ethnic Germans from Eastern Europe to Germany after the period of expulsion (the migration of so-called *Aussiedler* or ethnic German immi-grants). In this way *Aussiedler* were linked to their historical predecessors, expellees and refugees. (Kirchhoff et al. 1992: 15).[19] Issues regarding the legality and justice of expelling German populations from territories in Central Europe formerly belonging to Prussia at the end of the Second World War—an important controversy in West Germany in the post-war period—are rarely found in textbooks. Expellee interest groups and organizations thus did not manage to introduce their perspective into textbooks during the 1980s and 1990s.[20] Especially after *Ostpolitik,* the reconciliation between West Germany and socialist Eastern European countries, a revisionist depiction of history by individual interest groups no longer could be found in textbooks.

Representation of Privileged Migrants in East Germany

The representation of German refugees and expellees in East German textbooks was almost diametrically opposed to West German views. This holds true for quantitative coverage as well as for the interpretation and context of the depiction of refugee history. Despite the fact that about four million expellees forcibly migrated to the Soviet zone of occupation, this group was hardly mentioned in East German textbooks, if at all. Short references to the history of German expellees were made in textbooks until the early 1960s. Thereafter they disappeared for two decades and only reappeared briefly in the 1980s.

Compared to West German textbooks, a number of differences are striking. East German textbooks neither gave any numbers, nor did they explain the expellees' background, their countries and areas of origin. Only one textbook gave a total figure of 45-million Europeans who were evacuated, deported and resettled during and after the Second World War (*Staatsbürgerkunde 7* 1989: 17). The book did not specify the ethnic or regional origin of these people or disclose any further details concerning the reason or cause of evacuation, deportation, and resettlement.

The terminology in East German textbooks is strikingly different from their West German counterparts. The terms "expulsion", "expellees", "flight" or "refugees" were not used at all. Instead, the populations that were "transferred" westward were called "resettlers" [*Umsiedler*].[21] Thus, the forced element of this migration process was muted or even silenced.

The difference in the use of terminology was accompanied by completely different visual information concerning expulsion. East German textbooks lacked photographs of expellees and refugees, an element which figured prominently in many West German textbooks. The individual human experience or even tragedy of expulsion, which was central for the West German narrative, was thus not present at all in textbooks of the German Democratic Republic. Differences also are present when it comes to the depiction of post-war geopolitical changes after 1945. West German textbooks usually provided detailed maps, clearly marking the former Eastern territories of the German Reich before 1945 and the areas from which a considerable number of expellees stemmed. Maps in East German textbooks only displayed the post-1945 territorial boundaries. The territories ceded to Poland and the USSR were not mentioned at all.[22]

Finally and most importantly, the reasons why and the context in which expulsion was mentioned, were completely different from the West German view. Flight and expulsion were usually only mentioned in the context of the Potsdam Agreement and the new border it had implemented. Resettlement was legitimized as a logical and necessary consequence of shifting the Polish state westward, thus drawing a new German—Polish border along the Oder and Neiße river in order to provide international stability and security.[23] From the 1960s on, however, when the new border was labeled the border of peace: *Oder-Neiße-Friedensgrenze* (*Geschichte 10* 1964: 58), the "resettlement", was no longer mentioned when referring to the Potsdam Agreement. The Potsdam Agreement, including the "resettlement" of the German population, was again briefly mentioned in the 1980s: "The Germans remaining in Poland, Czechoslovakia and the Soviet Union are to be resettled" (*Geschichte 9* 1984: 183). In the 1950s, East German textbooks still provided a somewhat broader narrative of expellees, though with a strong moral judgment stigmatizing them as a group that deserved to be punished for German crimes committed before and during the war:

> The German war criminals exploited the ethnic Germans in these countries as a pretext to invade neighboring countries. For instance, the Sudeten German Nazi party was founded in Czechoslovakia and provoked conflicts with Czechs. This was the pretext for extreme rabble-rousing propaganda against Czechoslovakia. Therefore, the Allied powers decided to resettle the Germans living in Poland, Czechoslovakia and Hungary to Germany. The resettlement was intended to forestall future fascist violence."(*Lehrbuch für den Geschichtsunterricht* 1955: 293; my translation)

The main difference between West and East German textbooks was that the population, which was portrayed as victim in the early German Federal Republic, was (partly) portrayed as perpetrator in the early German Democratic Republic.[24]

Representation of Indonesian-Dutch in Dutch Textbooks

In comparison to French and German privileged migrants, Indonesian-Dutch repatriates were much less visible in Dutch textbooks. As in the French case, the narrative of the Indonesian-Dutch population in Indonesia and of Dutch repatriates to the Netherlands was deeply embedded in colonial history and the history of decolonization. This was depicted as the history of the fatherland or *Vaderlandse geschiedenis* (De Haas 1957: 202–203). However, Dutch textbooks did not depict repatriates as a distinctive, clearly identifiable group. Until the late 1980s the narrative was fairly straightforward, explaining the loss of the colonies and thus the repatriation of Indonesian-Dutch as an effect of the Second World War and Japanese occupation, international pressure after 1945 (from the U.S.A., the Soviet Union, Great Britain and the UN), and strong Indonesian nationalism under the leadership of Soukarno, who later on became president. Tendencies within Dutch society during the Second World War, especially the royal family's support for decolonization or at least for more autonomy in the colonies, were mentioned in Dutch textbooks. The narrative was one of political, state-centered history, that more or less excluded the colonial population and its social history. This picture, which dominated Dutch textbooks until the 1980s, neither provided much room for the internal dynamics which repatriates faced within the process of decolonization nor for the conflicts, namely the military actions and violence (euphemistically labeled as *politiële acties*, that is, police actions) and the atrocities against the Indonesian population.

The stratification of Indonesian colonial society, which consisted of a very small white colonial elite of about 40,000 people, a population of about 200,000 mixed Indonesian-Dutch, the pro-Dutch South Molukkans (mostly privileged members of the colonial military, the *Koninklijk Nederlands-Indisch Leger*), and the large majority of about 70,000,000 Indonesians, were not adequately represented in Dutch textbooks. The topic of repatriation and its problems, such as different access to Dutch citizenship for the various strata of Indonesians or Indonesian-Dutch, were not addressed at all. Representing the history of about 250,000 repatriates from Indonesia between 1945 and 1964 was limited to the events of 1957/58, when around 40,000 Dutch (mostly Indonesian-Dutch) had to leave Indonesia after their property had been nationalized as a response to the conflict over New Guinea between Indonesia and the Netherlands.[25] The conflict over New Guinea "was the reason why relations between the Netherlands and Indonesia became worse rather than better. In fact, they became so bad that in 1957/58 thousands of Dutch had to leave Indonesia against their will and were repatriated to the Netherlands" (Bakkum et al. 1958: 147).

Until the 1990s, Dutch high school students neither learned much about the history and the reason for the immigration of their "compatriots" from Indonesia to the Netherlands nor about the integration of these immigrants into Dutch society. The latter aspect was only referred to briefly and without much detail. "The repatriates who had to look for a new existence in the Netherlands were numerous," (Blonk 1969: 120). One could thus argue that forgetting, partial memory loss, or maybe even collective amnesia was the governing principle in representing these immigrants in Dutch textbooks and their incorporation into national curricula up to the 1980s.

This changed in the 1990s when Indonesian-Dutch, especially those who stemmed from mixed marriages, were suddenly represented in textbooks and were celebrated as "our Indonesians" or "our Indonesia" within the newly emerging credo of Dutch multiculturalism (Donk et al. 1990: 251). The new textbooks corresponded to a new interpretation of colonial history in which the Dutch were critically portrayed as the oppressor – [*onderdrukkers*] (ibid. 242). This new interpretation went as far as comparing the South African system of apartheid to Dutch colonial rule (ibid. 252). The criticism then even included issues of racism in Dutch society and prejudices of white Dutch people toward Dutch people of color: "In hindsight, it is surprising that they [the repatriates, R.O.] adjusted so quickly in the Netherlands. The opposite cannot always be said. There were sometimes Dutch people who wanted to grant Dutch citizenship only to people with white skin. What started already in the Dutch Indies continued in the Netherlands" (Ibid).

However, the textbook changes in the 1990s need to be seen in a larger context. They did not only effect repatriates or Indonesian-Dutch. The changes were linked to a general shift toward representing immigrants' issues in text-books in the Netherlands. Representing and giving a voice to colonial repatriates was just one small thread in the fabric of a new and more colorful patchwork of Dutch society and history (Immerzeel 1995: 251). In this text-book repatriates and labor migrants were covered within the same paragraph, drawing analogies and comparing the problems of integration.

Conclusion: Modes of Representing Privileged Migrants

The three case studies show striking differences as far as the representation of privileged migrants is concerned. Obviously, there is a difference between such countries that represented privileged migrants and those that did not. In the Netherlands, privileged migrants were practically forgotten until the late 1980s. The same is true for East Germany in the 1960s and 1970s. In contrast, privi-leged migrants were represented in West Germany, and later on also in the united Germany as well as in France, though in slightly different ways. The Netherlands represented these groups of people in their textbooks from the 1990s on and East Germany did so in the 1950s and 1980s.

There were marked differences also as far as the ascribed status of privileged migrants was concerned when it came to involuntary migration as a result of unfavorable and frequently violent political circumstances. This is also true when it came to atrocities or crimes in which these groups played a role either as perpetrators or as victims. Three forms of representation can be distin-guished: perpetrators, victims, or a multicultural community in the country to which they were repatriated.

In East Germany in the 1950s and partly in the 1980s, forced and privileged migrants were mainly seen as perpetrators. The "victim" perspective dominated in West Germany, partly also in united Germany after 1990 and in France until the 1980s. However, from the 1980s on, the image changed in West Germany as well as in France and became more differentiated, adding a critical tinge or even an element of perpetrator stories into textbooks. Only the Netherlands, starting in the 1990s, celebrated privileged migrants as a valuable addition to their multicultural society. How can these differences be explained? Which forces are at play when societies "forget" privileged migrants or when privileged migrants play a role in the national narrative? There are a number of socio-demographic, historiographical, and sociopolitical reasons for these findings.

Socio-demographic Factors

The sheer size of the immigrant group played a considerable role, whenever this group appeared in textbooks at all. In France and Germany, the number of migrants belonging to the ethnic majority was considerably larger (in absolute figures) than in the Netherlands. These migrants were immediately visible in French and German society and posed significant problems for the state and its social and welfare systems. In the Netherlands this was true to a much lesser degree. However, large population size and high visibility were also factors in East Germany, where expellees remained unmentioned in textbooks. Thus population size and visibility can determine the likelihood of whether privileged migrants will be represented in textbooks or not.[26] Moreover, when we compare the representation of privileged migrants in France and Germany with the Netherlands, another demographic factor also plays a role. Unlike France and Germany, the Netherlands continued to be a country of emigration in the 1940s and 1950s, and only became an immigration country from the 1960s on. Public discourse in the Netherlands focused on questions of overpopulation and unemployment. Such circumstances are rather unfavorable for (privileged) migrants who wish to enter the national discourse. Another factor also seems important: the population repatriated from Indonesia to the Netherlands was mostly of mixed origin, and this group was visible and could be singled out in the Netherlands on the basis of "race." This factor might have prevented considering this group as part of the national "self" before the 1980s, despite its Dutch citizenship. What brought about change and led to the representation of these groups in Dutch textbooks was the multiculturalization of society and public discourse.

Histiographical Factors

Important historiographical factors are public representations of privileged migrants and the ways in which professional historians view them. Since textbook narratives rely heavily on the work of professional historians—often historians write the textbooks or are consultants to the authors—it can be argued that textbook narratives mirror (yesterday's) state of the historical profession. What enters into textbooks has mostly trickled down from professional historiography with a certain time lag. An analysis of the ways in which Dutch, French, and German historiography has written privileged migrants into the national narrative allows for some far reaching conclusions. In West Germany, expellee history was researched from the mid 1950s on, when the government initiated a huge state sponsored research project, which was mostly carried out by professional historians (*Dokumentation der Vertreibung*). These documents and the narrative found an immediate and direct way into textbooks. In contrast, research on expellees was a taboo in East Germany throughout the state's existence. There was not a single book written on the topic by professional historians. In France, historiography on *pieds-noirs* also started early in the post-war era (Jordi 1993; Jordi 1995 and Miège 1973), though it never became as prominent as the writing of expellee history in Germany. The French government did not initiate this research: it was carried out independently by historians whose books, arguments and thoughts found their way into textbooks. In the Netherlands, historiography on the Indonesian-Dutch occurred rather late. There was state-sponsored research on the topic in the 1960s; however, these projects focused on issues of social integration and were not conducted by historians. Historians only started to discover privileged migrants in the 1980s (for the impact on the Indonesian-Dutch and their identity formation, see Willems 1999). Thus, the trickle down effect in textbooks could only be found starting in the 1990s.

Sociopolitical Factors

Sociopolitical factors for the differences in representing these migrant populations or repatriates into textbooks hint at the role that the privileged migrants played in constructing the national "self." Discourses were based on heroes or villains, national victims or perpetrators. The German case is particularly enlightening in this regard. In the French and the Dutch cases, important variations and limitations are at play. By helping to reconstruct national (West German) identity after the Second World War, one can argue that German expellees served a particular function. In the 1950s and 1960s, expellees were often portrayed as the nation's victims.[27] German *Flüchtlinge* and *Vertriebene* could thus be used to counterbalance the non-German victims whose plight was caused by Germans during the Third Reich. German expellees allowed for a kind of moral compensation. However, this kind of moral trade-off only worked until the 1960s. After a new discourse thoroughly investigated the Germans' role as perpetrators of the Second World War and the Holocaust, this kind of moral trade-off was no longer possible. In this discourse, the (Jewish, Gypsy and many other) victims of the Holocaust, and German military aggression became a central issue, through which the collective West German national "self" was reevaluated. In East Germany, different forces were at work based in the "national" founding myth of the GDR. East Germany also developed a kind of victim identity, but here it was the communists and anti-fascists, who were depicted as primarily having been persecuted during the Nazi period. In France and in the Netherlands the "victim mechanism" did not work quite as smoothly or as efficiently. A national awareness of being perpetrators and constructing one's "own" victims as a response was not as pronounced as in West Germany, although one could see a slightly similar pattern in France when it came to the war in Algeria. The case of the Netherlands is more complicated, since the Indonesian-Dutch played a different role, being in between the groups, or "racially" mixed.

Return migrants, repatriates and expellees are a comparatively privileged group of immigrants. They have easier access to the sources of society, and find more easily their way to the core of the national "self." Thus the question remains, a question which I am not able to answer in this context, of whether these ethnic migrants can be viewed as a model for the representation and incorporation of immigrants in general.

Notes

The research for this article was made possible by the German Research Foundation (DFG) within the *Forschergruppe Gesellschaftsvergleich* (Research Group on Comparison of Societies) at Humboldt University, Berlin. I thank Christal Morehouse for her careful editing of this chapter.

1. These privileged migrants belong to the ethnic majority of the country to which they immigrate. They are usually privileged in two or three ways: they gain access to "mother country" citizenship or they already possess it upon their immigration; they have the right of return migration; and they often have access to special integration programs after their immigration.
2. "Privileged migrant" will be used in this chapter as a crude term to signify the voluntary and forced migrant groups of return migrants, repatriates, and expellees in France, Germany, and the Netherlands. In the strict sense it was mostly not a "return" or "repatriation" of individuals who once had left their mother country, but rather a return after generations to the country of the ancestors.
3. In the French and German cases, I look at both history and geography textbooks; in the Dutch case, I only look at history textbooks. Distinguishing a clear difference of how privileged migrants are represented in the two distinct categories of books is difficult in the French case since many textbooks were used in both history and geography classes.
4. See Willems and Lucassen (1994: 9). In 1975, after Surinam became independent, 200,000 people from this former Dutch colony migrated to the Netherlands. Another 100,000 people came from the Dutch Antilles. This population, however, is not part of the analysis.
5. The Potsdam Agreement was signed on August 1, 1945 at the end of the Potsdam Conference (July 17 to August 2, 1945), which brought together the "Big Three" Allied powers (Great Britain, the Soviet Union, the United States). It stipulated, that

the "transfers should be effected in an orderly and humane manner" (paragraph 7 of the Protocol of the Proceedings). However, before this legal arrangement refuge and so-called wild expulsions had occurred.

6. This argument has also been brought up in the debate about postnational citizenship and postnationalism.

7. There were only two cases where the textbooks explicitly referred to other coethnic immigrants, namely one Dutch textbook which made references to German expellees and one German textbook which mentioned *pieds-noirs* when narrating the history of forced migration in twentieth-century history within the context of the history of German expellees: see Fontaine (1965: 90) for the Dutch case, and Gaigl and Jahn (1978: 42) for the German case.

8. See Berstein et al. (1975: 241), "Drames de la décolonisation" [Drama of decolonization]; Lambin et al. (1989: 124), "C'est un drame pour un million d'Européens (les pieds-noirs) installés en Algérie depuis un siècle" [It is a drama for one million Europeans (the *pieds-noirs*) who have been settled in Algeria for a century]; Brignon et al. (1980: 154), "La décolonisation: défaites militaires et drames humains" [Decolonization: military defeat and human drama]; Histoire Géographie 1980, 114 "Le drame des Répatriés" [The drama of repatriots] or also Perez et al. (1971: 256), "Un problème douloureux: l'Algérie" [A hurtful problem: Algeria].

9. The year 1997 represents the last year in this analysis and not an established cut-off date after which a new trend could be determined.

10. Désire, (1980: 92), "L'attitude la plus intransigeante fut celle de la France. (...) Dans l'Est de l'Algérie et à Madagascar, des émeutes sont suivies de terribles représailles (8,000 morts en Algérie)" [The French attitude was the most intransigent (...) In the east of Algeria and on Madagascar, uprisings are followed by terrible repressions (8,000 dead in Algeria)] and D. François et al. (1983: 270–76), "une minorité européenne exerce une domination économique, sociale, culturelle—la langue arabe est l'une des langues étrangères enseignée dans les lycées"; "une minorité européenne refuse toute évolution"; "les '*pieds-noirs*', qui n'ont pas compris la profondeur du sentiment national algérien" [a European minority exercises an economic, social, cultural dominance–the Arab language is a foreign language taught at school; a European minority refuses any evolution; the '*pieds-noirs*', who have not understood the depth of Algerian national sentiment] and Barbier et al. (1983: 140), "les gouvernements français (...) s'engagent dans une politique répressive [against Algerian moves toward independence, RO] qui mobilise des moyens de plus en plus importants et amène à recourir à des méthodes d'enquêtes et des représailles illégales et contestables" [the French governments (...) engage in a repressive policy (against Algerian moves toward independence, RO) which mobilizes ever more important means and entails to seek refuge in illegal and contested methods of enquiry and repression]; but see also Aldebert et al. 1980: 117, "Dans la métropole une part non négligeable de la population voyait dans la communauté pied-noire un group de priviléges: riches ci-devant propriétaires de grands domaines, qui par des mesures de précaution avaient su protéger à temps leur patrimoine. Les autorités, pour discréditer l'O.A.S. [Organisation de l'Armée Secrète, the French Algerian underground organization which fought against Algerian independence and became prominent with terrorist attacks in France, RO] s'étaient d'ailleurs servi de cette fausse image. C'est finalement leur courage, leur esprit d'initiative et leur dynamisme qui permirent à bien des *pieds-noirs* de recommencer leur existence avec succès" [In France an important part of the population saw in the *pied-noire* community a group of privileged people: rich former owners of great estates, who had managed to protect their property in time by measures of precaution. The French government authorities had used this wrong image to discredit

the O.A.S. (Organisation de l'Armée Secrète, the French Algerian underground organization which fought against Algerian independence and became prominent with terrorist attacks in France, RO). Finally it was their courage, their entrepreneurial spirit and their dynamism which allowed the *pieds-noirs* to start again with a successful life].

11. Numerous French colonists, the *pieds-noirs*, then abandoned their houses and their careers and returned to France where they tried to "reinstall" under often difficult conditions.

12. The narration of labor migrants' history and privileged migrants' history thus differs significantly. Whereas the former only starts with the act of immigration the latter usually ends with it.

13. Schäfer et al. (1972: 9), "Die verheerenden Auswirkungen *des 2. Weltkrieges* auf die Bevölkerungsstruktur" [the devastating impact of World War II on the structure of population] vs. Schäfer et al. (1979: 9), "Die verheerenden Auswirkungen *der nationalsozialistischen Politik* auf die Bevölkerungsstruktur" [the devastating impact of *national socialist politics* on the structure of population, my emphasis].

14. Lippold and Puls (1959: 4), "deutscher Volksboden" [soil of German people], "inselhafte Verteilung" [splintered distribution of population], "völkische Schütterzone Ostmitteleuropas" [zone of ethnically rubbled population in East Central Europe].

15. This was largely due to an early state-sponsored research project using interviews/oral history to document the history of expulsion in the 1950s, the *Dokumentation der Vertreibung* (Bundesministerium für Vertriebene, 1955–1961). Texts from this publication were used directly as sources in textbooks. For an analysis of the *Dokumentation* and its impact see M. Beer, "Die Dokumentation der Vertreibung der Deutschen aus Ost-Mitteleuropa. Hintergründe – Entstehung – Ergebnis – Wirkung, " *Geschichte in Wissenschaft und Unterricht* 2, 1999: 99–117; and M. Beer, "Im Spannungsfeld von Politik und Zeitgeschichte. Das Großforschungsprojekt 'Dokumentation der Vertreibung der Deutschen aus Ost-Mitteleuropa, " *Vierteljahreshefte für Zeitgeschichte* vol. 46, 3, 1998: 345–89.

16. See for instance Feldmeier et al. (1987: 6), who contextualized the history of German expellees within the continuity of resettlement and migration of ethnic Germans in the interwar period and during the Nazi era; see also Kirchhoff et al. (1992: 15), "Massenflucht, Vertreibung und Umsiedlung waren nichts völlig Neues. Ein 'Vorbild' hatte das Schicksal Griechenlands geliefert" [Mass flights, expulsion or resettlement were not completely new phenomena. A 'role model' had been provided by Greece] or Fink et al. (1997: 12), "Bevölkerungsverschiebung in Europa: In der größten Bevölkerungsverschiebung in der Geschichte wurden weitere Millionen von Europäern gezwungen, ihre Heimat aufzugeben." [Population Transfers in Europe: Within the largest population transfer in history, several million Europeans were forced to leave their homes].

17. Caspritz et al. (1989: 48), "die östlichsten Teile [des deutschen Reiches wurden] unter polnische oder sowjetische Verwaltung gestellt" [the Eastern parts of the German Reich were put under Polish or Soviet administration] or Becks et al. (1989: 88), "die deutschen Ostgebiete werden teils von Polen, teils von der Sowjetunion verwaltet und später diesen Staaten angegliedert" [the eastern German territories are partly administered by Poland, partly by the Soviet Union; later they were integrated into these states]; Deuringer (1993: 6), (chapter: Deutschland—Grenzen und politische Gliederung/Germany—Borders and Political Structure): "Als Folge von zwei verlorenen Weltkriegen kam es vor allem an der Ostgrenze zu großen Veränderungen des Grenzverlaufs" [As a consequence of losing two world wars borders were changed, particularly in the East].

18. The shift in German textbooks toward exclusion of the topic "expulsion" was partially a consequence of the German—Polish textbook talks, which started in 1972. The German—Polish Textbook Committee attempted to reach a consensus on the difficult and painful history of German—Polish relations. Topics where the commission could not reach a consensus were simply left out of the recommendations—upsetting the expellee associations and many politicians. Nevertheless, the German—Polish Textbook Committee was a remarkable institution. It was the only forum during the Cold War where scholars and teachers met, exchanged views, and formed personal bonds. The German-Polish Textbook Committee received much publicity, and still seems to be a model for conflict resolution in other parts of the world. The work of the Committee was reflected in the textbooks of the 1970s. In recognition of its work the Committee in 2002 was awarded a prize from the German and Polish governments for its special merits in promoting German-Polish relations. On the work and merit of the commission see Höpken (2002).

19. One homework question for students reads as follows: "Write to the German Foreign Office [sic] in Bonn and ask for information about the current situation of German speaking [sic] minorities in these states [Romania/Kazhakstan]." Actually, it is not the Foreign Ministry, but the German Ministry of Interior which is in charge of these issues; moreover, the majority of ethnic German immigrants from Kazhakstan (or Soviet successor states in general) do not speak German any longer.

20. An interesting document can be found in a 1988 Bavarian textbook, in which a statement by a British publisher of 1946 was cited condemning the expulsion of Germans. The textbook authors emphasized that the publisher was Jewish; see Glaß-Bernert et al. (1988: 50), "In 1946, the British publisher of Jewish belief Victor Gollancz judged the expulsion of Germans as follows: The Germans were expelled, but not only with a lack of exaggerated consideration, but with the highest degree of brutality one can think of"; (my translation).

21. *Neueste Zeit* (1957: 132), "Provisions of the *Potsdam Agreement* (…) 4. Germans from east of the territories of Oder and Neiße, from the CŠR and from Hungary are to be resettled to Germany" or *Geschichte 9* (1984: 183), "The territories east of the Oder and Neiße are given to Poland. The Germans remaining in Poland, the CŠR, Hungary and the Soviet Union will be resettled"; or *Geschichte 9* (1988: 203–205): "The new territorial conditions in Europe were fixed in the Potsdam Agreement. Of particular importance was the fixing of Poland's Western border along Oder and Neiße as well as the decision to resettle the parts of the German population which had remained in Poland, Czechoslovakia and Hungary"; (my translations).

22. On the other hand, West German atlases kept emphasizing the loss of territory in the East. They were originally marked with thick red lines as territories "currently under Polish or Soviet administration" (*Diercke Weltatlas* 1957 and 1964). From the 1970s on, the thick red lines vanished and were substituted by perforated lines (*Diercke Weltatlas* 1971). Moreover, temporary "Polish or Soviet administration" was no longer mentioned.

23. *Geschichte 10* (1960: 89), "Further important provisions of the *Potsdam Agreement*: 3. In order to guarantee Poland's claim for security, the Oder-Neiße Line is planned to be the future German-Polish border. 4. All Germans originating from east of the Oder and Neiße, from Czechoslovakia and from Hungary are to be resettled"; (my translation).

24. Austrian textbooks are an interesting case for comparison: The Austrian terminology shifted between the West German and the East German interpretation by using the terms *Heimatvertriebene* [expellees] and *Flucht und Vertreibung* [flight and

expulsion] as well as *Aussiedlung* (resettlement), sometimes even in the same book; see Heilsberg and Korger (1953: 157 and 1965: 167–171) and Absenger et al. (1982: 326) or Bielefeldt-Schredelseker et al. (1992: 11).

25. Indonesia claimed New Guinea after its independence was recognized in 1949. However, the Dutch government opposed this claim until 1963 when New Guinea was eventually incorporated into the Indonesian Republic after considerable international pressure had been exercised on the Netherlands.

26. This is especially true when immigration and the representation of ethnic migrants happens in unfavorable political circumstances, for example, when this group's interests collide with foreign-policy interests of the state as in the case of the GDR. A representation of expellees in the way West Germany did it would have been impossible without major conflicts with Poland, Czechoslovakia, and the USSR. Thus nonrepresentation or portraying them as perpetrators was the alternative.

27. To a certain extent this is also true for city dwellers who were bombed out in 1944 and 1945, for *Trümmerfrauen*, and for the surviving soldiers of the *Wehrmacht*, especially those who had served on the Eastern front. See Ahonen (2003: 239–40); Fure (2001); Hughes (2000); Moeller (2001) or Münz and Ohliger (1998) on the role of expellees; and Friedrich, (2002) on the commemoration of civilian German victims in German cities.

References

Absenger, Albert G. et al. 1982. *Der Mensch im Wandel der Zeiten. Lehr- und Arbeitsbuch der Geschichte und Sozialkunde*, 3. Teil, Wien: Österreichischer Gewerbeverlag.

Ahonen, Pertti. 2003. "The Impact of Distorted Memory: Historical Narratives and Expellee Integration in West Germany, 1945–1970." In *European Encounters: Migrants, Migrations and European Societies since 1945*, eds. Rainer Ohliger, Karen Schönwälder and Triadafilos Triadafilopoulos, Aldershot: Ashgate, 238–56.

Alba, A. 1947. *Histoire. 1789–1939*. Paris: Librairie Hachette.

——— 1954. *Histoire. 1789–1939*. Paris: Librairie Hachette.

Aldebert, Jacques et al. 1980. *Histoire Géographie. Livret du Professeur*. Paris: Delagrave.

Alter, Peter et al. 1992. *Grundriss der Geschichte. Band 2. Neuzeit seit 1789*. Stuttgart: Klett.

Askani, Bernhard et al. 1998. *ANNO 5/6, Das 20. Jahrhundert*, Ausgabe Sachsen, Doppelband 5/6, Braunschweig: Westermann.

Bakkum, P. et al. 1958. *Geschiedenis van Nederland*, Groningen: J.B. Wolters.

Barbier, D. et al. 1983. *La Guerre des Mondes 1939 à nos jours. Espaces et temps*. Paris: Magnard.

Becks, Friedrich et al. 1989. *Mensch und Raum 9. Erdkunde für Gymnasien im Saarland*, Berlin and Hannover: Cornelsen/Schroedel.

Beer, Mathias. 1998. "Im Spannungsfeld von Politik und Zeitgeschichte. Das Großforschungsprojekt 'Dokumentation der Vertreibung der Deutschen aus Ost-Mitteleuropa." *Vierteljahreshefte für Zeitgeschichte*, vol. 46, no. 3, 345–89.

——— 1999. "Die Dokumentation der Vertreibung der Deutschen aus Ost-Mitteleuropa. Hintergründe—Entstehung—Ergebnis—Wirkung." *Geschichte in Wissenschaft und Unterricht*, no. 2, 99–117.

Bernard P. and F. Redon. 1949. *Nouvelle histoire de la France et de la civilisation française*. Paris: Nathan.

Berstein, Serge et al. 1975. *Histoire. De la Révolution au monde d'aujourd'hui*. Paris: Hatier.

Bielefeldt-Schredelseker, Carola et al. 1992. *Spuren der Zeit 8*, Wien: E. Dorner.
Blonk, A. et al. 1969. *Hoofdwegen der geschiedenis II*, Groningen: Wolters-Noordhoff.
Borth, Wilhelm et al. 1988. *Zeiten und Menschen. Grundlagen und Entwicklungen der Gegenwart. Der Aufstieg der Supermächte und die Welt nach 1945*, Neue Ausgabe G, vol. 3. Paderborn: Schroedel.
Böttcher, Christina et al. 1998. *Geschichte Konkret 3. Ein Lern- und Arbeitsbuch*, Hannover: Schroedel.
Brière, Roger et al. 1980. *Histoire Géographie*. Paris: Librairie istra.
Brignon, Jean et al. 1980. *Histoire – Géographie classe de 3e*. Paris: Hatier.
Brucker, Ambros et al. 1991. *Europa. Raumnutzung, Raumstrukturen und Verflechtungen. Orbis. Erdkunde für die Oberstufe*. München: Oldenbourg.
Bundesministerium für Vertriebene. 1955–1961. *Dokumentation der Vertreibung der Deutschen aus Ost-Mitteleuropa*, ed. Theodor Schieder et al. 8 vols. Bonn: Bundesministerium des Inneren.
Caspritz, C. et al. 1989. *Erdkunde. Ausgabe G, Rheinland-Pfalz, Saarland*, vol. 3. Braunschweig: Westermann.
David, Ferré and Poitevin. 1953. *Histoire. Les grandes faits de la vie des français*. Paris: Fernand Nathan, Éditeur.
De Haas, G. 1957. *Vaderlandse geschiedenis*, Groningen and Djakarta: J.B. Wolters.
Désire, E.P. 1980. *Espaces & Civilisations*. Paris: Librairie Classique Eugène Belin.
Deuringer, Lorenz. 1993. *Fundamente. Jahrgangsstufe 11. Deutschland*. Stuttgart: Klett/Perthes.
Diercke Weltatlas. 1957. Braunschweig: Westermann.
———— 1964. Braunschweig: Westermann.
———— 1971. Braunschweig: Westermann.
Donk, Ronald et al. 1990. *Vragen aan de geschiedenis*. Groningen: Wolters-Noordhoff.
Dupaquier, J. and P. Guiot. 1971. *Géographie. L'Afrique*. Paris and Montréal: Bordas.
Feldmeier, Franz et. al. 1987. *Grundkurs Geschichte*, vol. 4, Viertes Kurshalbjahr. Freising: Stark-Verlag.
Fink, Hans-Georg et al. 1997. *Geschichte kennen und verstehen*. München: Oldenbourg.
Fontaine, P. 1965. *Van oermens tot wereldburger. Vierde deel B. De nieuwste geschiedenis, van 1789 tot heden*. 's Hertogenbosch: L.C.G. Malmberg.
François, Denis et al. 1983. *Histoire classes terminales*. Paris: Nouvelle Collection Fernand Nathan.
François, Josette et al. 1981. *Histoire – Géographie*. Paris: Nouvelle Collection Fernand Nathan.
Franze, Manfred et al. 1994. *Geschichte für Gymnasien*. München: Oldenbourg.
Friedrich, Jörg. 2002. *Der Brand. Deutschland im Bombenkrieg 1940–1945*. Berlin: Propyläen.
Froment, R. et al. 1980. *Histoire Géographie. Nouveau programme*. Paris: Bordas.
Fure, Jorunn Sem. 2001. "Gutes Zuhause, aber keine Heimat." War and Post-war Experience, Narrative Strategies and Memory of the German Expellees from the Eastern German Provinces after 1945. Ph.D. diss. University of Bergen.
Gaigl, Karl, and Walter Jahn. 1978. *Staat, Raum und Bevölkerung*. München: Blutenburg Schöningh.
Glaß-Bernert, Claudia et al. 1988. *Geschichte für morgen. Arbeitsbuch für bayerische Hauptschulen*, 9. Jahrgangsstufe. Frankfurt am Main: Hirschgraben.
Geschichte 10, 1960. Berlin: Volk und Wissen.
Geschichte 10, 1964. Berlin: Volk und Wissen.
Geschichte 9, 1984. Berlin: Volk und Wissen.
Geschichte 10, 1984. Berlin: Volk und Wissen.

Geschichte 9, 1988. Berlin: Volk und Wissen.

Grosche, Heinz et al. 1984. *Fragen an die Geschichte. Geschichtliches Arbeitsbuch für Sekundarstufe I. Die Welt im 20. Jahrhundert*, vol. 4, 4th ed. Frankfurt am Main: Hirschgraben.

Hahn, Roland et al. 1984. *Deutschland*. Braunschweig: Westermann.

Heilsberg, Franz and Friedrich Korger. 1953. *Lehrbuch der Geschichte für die Oberstufe der Mittelschulen*, vol. 4. Vienna: Hölder-Pichler-Tempsky/Ed. Hölzer/Österreichischer Bundesverlag.

Heilsberg, Franz and Friedrich Korger. 1965. *Lehrbuch der Geschichte für die Oberstufe der allgemeinbildenden höheren Schulen*, vol. 4. Vienna: Hölder-Pichler-Tempsky/ Ed. Hölzer/Österreichischer Bundesverlag für Unterricht. Wissenschaft und Kunst.

Histoire Géographie. 1980. Paris: Librairie Dealgrave.

Höpken, Wolfgang. 2002. Reconciliation through Textbooks: The German-Polish Experience, Paper delivered at the Stockholm International Forum on Truth, Justice and Reconciliation, Stockholm http://www.stockholmforum.com/dynamaster/file_archive/020423/93ff0c022477a7bbccc8caa7a9ffb259/hopken.pdf.

Hughes, Michael L. 2000. "'Through No Fault of Our Own': West Germans Remember Their War Losses." *German History*, vol. 18, 193–213.

Immerzeel, Bert et al. 1995. *Historia*. Utrecht: Meulenhoff Educatief.

Jordi, Jean-Jacques. 1993. *De l'exode à l'exil. Répatriés et pieds-noirs en France. L'exemple Marseillais, 1954–1992*. Paris: L'Harmattan.

——— 1995. *1962, l'arrivée des Pieds-noirs*. Paris: Autrement.

Kirchhoff, Hans Georg et al. 1992, *Geschichte und Gegenwart. Arbeitsbuch Geschichte. Ausgabe A. Band 5. Vom Ende des Zweiten Weltkrieges bis zur Gegenwart*. Paderborn: Schroedel.

Lambin, Jean-Michel et al. 1989. *histoire/géographie*. Paris: Hachettes Collèges.

Lehrbuch für den Geschichtsunterricht. 8. Schuljahr. 1955. Leipzig: Volk und Wissen.

Miège, Jean-Louis. 1973. *Expansion européenne et décolonisation de 1870 à nos jours*. Paris: Presses Université de France.

Milza, Pierre et al. 1975. *Histoire. De la Révolution au monde d'aujourd'hui*. Paris: Fernand Nathan-Éditeur.

Moeller, Robert G. 2001. *War Stories: The Search for a Usable Past in the Federal Republic of Germany*. Berkeley and Los Angeles: University of California Press.

Münz, Rainer and Rainer Ohliger. 1998. "Vergessene Deutsche – Erinnerte Deutsche: Flüchtlinge, Vertriebene, Aussiedler." *Transit: Europäische Revue*, vol. 15, 141–57.

——— 1998. "Long-Distance Citizens: Ethnic Germans and their Immigration to Germany. " In *Paths to Inclusion: The Integration of Migrants in the United States and Germany*, eds. Peter Schuck and Rainer Münz. Providence: Berghahn Books: 155–201.

Neueste Zeit. 1957. Berlin: Volk und Wissen.

Perez, Yves et al. 1971. *Histoire. L'Epoque contemporaine*. Paris: Mason et Cie.

Puls, Willi Walter, and Hans Lippold. 1959. *Wirtschafts- und Kulturgeographie Deutschlands. Mensch und Erde*. Frankfurt am Main: Diesterweg.

Schäfer, Wilhelm et al. 1972. *Erdkunde. Oberstufe. Gesamtband*. Paderborn: Schöningh.

Schäfer, Wilhelm et al. 1979. *Erdkunde. Oberstufe. Gesamtband*. Paderborn: Schöningh.

Schultze, Arnold et al. 1979. *Geographie 7.–9. Schuljahr*. Stuttgart: Klett.

Staatsbürgerkunde 7. 1989. Berlin: Volk und Wissen.

Todorova, Maria. 1997. *Imagining the Balkans*. Oxford: Oxford University Press.

Weber, Eugen Joseph. 1976. *Peasants into Frenchmen. The Modernization of Rural France, 1870–1914*, Stanford: Stanford University Press.

Willems, Wim. 1999. *No Sheltering Sky. Migrant Identities of the Dutch Nationals from Indonesia*, Amsterdam: IMES Amsterdam, manuscript.

Willems, Wim and Leo Lucassen, eds. 1994. *Het onbekende vaderland. De repatriëring van Indische Nederlanders (1946–1964)*. 's Gravenhage: Sdu Uitgeverij Koninginnegracht.

Chapter 3

❖─────

What Counts as History and How Much Does History Count? The Case of French Secondary Education

Jacques E.C. Hymans

World Society and National States

Sociology's world society school argues that global cultural and associational processes promote isomorphic nation-state rationalization in line with universally unquestioned "world models" of development and democratic justice (Meyer et al. 1997). The case of educational curricula has proven one of the most stunning confirmations of the power of world models (Meyer et al. 1992). In spite of major variations in levels of development, cultural heritage, and political ideology, nation-states around the world have chosen to structure students' school days in strikingly similar ways. World models have also exerted a profound impact on the nature of particular academic disciplines such as history. In their study of "what counts as history" in university curricula around the world over the entire twentieth century, Frank et al. (2000: 29–53) find that the history discipline has undergone a steady *social-scientization* (an increasing focus on contemporary history and on society as opposed to the state) and a steady *globalization* (an increasing focus on peripheral regions, transnational processes, and supranational units).

On the topic of education as on others, the world society approach has tended to focus on establishing correlations, instead of using case-study methods to trace the precise ways in which free-floating world models are connected to actual national educational practices.[1] Case study methods are particularly valuable for understanding the evolution of history teaching in advanced countries, as the world history school's expectations for such countries are ambiguous. On the one hand, advanced countries have the resources and the international legitimacy to set educational trends and might therefore be expected to be ahead of the world society curve (Meyer et al. 1992). On the other hand, the same countries tend to have entrenched educational professions and ideologies that can best resist the changes that world society demands (ibid). How do these tendencies interact, and in what contexts does one outweigh the other?

This chapter attempts to answer these questions in the case of French secondary school history education. It presents evidence that the basic content of French history curricula and schoolbooks has been rather slow to evolve toward the predominant world model. It then digs deeper into French educational practice as opposed to official policy preferences, through a study of 100 years of essay questions from the history entrance exam to the Ecole Normale Supérieure (ENS), the most academically prestigious of France's elite *grandes écoles*. The slow evolution in the content of these questions generally parallels that of the secondary curricula. Finally, the chapter attempts to find clues to the persistence of French distinctiveness through a study of the largely stillborn history curriculum reform effort of the 1950s. This study suggests a hypothesis for further testing: that the 1958 return to power of Charles de Gaulle renewed the domestic legitimacy of the secondary school history teachers' traditional, "Jacobin" vision of history against the social-scientizing, globalizing push of the *Annales* school.[2]

Should France have been the Engine or Caboose of History Curriculum Change?

When we add the national level of ideas and institutions to the basic world society framework, the expected evolution of the French secondary school history curriculum becomes ambiguous.

From one perspective, France appears a perfect candidate for a vanguard role in the social-scientization and globalization of history education. Intellectually, France has been at the forefront of the evolution of the discipline of history since at least Jules Michelet. More recently, it was the French *Annales* school in history that did much to initiate the worldwide trends toward social-scientization and globalization. If French historians had such an impact on world society, one might expect them to have had at least as much influence on French society. Moreover, institutionally France is the ideal-typical strong state, with a tradition of professional and technocratic state administration and intense centralization of policy making, not least in the education field.[3] All of these factors would seem to provide a perfect context for the clear reception and quick implementation of world norms.[4]

On the other hand, other general characteristics of the French nation-state might lead it to resist evolving world society norms of history. On the level of ideas, a national, "Jacobin" vision of history has long been seen as a crucial support to the French republic's legitimacy claims.[5] Indeed, the study of history (along with the French language) was the key to Jules Ferry's dramatic drive to use universal, free, and compulsory education to produce a unified, rational, secular, and republican citizenry.[6] One might therefore expect French politicians, if not technocrats, to resist any shift away from this tradition. Moreover, on the level of institutions, the venerable age of history teaching and of history teachers' associations in France—the professional *Société des Professeurs d'Histoire et de Géographie* [History and Geography Teachers' Society] was founded in 1910—might be expected to contribute to a certain inertia. And more broadly, the same strong state/weak society mix that can lead to rapid and major shifts in policy can also diminish the effects of world models if the state opposes them.

Both hypotheses are convincing: which is right? It is time to turn to a description of the actual evolution of "what counts as history" in France. I begin with some evidence from secondary school curricula and textbooks.

French Secondary School History Curricula and Textbooks: *plus ça change…*

In this section I offer some evidence from France on the four main world society expectations given above: increasing focus on contemporary history; increasing focus on "social" rather than "political" topics, increasing focus on "peripheral" regions, and increasing focus on transnational processes and supranational units. I focus in particular on the history "*programmes*" [curricula] that are produced by the Ministry of Education for general (as opposed to technical) secondary schools.[7] I also present some evidence from a close analysis of Hachette's *Malet-Isaac* series of textbooks (see Hymans 1998), which held a market position that approached monopoly for most of its run from the 1920s to the early 1960s.[8]

First of all, it is important to note that in France, unlike many other countries (Meyer et al. 1992: 124–38), the subject "social studies" has not eclipsed the subjects "history and geography" as the primary mechanism introducing secondary school students to the human sciences.[9] Most students in France are currently required to study three hours per week of history, geography, and civics, rather than "social studies," in the early secondary years from *sixième* to *seconde*. Then, for *première* and *terminale,* their last two years of secondary education, students can choose one of three different tracks: "literary," "scientific," or "economic and social." In the first two, again only history and geography are required: four weekly hours for both years of the literary track, and 2.5 and then 2 weekly hours for the scientific track. The economic and social track is the only one in which "economic and social sciences" is required subject matter, accounting respectively for four and five hours in *première* and *terminale.* But this requirement is in addition to, not instead of, four hours of history and geography both years.

So overall, it is fair to say that what French students learn in school about history, they learn in history class. On the other hand, the total time allotted to the study of history in French schools has declined substantially over the past decades. It is important to ask not only "what counts as history" but also "how much history counts" among national educational priorities. Indeed, the end of the chapter puts forth the hypothesis that the centrality of history in French education has waned in part as a *consequence* of the history teachers' failure to maintain the discipline's fit with world models. But first it is necessary to make the case that French history education is indeed a laggard in terms of its acceptance of these world models.

History: How Contemporary?

The first finding of the world society school is that there has been a shift toward contemporary history and away from earlier periods. Is this true of the history taught in French secondary schools? On the evidence of the *programmes*, it is not.[10] For most of the twentieth century, the French *programmes* simply asked students to plod their way chronologically through the story of civilization. Thus Ancient Egypt, Greece, and Rome, and the beginnings of Christianity were covered in *sixième* and never again, and by *terminale* the students would finally arrive at the contemporary era. French history education's obsession with maintaining chronology—a topic to which I will return below in my discussion of the attempted reforms of the 1950s—may have been "old-fashioned," but in one sense it led to a "progressive" result. Younger students learned about classical and medieval history too early in their schooling for these topics to be covered with any sophistication. The more mature students focused uniquely on the modern and contemporary periods.[11] By contrast, starting with the *programmes* of 1995 there was a break with this tradition of respect for chronology (*Bulletin Officiel de l'Education Nationale* 1995). Since then, after first covering the entire history of the world chronologically between *sixième* and *troisième*, students in *seconde* are treated to a "greatest historical hits" tour that covers fifth century Athens, the birth of Christianity, and the Mediterranean of the twelfth century, as well as the Renaissance, the French Revolution, and Europe in the first half of the nineteenth century. Finally, *première* and *terminale* go back over the contemporary period (the mid-19th century to the present).[12] In short, because of the decision to break with the traditional respect for chronology, for the first time students are being exposed to ancient and medieval history in *seconde*, part of the intellectually weightier *deuxième cycle*. So although today's French secondary school history curricula are certainly very heavily weighted toward contemporary issues as the world-society school would expect, the contemporary bias is arguably less severe than it was fifty years ago. Thus France clearly bucks the world trend on this dimension.

Political versus Social History

The second world society finding is that "political" history (broadly construed to include diplomatic and military history) has been eclipsed by "social" history (broadly construed to include economic and cultural history). Is this true for secondary education in France? The French *programmes* of today do offer significantly more emphasis on social history than was the case in the early twentieth century. The *programmes* of the late 1940s, for instance, still offered little respite from the traditional steady diet of war, revolution, and political institutions. But a quite strongly social dimension was already instituted beginning in the mid-1950s, and the more recent *programmes* have in fact not moved very far beyond those landmark reforms.

It is difficult to determine precisely the balance between "political" and "social" topics in today's history classrooms, because much depends on the preferences of individual instructors. However, we can make some general assessments from the *programmes'* descriptions of the broad teaching units. On this evidence political topics appear still to have the upper hand in French secondary school history education. For instance, in *collège* (from *sixième* to *troisième*), the balance between "political" and "social" topics is roughly as follows. In *sixième* the balance of time is roughly two-thirds on the political side (e.g., "Alexander the Great"), versus one-third on the social side (e.g., "The Beginnings of Christianity"). In *cinquième*, the balance of time is roughly one-half on the political side (e.g., "The French Kingdom of the 16th Century: the Difficult Affirmation of Royal Authority") and one-half for the social side (e.g., "Humanism, Renaissance, Reforms"). In *quatrième*, the balance of time is roughly three-quarters on the political side (e.g., "The Absolute Monarchy in France") and one-quarter on the social side (e.g., "The Industrial Age"). Finally, in troisième the balance of time is also roughly three-quarters on the political side (e.g., "The Second World War") and one-quarter on the social side (e.g., "Economic Growth, Demographic Evolution and their Social and Cultural Consequences").[13]

The fact that France appears to be lagging behind world trends on this indicator is surprising. As early as the 1930s, French history teachers and textbook authors were going beyond the official *programmes* to inject a strong socioeconomic dimension into the study of history. The most spectacular example of this is the 1930 edition of the Malet-Isaac *Histoire Contemporaine* (Malet, Isaac et al., 1930), written for the final year of high school. Jules Isaac chose to open that book with a major chapter on the economic and technological revolutions of the twentieth century, explaining in the preface, "It may surprise to find the last volume of the *Cours* (course of study) begin with a chapter that is not mentioned in the *programme*. But it seemed to me impossible, in discussing contemporary history, to be silent on the capital fact that dominates it and all of its avenues: that is the economic revolution, which is itself the product of scientific progress" (ibid.: vii). Isaac's focus on socioeconomic factors was not limited to that first chapter, but rather was carried throughout his books, increasingly so in later editions.[14] As was mentioned above, in the 1950s the ministry's *programmes* finally caught up with the teachers and textbook authors. But subsequently this movement slowed.

The West versus the Rest

The third finding of the world society school is that there has been a shift away from a focus on the West and toward other world regions. Does French secondary school history education reflect this trend? As a former colonial empire with continuing world responsibilities and a major immigrant population, one might expect France to be far ahead of the curve in terms of the globalization of history taught in schools. But in fact, one of the remarkable aspects of French secondary school history is how little it has opened up to the world beyond the West.

In the currently operative *programmes*, in *sixième* we find the same ancient civilizations (Ancient Egypt, Biblical peoples and the origins of Christianity, Greece, and Rome) that have been covered in that class for decades. This list has not expanded to include, for instance, ancient pre-Colombian or Chinese civilizations. *Cinquième* is almost entirely devoted to European history through the Renaissance, with only a brief excursion to the Muslim world. *Quatrième* and *première* concentrate on European history in modern times, only taking in other world areas as part of the history of European imperialism. *Troisième* and *terminale* do devote about one third of the total time to the study of broad world trends since 1945, but the bulk of their focus is on twentieth century Europe and North America. Finally, the whirlwind "greatest hits" tour of *seconde*, described previously, includes a doff of the cap to Braudel ("The Mediterranean in the Twelfth Century") but otherwise has a traditional Eurocentric focus. In sum, French students, almost as much as in 1920, study European and not world history.

The most marked shift in emphasis over time has been the greater attention paid to the United States. This increase was already occurring during the lifetime of the Malet-Isaac series. A laborious paragraph-by-paragraph count of the number of references to the U.S. shows that such references as a percentage of total references to external actors doubled from 5 percent in the 1920s Malet-Isaac edition to 10 percent in the 1960s edition.[15] It is hard to make such precise comparisons across different textbook series, but to all appearances the focus on the U.S. has continued to increase in recent decades. This suggests that it is not just geographical proximity, but also perception of power that determines the level of focus on various external actors. If the French books were and still are largely Eurocentric, it is not simply because France happens to be located in the continent of Europe, but also because world power has been historically focused in Europe. Again, as will be detailed below, the "Braudelian" reform effort of the 1950s would have radically changed this state of affairs, but the effort was snuffed out.

National versus Supranational Frames

The final general finding of the world society school is the growing use of transnational and supranational frames to analyze the course of events. In the European Union context, clearly the most interesting question under this heading is the extent to which national educational systems are beginning to move beyond the national to a European frame. Since the implementation of the 1995 *programmes*, French secondary curricula have, indeed, very much begun to reflect this. In particular, Europe is the dominant frame of reference in *quatrième*, which covers the period from the seventeenth century to 1914. After *quatrième*, the European frame remains fairly prominent. For instance, the *programme* for *terminale* that goes into effect in the fall of 2004 is divided into three sections: the world (22 hours), Europe (10 hours), and France (18 hours). Clearly, then, Europe is not dominant, but it is much more present than it was in earlier decades.

Do these increasingly "European" *programmes* reflect a mere relabeling, or do they really suggest some significant change in the way that history is conceived and taught? The evidence suggests the former rather than the latter. For instance, in the apparently highly "European" *quatrième*, one of the main topics is the "Revolutionary Period, 1789–1815." Under this seemingly denationalized heading, however, we find the traditional French concern with the French Revolution (which is allotted 7–8 hours of the 9–10 total hours for this unit). Even a "mere relabeling" has significance, of course, in that it demonstrates how apologetic a European state must be nowadays when it chooses to focus on national history. Nevertheless, French secondary education seems not to have pushed beyond relabeling.[16] Such is the conclusion of a report on "Europe in the Teaching of History, Geography and Civic Education" (Inspectorate-General of the Ministry of Education 2000). Indeed, not only does the report strongly argue that history education's discursive turn to Europe has so far reflected mere "intentions that cost nothing"; it also does not view this as problematic. For the report stresses that from a political and a scientific perspective, the jury is still out on the reality of "Europe," and therefore teachers cannot be criticized for showing a reluctance to reorient their teaching around it. In sum, the French state is clearly not pushing "Europe" on sullenly national-minded teachers. Rather, there is a minor rhetorical shift that seems to be having little effect on the ground.

The Ecole Normale Supérieure Concours

The previous section demonstrated that progress toward adoption of world models in French secondary school curricula has been sluggish. But I have previously indicated that history teaching, even in France, does not necessarily reflect the diktat of the education ministry. Textbook writers and individual teachers choose to emphasize some subjects and to deemphasize others according to their tastes and to the tastes of the "market." Might it therefore be the case that while on the official level France is digging in its heels against the globalizing and social-scientizing world model of the history curriculum, inside actual classrooms this model is nevertheless having a powerful effect on "what counts as history"—and would have a greater effect were it not for those bureaucrats?

To study the actual French practice of history teaching would require the use of anthropological techniques involving the close observation of individual classrooms. However, we can gain some insight into the mind of the French history profession by looking at the essay questions in history that are given in the written entrance exam [*concours*] for the most academically prestigious undergraduate institution in France, the *Ecole Normale Supérieure* (ENS) of the rue d'Ulm in Paris.[17] The questions for this exam are set by the exam "jury," typically made up of professors from the ENS and other ENS alumni who teach at prestigious academic institutions. Prospective candidates study in special preparatory classes (*classes préparatoires*) for two or more years after finishing high school to prepare themselves for the ENS exam. The course of study for the *classes préparatoires* is driven entirely by the expectations of what will be asked in the exam. These expectations are based on the vague *programme* set by the ENS—not the Ministry of Education. Since 1992 that *programme* for the subject of history has been "France since 1848, and the US, USSR, China, and Germany since 1918."[18] Within those broad parameters, any question is fair game.

In short, looking at ENS exam questions allows us a separate test of the power of world models in France. Whereas the content of secondary school curricula and textbooks is heavily dependent on education bureaucrats, the ENS *concours* is largely independent of such interference. So if the evidence from the *concours* parallels that from secondary curricula and textbooks, this would suggest that the resistance to world models in history education is shared both by French educators and by the state.[19]

At the ENS library I located approximately 100 years of ENS exam questions: from 1852–1860 and from 1891–1988, with only eight missing years over that latter time span. Prof. Gilles Pécout of the ENS also provided me with the questions from the years 1992–2003. There is one question for each year.[20] The exam questions are very broad and give little indication of how they should be analyzed by the student. Often the question is a mere statement of the historical event that the student is to discuss (sometimes a short list of key sub-topics is also offered). For instance, in 1894 the question was "The Congress of Vienna and its handiwork." In 2003 the question was "French society and economic growth from the end of the Second World War to the start of the 1980s." This limited data clearly does not allow us to perceive the evolution in standards for a good answer. But through it we can nevertheless develop a first-cut analysis of "what counts as history" at the ENS. I consider the same four hypotheses as in the previous section.

History: How Contemporary?

The first world society finding is that there is a shift toward contemporary history and away from ancient history. On the level of curricula and textbooks France seems to have resisted this trend to some extent. What about the ENS *concours*? I carried out a simple quantitative study of this issue. For each exam question I took the date the exam was given and subtracted it by the latest historical date the student was being asked to cover. For instance, in 1963 students were quizzed on "French Catholics under the Third Republic (1871–1914)." So in this case, there was a gap of 49 years between the exam date and the latest historical date covered by the exam (the interested reader can refer to the appendix for complete coding rules). Looking across all the exams, then, has there been a trend toward smaller gaps? Figure 3.1 answers this question.

Figure 3.1 *Average Difference in Years between Date Exam was given and latest Historical Date covered on Exam*

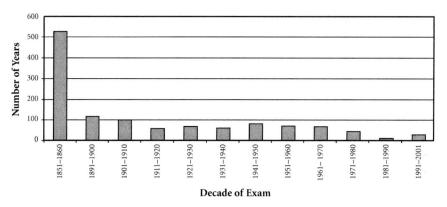

Data (count of questions): 1851–60: 8 (2 missing); 1891–1900: 8 (2 missing); 1901–10: 6 (4 missing); 1911–20: 9 (1 missing); 1921–30: 10 (0 missing); 1931–40: 9 (1 missing); 1941–50: 11 (1 extra: different questions for females and males in 1950); 1951–60: 11 (1 extra: different questions for females and males in 1951); 1961–70: 10 (0 missing); 1971–80: 10 (0 missing); 1981–1990: 8 (2 missing); 1991–2003: 12 (1 missing).

Source: Exam questions on file at the Bibliothèque des Lettres de l'Ecole Normale Supérieure, rue d'Ulm, and Prof. Gilles Pécout.

Figure 3.1 contains mixed support for the notion of a growing "contemporization" of the exam questions in recent decades. World society trends toward social-scientization and globalization should be most prominent since the Second World War. But this figure demonstrates that as far as the ENS *concours* go, the fields of ancient and medieval history had already died out *by 1900*. At no point since 1891 has an exam question covered the period before 1328, and at no point since 1897 has a question been given on the period before 1715. On the other hand, in support of the world society school, throughout the twentieth century there has been a continuing trend toward ever more contemporary questions. For instance, although even as early as the decade 1911–1920 80 percent of the questions already focused on the post-1789 period, not since 1977 has a question even reached back as far as 1789 (the question in that year was "Progress and problem of national unity in France 1789–1914"). Meanwhile, one has to go as far back as 1964 to find a question that actually focused on the revolutionary period (the question in that year was "Theory, utopia and realism in the work of the French Revolution 1789–1799"). In sum, although contemporization has been a reality for over a century, the shift toward the present has not abated. This is in line with current world models of what counts as history, and it stands in contrast to the continuing strong presence of antiquity in secondary school curricula.

Political versus Social History

The second world society finding is that there has been a shift from political to social topics as the focus of historical research and education. On the level of curricula and textbooks, France seems to have been a leader in this shift until the 1950s, but then progress in this direction slowed. What about the ENS *concours*? I have divided all exam questions into one of two categories, "political, diplomatic, and/or military history" on the one hand, and "social, economic, and/or cultural history" on the other. For instance, I count the 1941 exam question, "Characteristic traits of Napoleon III's foreign policy," in the former category, whereas I count the 1951 question, "Show how the economic evolution from 1850 to 1914 favored the development of cities in Western Europe," in the latter category (see appendix for complete coding rules). The results are summarized in Figure 3.2.

Figure 3.2 *"Social" versus "Political" Questions on Exams*

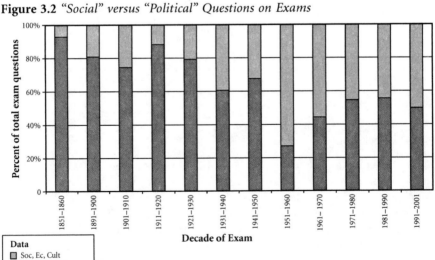

(**Data and sources:** see Figure 1)

As can be seen, the story of the ENS *concours* is quite parallel to the general story of French secondary school curricula and textbooks on this dimension. Questions covering social, economic, and/or cultural history arrived in abundance in the 1930s, accounting for approximately 40 percent of the total questions in that decade. There was another forward surge in the 1950s, with such questions accounting for nearly 75 percent of the total. But after that decade, political, diplomatic and/or military history staged a comeback. Since the 1970s, the exam questions have struck an approximately even balance between the two areas. The authors of the 1948 question "English power on the eve of 1914," would have been completely comfortable with the question selected for the 1993 *concours:* "The power of the United States in the world, 1945–1980."

It is certainly possible that the seeming similarity of the 1948 and 1993 questions is misleading, for the juries in those different decades may have had very different ideas of how best to analyze those questions. Ostensibly "political" topics may well require a more "social" analysis today than they did in 1948. But even if this is the case, the fact that about half the questions in the ENS *concours* focus on political history offers further evidence of France's resistance to world models.

The West versus the Rest

The third world society finding is that there is a shift away from a focus on the West and toward non-European peoples great and small. On the level of curricula and textbooks, France has not made such a shift. What about the ENS *concours*? I have surveyed all of the exam questions for whether their explicit references are limited to Europe and the US or whether they look beyond there to the rest of the world (see appendix for complete coding rules). The results are summarized in figure 3.3.

Figure 3.3. *Exam Questions Focusing on Europe/U.S. versus Questions Including the Rest of the World (ROW)*

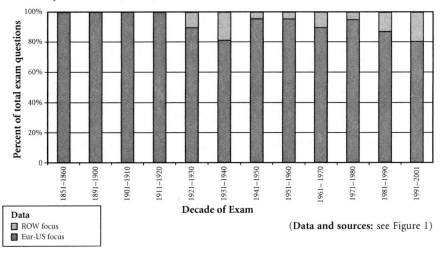

(**Data and sources:** see Figure 1)

This figure shows very clearly that just as in the case of curricula and text-books, countries dominated by people of European stock continue to serve as the focus of questions for the ENS *concours*. There has been, admittedly, some evolution in the last two decades toward a greater focus on the rest of the world, but this evolution has been quite timid. It is not too much to say that the *concours* are as Eurocentric today as they were in the 1930s. As noted previously, the broad *programme* set for the exam by the ENS focuses uniquely on great powers and includes only one non-white state, China. Unless that is changed, the Eurocentrism of the *concours* will persist.

National versus Supranational Frames

The final general finding of the world society school is the growing use of transnational and supranational frames in describing the course of events. In the cases of curricula and textbooks, France has taken only moderate steps to move beyond its traditional focus on the national framework. What about the ENS *concours*? To answer this question I have divided the relevant exam questions into two groups: those that focus exclusively on France, and those that do not focus exclusively on France. So, for example, the 1945 question "The Girondins," counts as focused exclusively on France, whereas the 1956 question, "National idea and national sentiment in France and Germany from 1848 to 1914," does not (see appendix for complete coding rules). The results are summarized in figure 3.4.

Figure 3.4 *Questions Focusing Exclusively on France versus Questions not Doing so*

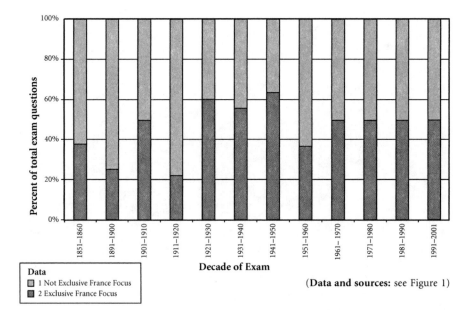

(**Data and sources:** see Figure 1)

This figure shows that the ENS *concours* have not tended to move away from the French national framework. Since the 1960s, the jury has been consistent in giving precisely 50 percent of the *concours* over to "Franco-French" questions. Indeed, purely French topics are more prominent now than they were in the decades leading up to World War I.

Nor has the *concours* jury begun to request that students apply a European frame of reference. Indeed, the last exam question to use the word "Europe" was in 1976 ("Public opinion in Europe 1914–1945: formation, expression, influence in international and internal relations"). Even in the few cases where the term "Europe" does appear, it is not clear that it represents anything more than a geographical expression. One can find the word "Europe" in the exam questions as early as 1854, probably not because the *concours* jury at that time was looking forward to supranational integration.

To summarize this section, in general the ENS *concours* appear even more resistant to contemporary world models than French secondary school curricula and textbooks. This indicates that if anything, the world society tide is being resisted in France even more by the history profession than by state elites. The evidence from this broad quantitative approach is reinforced by my case study of the 1950s efforts to reform the secondary school history curriculum, to which I now turn.

The 1950s Reforms and their Aftermath

This chapter has on a number of occasions made reference to a 1950s surge in French conformity to the worldwide social-scientization and globalization of history teaching—a surge that subsequently faltered. What happened? Who were the actors for and against these trends, and why did the forces favoring the world models stall in France? A historical study of the reform efforts of that era, seen through the lens of the journal of the professional Société des Professeurs d'Histoire et de Géographie (henceforth SPHG) can shed some light on these questions.

As early as 1951, a strong movement was afoot in the Ministry of Education to promote an evolution of secondary school history toward the new world model promulgated internationally by the United Nations Educational, Scientific, and Cultural Organization (UNESCO) and at home by the *Annales* school and its most prominent exponent, Fernand Braudel.[21] This move was strongly opposed by the legendary textbook author Jules Isaac. Isaac warned in an open letter to the SPHG—of which he was one of the founding members and a permanent member of the executive committee—against any move away from the traditional narrative history, known as *histoire événementielle*. Strict adherence to the chronology of historical events was, in his eyes, the "backbone" of history teaching, "all that gives it movement and life" (*Bulletin* 1951: 216–19). To dilute this with the proposed focus on "civilizations" in the upper grades, Isaac warned, would undermine the teaching of French political history and even the jewel in the crown, the history of the French Revolution: "The role, the place of the French Revolution must not in any way be diminished. The event—[and especially] *that* event—must remain at the core of our teaching. It is complex, it is turbulent and tragic; one cannot simplify it excessively without running the risk that the students will understand nothing and retain nothing" (ibid: 219). In sum, in this letter, Isaac neatly summarized the two rallying cries—to maintain the principle of chronology and to produce a patriotic and republican citizenry—that would be central to the actions of the SPHG in the 1950s and 1960s, and even into the 1990s.[22] He also identified the key republican symbol or *lieu de mémoire* [site of memory] that the SPHG would invoke to defend its position: the teaching of the French Revolution.

Despite Isaac's early objection, the ministerial intention to introduce the study of "civilizations" into French secondary education was concretized in a ministerial draft for a new history *programme*, sent to the SPHG for comment in November, 1955 (*Bulletin* 1955: 138). This draft—already a big step away from Braudel's much grander initial vision—envisaged devoting *seconde* to a social-scientized and globalized study of great world "civilizations." The other grades would remain focused on the traditional chronological sweep from Greece and Rome to the present day. This idea received a negative reception from the SPHG. Its members countered with three alternatives, authored by professors Schwab, Marc-Bonnet, and Alba (*Bulletin* 1956: 167–76). The Schwab project was merely cute—it said, in essence, that we will teach your civilizations if you give us a bigger share of classroom hours. The Marc-Bonnet project admitted the utility of a focus on "civilizations" but worried about the violation of the principle of chronology. It therefore proposed a strange hybrid between the two, which would have undoubtedly left students reeling had it ever been inflicted on them. The Alba project—the best reflection of the weight of SPHG opinion—flatly rejected the idea of studying "civilizations." After first tarring the proposal as being essentially a return to the failed Vichy France curriculum reform project of 1941, Alba (who was one of Isaac's coauthors) offered a stirring defense of the principle of chronology. In particular, Alba wrote, the very juncture at which the ministry was proposing to introduce the study of "civilizations" was the point of inflection of the whole curriculum—the study of the French Revolution. Alba wrote:

> I said that [in the ministry's proposals] the principle of historical continuity is broken and one must, I think, insist on this important fact. Having arrived, at the end of *troisième*, at the convocation of the *Etats généraux* [Estates General], the student will not study that history until fifteen months later, after first going backward several millenniums. What will he retain of the long eighteenth century prelude when he studies the Revolution? (*Bulletin* 1956: 170)

By 1957, a compromise had been reached (*Bulletin* 1957: 131–32). The study of "civilizations" was to be included in the *programme* but limited to the last two trimesters of *terminale,* too late to be included as a topic for the *baccalauréat* (and besides that, consigned to a period in which most students could be expected to have what Americans call "senioritis"). As a parting shot, to Braudel's great consternation the SPHG annual assembly unanimously approved Alba's proposal that the study of "civilizations" be limited to a "precise historical time period, from 1914 to the present" (ibid.).[23]

The new *programmes* for *terminale* were published in the ministerial *arrêté* [order] of 9 June 1959 (*HOPI* 1959: 11). One trimester would be devoted to the "Western" civilization and one to the "European Communist" civilization; the other trimester would cover "the Muslim world," "the world of the Indian and the Pacific Oceans," and "the black African world." Partial as it was, the reform represented a beachhead that reformers expected to expand throughout the curriculum. And it had one quite dramatic, immediate, practical consequence, which was to sound the death knell for the long-dominant "traditionalist" history textbook series: Hachette's Malet-Isaac. Jules Isaac was too old to undertake personally such a significant revision as demanded by the reforms, and his editor at Hachette told him that, in any case, times were changing and the market was demanding a fresh approach.[24] Braudel himself jumped into the void, penning a twelfth-grade text, but it failed to win much market share and was finally remaindered in 1970 (Daix 1995: 350).[25]

In fact, Braudel's personal failure mirrored the broader failure of his reform vision. A notable change in 1965 was the deleting of the black African world (as well as Indonesia, Indochina, and Madagascar) from the study of "civilizations" in *terminale* (*HOPI* 1965: 61). Braudel was livid about this: "In the middle of decolonization, when the new independent states tried, not without courage, to write their own history, an *arrêté* eliminated purely and simply the African world" (Braudel 1987, cited in Daix: 349). The real disappointment for Braudel, however, was not this minor setback, but rather the more general failure of social-scientizing and globalizing history to make a more profound penetration into the curriculum. The proponents of the old chronological and national vision had been able to contain these newfangled notions to the last two trimesters of the twelfth grade. It was only with the 1995 *programmes* that a semblance of the original 1955 proposal for *seconde* was implemented. Why did the reformers' momentum evaporate in the late 1950s?

The obvious hypothesis that presents itself is that the reform momentum was stopped by the return to power of Charles de Gaulle and the regime change to the Fifth Republic in 1958. This hypothesis, which certainly requires further research to be confirmed, would run as follows. While Braudel was clearly important in providing the intellectual framework for the

1950s reform effort, the real powers pushing the effort were the state technocrats, who undoubtedly were also heavily influenced by the world society through such mechanisms as UNESCO and Council of Europe education conferences (Schüddekopf et al. 1967). These technocrats were in the drivers' seat in the fractious and unstable parliamentary system of the Fourth Republic.[26] In such an institutional framework, the generally Jacobin teaching corps could not rely on its natural allies, republican politicians, to provide much political heft against the technocratic carriers of the new world model of history education. But the political balance of power was altered by the Fifth Republic's return to a strong presidency and more stable parliaments under de Gaulle. The technocrats' political chiefs were once again their masters. In addition, de Gaulle himself incessantly articulated the traditionalist narrative of the French Republic's distinctiveness and destiny (Hoffmann and Hoffmann 1973: 63–70). A powerful alliance with the traditionalist *professeurs* was in the cards, and therefore by the early 1960s the technocratic momentum on curricular reform had been stopped.

But the Fifth Republic technocrats have taken their pound of flesh nonetheless, by drastically cutting the amount of time dedicated to the teaching of history. It is not so much in "what counts as history" as in "how much history counts" that we see the real impact of world models on the French case. History and geography have ceded ground to more "useful" skills, especially in math and science. As mentioned previously, repeated reforms have significantly reduced the traditional four classroom hours per week devoted to history and geography. The most striking case is the "scientific" track in *première* and *terminale,* which grant the subjects only 2.5 and 2 hours per week respectively. For scholarly observers of the Fifth Republic, this paradoxical mix of a fierce rhetorical maintenance of old traditions combined with a gradual undermining of their real place in French society is an old story. The Gaullist state's fervent desire to protect the core elements of French national self-definition led into a frightened chase after the saviors of science and technology, which eventually became in fact more central to French reality than the increasingly hollow rhetoric commemorating the revolutionary and republican past. As Philip Cerny (1980: 272) has written: "[De Gaulle] industrialized France while arguing the evils of machine civilization. He presided over an era which effectively fitted France for participation in the interdependent world of advanced industrial societies, while calling for national pride and consciousness." This Gaullist paradox is all too evident in the fate of the discipline of history. History may still be the monarch of the human sciences in France, but it rules a vastly diminished kingdom.

Appendix: Coding Rules for Figures 3.1–3.4

Figure 3.1 Average Difference between Date Exam Was Given and Latest Historical Date Covered on Exam

How far back do exam questions look?
1. Assume each exam question to be temporally bounded. First look for explicit bounds (e.g., the 1895 question "Religion in Holland 1648–1713").
2. If there are none, then some interpolation is necessary. If a group or individual is listed, their birth and death dates may be taken as the temporal bounds. For instance, the 1944 question "Portrait of Victorian England," can be said to end with the death of Queen Victoria in 1901. If the end date of a question seems open ended, for instance the 1987 question "French and Germans facing peace and war from the 1920s to our times," then the end date is the date of the exam (1987 in this case).
3. Having constructed the data base, take the date of the exam and subtract it by the latest date covered in the exam question. Then group these by decade and calculate the means.

Figure 3.2 "Social" versus "Political" Questions on Exams

Proportions of exam questions by issue area.
1. Look for keywords to code the questions as "political/diplomatic/military" or "social/economic/cultural." Keywords indicating a "political/diplomatic/military" focus include references to states, empires (including decolonization), state institutions, political parties, wars, revolutions, foreign policy, domestic policy, kings, politicians, state bureaucrats. Keywords indicating a "social/economic/cultural" focus include references to religion, the Church, social classes and relations (including their "revolutionary potential"), high and low culture, ideas and ideologies (including political ones), trade and commerce, and socioeconomic "development."
2. For each exam question, assign one point to either "political-diplomatic-military" or "social/economic/cultural" category. In some cases the vagueness or complexity of the question makes it difficult to assign it to one or the other category. In such cases, give a half-credit to each.
3. Having constructed the data base, group it by decade and calculate the means.

Figure 3.3 Exam Questions Focusing on Europe/U.S. versus Questions Including the Rest of World (ROW)

Proportions of exam questions by geographical placement.
1. Assume that every question has a definite geographical focus. Look for explicit mentions of geographical entities or their inhabitants (e.g., reference to "Girondins" counts as a reference to France).

2. The category "Europe-US" includes all of geographical Europe, Russia and the Soviet Union, and North America. The category "Rest of World" includes all other regions and the world taken as a whole.

3. References to broader geographical entities than nations or states are counted only if they are more than mere foils for the primary focus of the question. For instance, there are two such entities (West and Far East) in the 1954 question "Reciprocal influence of the civilizations of the West and the Far East," but only one (USSR) in the 1985 question, "Strategy of the Soviet Union facing the outside world."

4. For each exam question, count the mentions of the various geographical entities. Then for each question, divide 1 point between "Europe-US" and "Rest of World" according to the balance of explicit mentions. So, for instance, for the 1954 question, 0.5 points would be assigned to each category, whereas for the 1985 question, 1 full point would be assigned to the "Europe-US" category.

5. Having constructed the data base, group it by decade and calculate the means.

Figure 3.4 Questions Focusing Exclusively on France versus Questions not Doing so

1. As for Figure 3.3, assume that every question has a geographical focus. If only France or its inhabitants are explicitly mentioned, then assign a score of 0. If areas or inhabitants from outside France are mentioned, assign a score of 1. The only exception to this is questions relating exclusively to the French empire prior to decolonization, which receive a score of 0 (N.B. this exception turned out to have almost no effect on the overall results).

2. For instance, the 1942 question "Evolution of the Napoleonic Regime in France from 1799–1814" receives a score of 0, but the 1987 question "French and Germans facing peace and war from the 1920s to our times" receives a score of 1.

3. Having constructed the data base, group it by decade and calculate the means.

Notes

Thanks to Gilles Pécout for research guidance and for locating recent ENS exam questions. Thanks also to Ange Ansour, David Frank, Rieko Kage, Tomila Lankina, Thomas Lienhard, John Meyer, Sylvain Perdigon, Francisco Ramirez, Jeremi Suri, the editors of this volume, and the other participants at the conference on "Teaching Europe," European University Institute, Florence, 15–16 June 2001, for comments on earlier drafts of this chapter.

1. An exception is Yasemin Nuhoğlu Soysal (1998:53–61). She argues that the unique German historical experience, particularly the "collective guilt" over the Nazi period, combined with domestic corporatist educational structures can explain why Germany has been so much in favor of the social-scientizing and globalizing world model of history education.
2. The *Annales* school of historiography emerged in mid-twentieth century France. As Michael Harsgor puts it, the *Annales* approach enshrined a "secular trinity of seri-alism, structuralism, and functionalism" (Harsgor, 1978: 3).
3. On the notion of strong and weak states and societies, see Katzenstein (1978).
4. In general, the world society school argues that states should generally be more "progressive" than societies because of the material and normative pressure placed on them by the anarchic nature of the international system. See Meyer et al. (1997: 163–64).
5. For more on the persistence of Jacobinism in the French study of history, see Jean-Pierre Rioux (1987: 195–212).
6. For a panoramic view of French educational history, see Prost (1968).
7. It is true that Frank et al.'s "What Counts As History," is based on a study of university curricula, not secondary education. However, their hypotheses are not limited to higher education.
8. The *Malet-Isaac* series of textbooks went through many editions in its long lifetime. The final 1960 edition was recently reprinted (Isaac et al., 2002 [1960]).
9. Although the subjects of history and geography have for many years been deeply intertwined in French secondary education, this chapter chooses to focus more narrowly on history alone.
10. The most efficient way of collecting French *programmes* starting from the 1930s is to look at the privately published *Nouveaux Horaires et Programmes de l'Enseignement du Second Degré* (Paris: Librairie Vuibert), referred to subsequently as 'HOPI.' The *programmes* were also published in the state *Bulletin Officiel de l'Education Nationale.*
11. The "return to antiquity" was paradoxically an argument used in favor of the "progressive" 1950s reforms of the *programmes.* See below in this chapter, and also *Bulletin* 1956.
12. The secondary *programmes* have gone through another round of updating since the major reforms of 1995. Links to the currently operative *programmes* can be found at http://www.histoire-geographie.org/programmes.html.
13. The *programme* revisions of 2002 (*Bulletin Officiel de l'Education Nationale*, 2002a, 2002b) for higher secondary education (*lycée*) are not as explicit as their 1995 counterparts about the time allotments within each unit. The 1995 programmes for the upper grades were heavily weighted toward political history: 2/3 in *seconde*, 2/3 in *première*, and in *terminale* (*Bulletin Officiel de l'Education Nationale*, 1995).
14. Hymans (1998) reports many quantitative measures of the evolution of the Malet-Isaac books.
15. References to "external actors" include countries other than France, plus larger units such as the world as a whole.
16. Soysal and Bertilotti (2001) point out that this relabeling is particularly easy in the French case, given the long tradition of universalism at the heart of French national identity.
17. It would also be of interest to consider the questions given in the oral exam that follows the written one. Unlike the written exam, however, the oral exam questions are not standardized across all students. Moreover, the written exam is more relevant to the study of French history education, for most students never make it beyond the written exam.

18. Previously, the list also included the United Kingdom and Italy. Thanks to Thomas Lienhard, an ENS history alumnus, for this information.
19. Of course, teachers in higher and in secondary education are not necessarily like-minded (see Prost, 1968).
20. Except for two years in which there were different questions for boys and girls.
21. As will be noted below, Braudel himself was heavily involved in the curricular reform movement throughout the 1950s.
22. Indeed, even the 1995 *programme* reforms were a compromise after a more thorough-going reform proposal was beaten back by the SPHG, now known as the *Association des Professeurs d'Histoire et de Géographie*.
23. For Braudel's reaction to this vote, see Daix (1995: 349).
24. For more on the end of the Malet-Isaac series, see Hymans (1998).
25. Part of Braudel's textbook was later republished as a mass-market history, under the title *Grammaire des civilisations* (Braudel 1987).
26. For one of the clearest arguments for the primacy of technocrats in the Fourth Republic see Hitchcock (1998).

References

Braudel, Fernand. 1987. *Grammaire des civilizations*. Paris: Arthaud-Flammarion.
Bulletin. 1951. "Correspondence: M. Isaac." *Bulletin de la Société des professeurs d'histoire et de géographie*, no. 126 (March): 216–19.
——— 1955. "Enquête sur les programmes." *Bulletin de la Société des professeurs d'histoire et de géographie*, no. 144 (November): 138.
——— 1956. "La réforme des programmes d'histoire." *Bulletin de la Société des professeurs d'histoire et de géographie*, no. 145 (January): 167–76.
——— 1957. "La réforme des programmes." *Bulletin de la Société des professeurs d'histoire et de géographie*, no. 153 (December): 131–32.
Bulletin Officiel de l'Education Nationale. 1995. Hors-série No. 12, 29 June 1995, at www.ac-grenoble.fr/histoire/programmes/lycee/classique/general/presen_lyc.htm.
——— 2002a. "Histoire et Géographie en Classe de Seconde Générale et Technologique." Hors-série no. 6, 29 August 2002, at www.education.gouv.fr/botexte/hs06020829/MENE0201544A.htm.
——— 2002b. "Programme de l'Enseignement de l'Histoire-Géographie dans le Cycle Terminal des Séries Générales." Hors-série no. 7, 3 October 2002, at www.education.gouv.fr/botexte/hs07021003/MENE0201714A.htm.
Cerny, Philip G. 1980. *The Politics of Grandeur: Ideological Aspects of de Gaulle's Foreign Policy*. Cambridge: Cambridge University Press.
Daix, Pierre. 1995. *Braudel*. Paris: Flammarion.
Frank, David John, Suk-Ying Wong, John W. Meyer and Francisco O. Ramirez. 2000. "What Counts as History: A Cross-National and Longitudinal Study of University Curricula." *Comparative Education Review*, vol. 44, no. 1, 29–53.
Harsgor, Michael. 1978. "Total History: The *Annales* School." *Journal of Contemporary History* 13, no. 1, 1–13.
Hitchcock, William. 1998. *France Restored: Cold War Diplomacy and the Quest for Leadership in Europe, 1944–1954*. Chapel Hill: University of North Carolina Press.
Hoffmann, Stanley and Inge Hoffmann. 1973. *De Gaulle: artiste de la politique*. Paris: Editions du Seuil.
HOPI. 1959. *Nouveaux Horaires et Programmes de l'Enseignement du Second Degré*. Paris: Librairie Vuibert.

Hymans, Jacques E.C. 1998. "Teaching the Nation: Schoolbooks and the State in 20th Century France." Paper presented to the Conference on "Military Culture in European Societies." Center for European Studies, Harvard University, Cambridge, USA, February 1998.

Isaac, Jules et al. 2002 [1960]. *L'Histoire*. 4 vol. Paris: Hachette.

Katzenstein, Peter J. 1978. *Between Power and Plenty: The Foreign Economic Policies of Advanced Industrial States*. Madison: University of Wisconsin Press.

Malet, Albert, and Jules Isaac, with the collaboration of André Alba. 1930. *Histoire Contemporaine depuis le Milieu du XIXe Siècle* (classes de Philosophie-Mathématiques). Paris: Hachette.

Meyer, John W., John Boli, George M. Thomas and Francisco O. Ramirez. 1977. "World Society and the Nation State." *American Journal of Sociology*, vol. 103, no.1 (July), 144–81.

Meyer, John W., David H. Kamens and Aaron Benavot, with Yun-Kyung Cha, and Suk-Ying Wong. 1992. *School Knowledge for the Masses: World Models and National Primary Curricular Categories in the Twentieth Century*. Washington, DC: The Falmer Press.

Ministère de l'Education Nationale, Inspection Générale, Groupe Histoire et Géographie. 2000. "L'Europe dans l'enseignement de l'Histoire, de la Géographie et de l'Education Civique: Rapport sur le theme d'étude de l'année 1999–2000." September 2000, at www.education.fr/syst/igen/rapports.htm.

Philippe, Robert, Fernand Braudel, and Suzanne Baille. 1963. *Le monde actuel: histoire et civilizations (classes terminales, propédeutique, classes préparatoires aux grandes écoles)*. Paris: E. Belin.

Prost, Antoine. 1968. *L'Enseignement en France 1800–1967*. Paris: Armand Colin.

Rioux, Jean-Pierre. 1987. "Twentieth Century Historiography: Clio in a Phrygian Bonnet." In *Contemporary France: A Review of Interdisciplinary Studies*, eds. Jolyon Howorth and George Ross. London: Frances Pinter: 195–212.

Schüddekopf, Otto-Ernst, with Edouard Bruley, E.H. Dance, and Haakon Vigander. 1967. *History Teaching and History Textbook Revision*. Strasbourg: Council for Cultural Cooperation of the Council of Europe.

Soysal, Yasemin Nuhoğlu. 1998. "Identity and Transnationalization in German School Textbooks." *Bulletin of Concerned Asian Scholars*, vol. 30, no. 2 (March), 53–61.

Soysal, Yasemin Nuhoğlu and Teresa Bertilotti. 2001. "Rethinking the Nation-State: Projections of Identity in French and German History and Civics Textbooks." Paper presented to the conference on "Teaching Europe." European University Institute, Florence, 15–16 June 2001.

Chapter 4

❖————

The Decline and Rise of the Nation in German History Education

Julian Dierkes

Many observers have found global and transnational trends to be in evidence in changes in history curricula. Although large-scale quantitative comparisons have shown evidence for such trends, little is known about the transmission of transnational trends to the national level and the possible blocks to such transmission.

I will show that the focus on national history has declined since 1945 in West German history education. I argue that these developments follow post-war global trends and were championed by teachers within the West German educational policy-making regime based on their identification with academic historians. A comparison with East German curricula, however, points to some of the limits of the impact of transnational trends on curricula. Immediately after the Second World War, East German historiography was at the vanguard of global trends toward an increasingly social-scientific orientation of history writing, but the 1970s shift toward an increasing emphasis of the (East) German nation calls into question the impact of global trends. At the same time, however, the East German party leadership used its power over educational content to follow the example of other Soviet bloc countries in implementing a general shift toward a national orientation of historiography.

The comparison of the East and West German cases suggests a more general model that includes institutional characteristics of educational policy-making as a mediating element between the world polity and other transnational factors, and the implementation of educational policies in national policy-making. As I will show below, the interaction between the educational policy-making regime and the collective interests of dominant actors explains shifts in the historiographical orientation of German portrayals of the nation in reference to global trends.

The Decline of Nationalistic Historiography

In 1973 Paul Kennedy observed a decline of nation-centered historiography in Europe and North America for most of the twentieth century. He concluded that in the span of two generations of historians, history writing concentrating on the historian's own nation and a positive portrayal of its history, was replaced by an increasingly materialist, social-scientific, and internationalist outlook in historiography. German academic historiography as the "birthplace of modern 'scientific' historical scholarship" (Kennedy 1973: 78) served as one of the main examples of the developments Kennedy traced. He pointed to three specific movements within academic history as the primary factors in this development (ibid: 91–95): (1) the internationalist outlook of Marxist approaches; (2) the attempts of "cyclical systematizers," like Spengler and Toynbee, to extract long-term developments in world history; and (3) the increasing materialism of economic historians. In addition, Kennedy speculated about the professionalization of history writing and the changing status of history education as additional, broader factors in the decline of nation-centered discourses.

The Global Rationalization of Historiography

An examination of the factors contributing to the trend away from nation-centered historiography, which Kennedy only touched upon briefly, has been one of the main concerns of the sociology of education and, specifically, the "world polity" approach within this field. Researchers have argued from the world polity perspective that the content of education around the world is determined partly by globally prevalent models of nationhood (Meyer et al. 1997). As the nation-state has become the exclusive form of collective organization for a people recognized by the international community, nations around the world have adhered closely to evolving criteria of recognition. The status of the nation has changed from a "natural" form of social organization to one that is grounded in "rational" arguments for its existence. Nation-states have come to be "organized around universally available rational-legal principles, rather than a distinctive high cultural heritage" (Frank et al. 2000: 33). In the process of this "rationalization" of nationhood, structural differences between nation-states have eroded, and today many of the basic features of nation-states are characterized by an increasing isomorphism. Comparative research has not only uncovered structural similarities, but has increasingly focused on similarities in the content of education as well.

In replacing ethnic, linguistic or cultural homogeneity in historical narratives, recent curricula emphasize causal interrelations between aspects of social systems and historical developments and thus present an increasingly rationalized view of the nation. "With the rise of more rationalized forms of society … legitimacy came to reside in functional operations of the empirical present…. Focus shifted from the glorious past to the operational present" (Frank et al. 2000: 34). On the basis of this shift Frank et al. hypothesized that history curricula increasingly presented "more social scientific and contemporary depictions of society" (ibid: 38) in the course of the twentieth century.

Both of the above arguments, Kennedy's and the world polity approach, are pitched at a global level for long-term processes. Though an examination of post-war developments in East and West Germany alone cannot formally test such broad arguments, one would expect these global developments to exert some discernible influence on shorter periods and more specific cases. For both German nation-states, these arguments suggest that educational materials should exhibit a decline of nation-centered narratives and their replacement with rationalized, scientific historical justifications for the existence of the nation.

An Institutional Power Perspective on History Education

Modifying world-polity models by adding mechanisms for the diffusion of global precepts, I identify specific institutional forces leading to changes in officially sanctioned portrayals of history. Over the course of the post-war period, West German history education moved from an emphasis of a teleological national development and the importance of "great men" to a portrayal of history that focused less on national history and more on the agency of subnational collective actors, such as women or the working class, in shaping historical developments. East German curricula, meanwhile, were thoroughly materialist in their explanation of human development. In the 1970s, however, East German historiography reemphasized the nation as a focal point for history instruction. I argue that two factors in particular determine these outcomes: the educational policy-making regime, and the construction and perception of the collective interests of those involved in policy making.

The post-war West German policy-making regime was above all characterized by federalism and professional authority. The nominal control over educational content wielded by state ministries of culture was generally ceded to committees of experts, though the make-up and constitution of these committees varied by state. The most powerful collective actor in these committees, teachers, saw their authority as legitimated by their status as academics. Paradigmatic shifts in academic historiography, which paralleled global shifts, were therefore quickly transmitted to secondary education to maintain a connection that was deemed to be in teachers' best interest.

East German education was controlled by the Socialist Unity Party to the same degree that all policy decisions in the GDR were subject to party influence. All individuals and collective bodies involved in curriculum drafting were vetted by the party, and thus represented a party view in their deliberations. Given the party leaders' focus on the legitimacy of their power based on the Soviet Union, the leadership saw it to be in their interest to follow quite closely the example of the Soviet Union and the Soviet bloc in general. While the nation was increasingly reemphasized in Soviet bloc policies and rhetoric after the death of Stalin and after Khrushchev's critique of Stalin's nationalities policies, the East German leadership initiated the heritage debate [*Erbe-Debatte*] of the 1970s, which reevaluated the status of German history in general and Prussian history in particular.

Analyzing Portrayals of German National History

In order to evaluate the impact of global trends in historiography, I have collected middle school curriculum portrayals of national history in the Federal Republic of Germany (FRG) from 1945 to 1995, and in the German Democratic Republic (GDR) from 1945 to 1989. In both German states, these curricula were the legal and formal basis for history instruction and also served as guidelines for textbook authors. For West Germany, I chose the *Sekundarstufe I* (or *Realschule*), the middle tier of secondary education, and for East Germany, the *Oberschule* in its various incarnations, because these are the levels of compulsory schooling at which students were exposed to systematic treatments of national history for the first time. (The *Oberschule* in GDR in fact encompassed both: *Sekundarstufe* I and II).

West German curricula are revised and published at irregular intervals by the state ministries of culture. For the present analysis I have included the curricula from three states: Bavaria, Hesse and Northrhine-Westphalia (NRW). East German curricula went through four major revisions between 1945 and 1989, yielding five curricula for the analysis.

I have analyzed these curricula regarding the changes in their structure and content. While analyses of the preambles of curricula and of some of their content focus on an interpretive reading of these materials, wherever possible I have also constructed metrics to compare the inclusion of particular episodes and historical developments.

Historiographical Shifts in West German History Curricula

West German curricula shifted radically in their format during the post-war era. While early post-war curricula outlined the topics to be covered in particular grades in some narrative detail, since the 1970s curricula have been mainly concerned with stating the overarching goals of history education. While early curricula thus made no explicit judgments on the status of particular develop-ments and seemed to assume the desirability of historical erudition in general, later curricula spelled out the importance of an understanding of history (as opposed to knowledge thereof) and the general applicability of skills learned through history education. Similarly, curricula became more broadly prescrip-tive in their aims, in contrast to specific prescriptions for the portrayals of particular historical events.

The general shift in the format of curricula brought a number of substan-tive shifts with it. First, a gradual increase in the emphasis of more recent historical periods and of non-German history can be observed, although this shift is difficult to analyze given the schematic nature of later curricula. The increasing focus on more recent periods was accompanied by a pedagogical shift from an emphasis on the memorization and knowledge of history to an understanding of historical interconnections. In more recent curricula (late 1970s and 1980s), this shift continued to emphasize the relation of history education to academic historiography, the importance of scientific methodol-ogy, and the weighing of competing explanations for historical phenomena. These later curricula also took steps toward the dissolution of chronological organization and its replacement by thematic modules. Curricula of the 1990s took the "rationalization" of curricula through scientific methodologies a step further, and advocated multiple perspectives on history and on historical inter-pretation.

Shifts in the Pedagogical and Historiographical Orientation of Curricula

The most visible shift in West German post-war education and pedagogy was the demise of humanism as a fundamental perspective on education. Having dominated German education throughout the modern era, humanism was the dominant pedagogical paradigm in the 1940s and 1950s. With its dominance of pedagogical discourse, humanism also characterized the preambles that usually preceded specific course guidelines in curricula. The 1955 NRW curriculum thus offered the following appeal for coordination of history with other subjects in secondary education "In particular the word of the poet should not be neglected in interpretations of historical events"[1] (NRW 1955: 17). Such appeals reflected humanism as well as the dominant interpretation of history as cultural history [*Kulturgeschichte*].[2] The most obvious connection that curriculum authors saw was with literary statements as sources of histor-ical judgments.

The second dominant stream paralleling cultural history was *Historismus*. *Historismus* had been the dominant historiographical paradigm among German historians since the early nineteenth century when it replaced Renais-sance approaches to history. Jaeger and Rüsen (1992, cited in Conrad 1999: 38) have offered the following elements as defining *Historismus* in Germany: (1) scientific objectivity; (2) an idealist conception of history; (3) the reconstruction of continuities in past events; (4) epic narratives; and (5) the construction of a national identity as the historian's aim. In practice, this implied a clear focus on national history and on a teleological narrative of the development of the nation. The idea of the nation as one of the driving forces in historical developments was joined by an emphasis of the significance of particular actors. When the 1955 NRW curriculum described the foundation of the German Empire in 1871, it exemplified some of the tension between a focus on important actors and the power of ideas: "Bismarck's ingenious abilities as a statesman should be honored, but it should also not be overlooked that a solution to the German question precluded the inclusion of the Habsburg Empire on the basis of a central European federalism"[3] (NRW 1955: 18).

Shifts in the Importance of Historical Episodes in Curricula

Despite the increasing lack of specificity in curricula, even the latest versions contained some framework outlining the historical developments to be covered in particular grades (or in the course of a succession of grades). The number of curricula per state (Bavaria: four; Hesse: three; NRW: six) and the irregular interval at which these curricula appeared make it difficult to plot this shift or to compare shifts between curricula. However, of the thirteen curricula, only five devoted an entire year to recent history, from nineteenth-century imperialism on until the present: Bavaria 1981; Hesse 1982; and NRW 1966, 1973, and 1978.[4] In contrast, the longest time span to be covered by the final year of history education was prescribed by the 1950 Hessian curriculum and stretched from the Congress of Vienna (1815) to the present. Later curricula were thus much more likely to devote greater attention to more recent history than earlier curricula had.

From National to Thematic History

Early curricula were structured by the chronology of German history which provided the dominant periodization of historical episodes. Typical cutoff points for the end of a particular grade's course were thus the establishment of the Franconian empire under Charlemagne (Bavaria 1961; Hesse 1957; NRW 1966) or the bourgeois revolution of 1848 (NRW 1949). Non-German history was discussed only in relation to events in Germany. This periodization in reference to German history and the overall share of German history in the curriculum waned in the 1970s. The lack of a common and constant structure among the curricula makes it difficult to compare these formally in terms of the share of history devoted to Germany, but some of the developments in the preambles of curricula signal a clear shift away from national history (for example, the introduction of multiple perspectives and thematic units in the most recent curricula). The addition of subjects to the history curriculum also indicates a shift in emphasis. The most prominent recent additions to curricula tend to be either thematic or on countries/regions other than Germany. Thus, the 1993 NRW curriculum included such thematic units as "environmental history," "Islam as a cultural and political force," "Judaism as a cultural and political force," and "migration in history" in the nineteen prescribed units. This curriculum in fact introduced a thematic unit specifically devoted to the "history of the German nation-state" signaling that this topic was not covered by default in other thematic units. Surprisingly, none of these nineteen units were devoted to a specifically European theme.

Wissenschaftlichkeit as a Goal of History Instruction

Curriculum authors increasingly laid claim to *Wissenschaftlichkeit* (scientificness) as the basis of the curriculum and also as an aim of history education. Whereas earlier curricula emphasized knowledge of history as the overriding goal, later authors were aiming for students' understanding of historical developments. As an example of the emphasis of knowledge, the 1957 Hessian curriculum included a listing of important dates, explaining that this should serve as a canon of topics to be memorized (Hesse 1957: 343).

Such calls for knowledge and memorization of important historical events had disappeared entirely from the curricula by the 1960s. Knowledge of history as the overarching goal of education was replaced by an understanding of history through the application of historical methods. For example, the 1978 NRW curriculum listed the following as one of five main subject-specific goals: "History instruction should awaken the ability and willingness in students to transcend non-scientific identification and indoctrination on the basis of knowledge of historical interrelations"[5] (NRW 1981: 13). Similarly, the 1993 NRW curriculum emphasized criticism of ideology as a task[6] for history education. This trend away from knowledge of historical facts toward a broader, analytical understanding of history, is an important example of the overall rationalization of portrayals of national history in that such an understanding was intended to be universally applicable, unlike earlier narratives that were specific to a given territorial or political unit.

Scientific methodology and an understanding thereof was of particular importance in the preambles of recent curricula. Emphasizing the role of the teaching of scientific methodology, the 1982 Hesse curriculum's note on "scientific orientation" explicitly included methodological training among the goals of history education: "In addition to the realization of an increase in knowledge through science, instruction should enable the student to learn the elements of scientific methods and to apply them"[7] (Hessin 1982: 9).

Shifts in academic paradigms were mentioned explicitly in recent curricula. The 1981 NRW curriculum stated: "Academic historiography supplies the scientific bases for history teaching. In recent years the emphasis in historical research has shifted to structural historiography"[8] (NRW 1981: 7). Or, even more explicitly, in 1994: "History teaching must be guided by scientific paradigms. It has to be taken into account that historiography – like all other sciences – is characterized by a multiplicity of perspectives and emphases, which are constantly shifting"[9] (NRW 1994: 43–44). The paradigm shift from *Historismus* to more structuralist historiography was presented as leading to a more "rational" history in this context (Hessin 1982: 31).

Along with the orientation toward scientific method, teachers were admonished to use history and past events to allow students to see the roots of current social conditions, and also to evaluate these conditions in their own right. The present was seen in the light of the future in such calls. History instruction "should lead students to the realization that human thoughts and deeds in all historical periods have been and will be shaped by the past"[10] (NRW 1994: 38).

Shifts in the Portrayal of Bismarck and the German Empire

As *Historismus* was replaced by *Sozialgeschichte* (originally, social history; later to include cultural history, history from below, women's history, etc.) in the 1960s, the focus on "heroes" of German history was reduced noticeably. The portrayals of the creation of the German empire are a particularly useful site to measure this decline of personalistic history, given the importance of this episode to national history and the significant role of Otto von Bismarck in this development.

In the 1949 NRW curriculum, the section on the proclamation of the empire in 1871 was divided into four subsections. Of the titles of these four subsections, three begin with the word "Bismarck" and focus almost exclusively on Bismarck and his politics (NRW 1949: 25–26).[11] Contrast this with the 1981 Bavarian curriculum which suggested that interpretations of caricatures of Bismarck might be a useful way to evaluate students' understanding of "The Era Bismarck – The German Empire" (Bavaria 1981: 1027).

With the above analyses and examples, I have shown that the status of national history in West German curricula shifted significantly over the fifty years since the Second World War. There are some indications for a decline of the significance of national history and its share of the history curriculum. More clearly, we can observe a broad pedagogical and historiographical reorientation of history education away from knowledge of a teleological account of national history, driven by the idea of the nation and great leaders, toward an understanding of history and historiographical methodology as the root of today's social relations.

West German Teachers as Transmitters of Global Precepts

The observations of broad changes in West German curricula in accordance with transnational trends beg the question of who might have championed such a shift from grand national narratives to socio-scientific historiography de-emphasizing the nation. With their powerful position within the educational policy-making regime, West German teachers had the authority to initiate such a shift. They were motivated in this by their identification with academic historians who had themselves undergone a paradigm shift toward social-structural approaches in the early 1960s.

Comparative studies of German education during the Allied occupation years have pointed to the importance of a strong, pre-existing educational tradition in Germany (Halbritter 1979; Lange-Quassowski 1979; Rosenzweig 1998; and Ruge-Schatz 1977). German teachers in the Western occupied zones successfully resisted the break-up of the three-tiered system of secondary education which had been one of the main goals of Allied occupation policies. Resistance was possible in Western Germany because teachers, parents, and administrators all relied on their pre-war experiences in arguing for the continuation of German educational policies.

The experience of the Nazi period only strengthened arguments for continuity in that Nazi educational policy in the post-war years was perceived to have been primarily directed at the creation of mechanisms of indoctrination outside of schools rather than the reform of schools to conform with Nazi ideology.[12] Attempts by the Nazi regime to create alternative institutions outside the education system also left education relatively "untainted" once these alternative institutions and officials, teachers, and educational materials in traditional institutions of learning had been nominally censored, allowing a substantial continuity in teaching personnel and educational content from the pre-war era. Apart from the specific situation regarding educational policy, Levy and Sznaider (2001: chap. 4) have shown that purported institutional requirements for reconstruction led to bureaucratic continuity in many areas of policy making.

Continuity was also reinforced by the lack of coordination of educational policy between the Western allies and the federal political structure of the administration of education in the Federal Republic. State bureaucracies in the Federal Republic yielded control over questions of educational content to the teaching profession, as they had done during the Weimar Republic. West Germany thus institutionalized professional control over educational content. Teachers' authority over educational content was only rarely questioned by the presence of particularly active state ministers of education.

Given teachers' control over educational content, two additional factors contribute to the use of this power to redirect historical narratives in the 1970s: demographic changes, and the construction and perception of the collective interests of teachers, coupled with developments in academic historiography.

Some of the demographic developments prevalent in the industrial world during the late 1960s were of particular significance in the West German context. The birth cohorts of the beginning of economic recovery in the FRG were passing through the education system, leading to an expansion of this system. The late 1960s was also an era of relative abundance of public funds. Given that Social Democrats came to power for the first time in the post-war era during the 1960s, some of this abundance was earmarked for the improvement of educational opportunities, resulting in an expansion of higher education. Economic stability and tight labor-market conditions also led to an increase in academic interest within the expanded system of higher education. Because of the combination of these factors, university enrollments in history increased significantly. The entry of cohorts into higher education who had not witnessed the Second World War themselves, and who had been radicalized by the political atmosphere on university campuses in the late 1960s, brought about wide-spread attacks on previous generations because of their role in the war. In addition, the so-called "Auschwitz trials" focused such generational attacks on the Holocaust (Bude 1998).

The upheaval caused by generational changes led to specific transformations in the historiographical orientation of curricula because of the construction and perception of history teachers' professional interests. Preparation for secondary teaching in Germany always involved a course of academic study, leading to the equivalent of a master's degree [*Staatsexamen*], coupled with pedagogical training. Students preparing to become history teachers were thus exposed to academic historiography in their studies. Through this exposure and the prestige attributed to teachers as academics, the dominant professional identity of West German teachers was as much bound to teaching as it was to history as an academic field. The prestige accorded to a journal self-consciously directed at teachers and academics—History in Teaching and Academia [*Geschichte in Unterricht und Wissenschaft*]—might serve as an indicator of this tight coupling between teaching and academic historiography (Conrad 1999: 30).

Younger West German historians swept into the profession with the expansion of the educational system, championing forms of historical research that were very much in tune with global developments, both in history itself, as well as in an increasing rationalization of the nation-state. In the FRG, this gave rise to "social history," "history from below," "women's history," etc., all of which emphasized universalistic as opposed to particularistic aspects of national historiography. All of these movements paralleled changes in academic curricula and in pedagogical theory more generally in other countries (Frank et al. 2000), and represent in part a reaction to the international dominance of the *annales* school in academic history writing (Erbe 1981).

My findings regarding the changes in the historiographical orientation exhibited by West German curricula thus support the findings of world polity researchers on global developments of history curricula, and suggest that West

German history teachers acted as agents of transmission of global precepts within the educational policy-making regime, along the lines found by Frank et al. (2000). Teachers were motivated in championing this shift by their identification with academic historians. This identification not only assigned them power over educational content within the policy-making regime, but it also provided the substantive impetus for the changes I have described above, based on the paradigm shift from *Historismus* to social history in the 1960s.

The Reemergence of the Nation in East German Curricula

Compared to West German curricula, the documents promulgated by the East German government remained remarkably stable in their structure, format, and even their content over the forty years of the existence of the GDR. They were relatively lengthy documents (the 1951 curriculum[13] was the longest at 109 pages) that included elaborate preambles presenting a forceful case for a Marxist orientation in history education and for the importance of education to the construction of a socialist nation. In addition to their role in specifying periods to be covered and the valuation they were to be treated with, the curricula thus served as a lengthy lecture to history teachers on how to conduct their classes, and also as documentation of official attitudes toward history.

Because of the high degree of standardization of the East German curricula, it is possible to construct some metrics for over-time analyses of changes. East German curricula specified a well-defined canon of historical knowledge in the listings of important dates that students were expected to memorize. Standardization of the curriculum format meant that the scope of this canon remained the same over forty years of East German educational policy making. Attention to more recent historical periods jumped markedly in the post-war period, but I also show below that the importance of German history in general, and East German history especially, increased steadily in the curricula.

The Pedagogical and Historiographical Orientation of Curricula

East German materials presaged some post-war global trends and contradicted these trends at other times. The most noticeable characteristic that distinguished East German from West German narratives was their strict adherence to a class-analytic interpretation of history. Except for later hagiographical elements describing the role of socialist leaders, East German narratives were thus not histories of great national heroes, nor did they present grand national narratives. Throughout the forty years of the existence of the GDR, all educational materials in general and those for history education in particular presented historical developments in the context of class conflict and materialist historical science. These narratives were thus social-scientific in that they interpreted historical developments in the context of a social system before this focus became dominant at the world-polity level.

Material forces and class struggle are the great dynamic of Marxist understanding of human development and history. Even in the earliest, least doctrinaire versions of the curriculum, these forces already formed the backbone of the discussion of historical developments, as the "hidden connections between historical events"[14] (1946: 5). All sections on specific historical episodes focused on the material forces that characterized this period. From treatments of the first signs of the gathering of humans into a nascent society, to accounts of the postwar division of the world into socialist and capitalist camps, historical accounts were permeated by attention to material forces. In describing early human societies, the 1954 curriculum, for example, admonished teachers to illustrate to students how increasing productivity based on improved farming techniques "led to the creation of private property and how social groups that had originally been formed through genealogical lineages began to split into classes"[15] (1954: 5). The Lutheran Reformation was described as an early bourgeois revolution and the subsequent (or resulting, to follow the East German portrayal) Peasant War as the "high point of the class struggle of peasants against the ruling feudal nobility and directed against feudal exploitation and subjugation"[16] (1966: 71).

In the course of the forty years of East German history, pedagogy underwent a modernization and increased its focus on the dogmatic and ideological elements of history education. This shift was more gradual than some of the substantive shifts summarized below, but no less noticeable. While earlier curricula were more likely to advocate pedagogical methodologies that were viewed as appropriate to learning at particular ages, the shift toward more dogmatic instruction in later curricula brought a homogenization of pedagogical strategies that made less of a distinction between ages and their ability to absorb historical information. The last curricula were thus almost completely devoid of references to "historical illustrations"[17] that had characterized discussions of early history education in the first curricula. Using such illustrations, earlier curricula conceived of instruction grades five and six as a gradual introduction to historical thinking with more systematic attention to follow in the upper grades of secondary education[18] (1946: 14), while later curricula emphasized a more analytical approach from the beginning of the history course.

The listing of important dates for memorizing in the curricula suggests that despite the analytical focus of Marxist historiography, East German history education placed a great premium on the knowledge of historical facts. All curricula listed dates to be memorized for a particular section of the history course either right before or right after the listing of the topics to be covered. In the later curricula the dissemination of factual knowledge was given even greater priority by listing dates to be memorized by content unit (typically between one and four hours of instruction) and thus tying the memorization directly to particular units. Such lists of dates ranged from very short lists per grade for the younger students' instruction on pre-history (for example, "around 3,000 before the current era: development of first states in Mesopotamia" (1988: 14)) to lists of over twenty events for instruction on most recent history (for example, "1986: XXVII. Party congress of the CPSU" (ibid: 94)). As the time devoted to history instruction increased over successive curricula (from four grades until 1954 to five grades thereafter) the total number of dates to be memorized also increased, suggesting a shift in teaching methodology toward a more rigid model of the imparting of a canon of knowledge rather than an understanding of historical events.

Shifts in the Importance of Historical Episodes in Curricula

Measured by the proportion of memorization dates drawn from recent history, modernity gained in prominence in the historical narratives presented by the curricula. The period of the modern German nation-state since 1871 thus contributed only 20 percent of the memorization dates included in the 1946 curriculum, but this share had risen to 60 percent by the late 1980s. Although much of this rise can be attributed to dates drawn from very recent history, early modern periods also contributed an increasing share of the memorization dates. The privileging of recent historical periods was thus not merely an artifact of the addition of post-war history to the curriculum as the historical distance from 1945 grew. The dates drawn from the period 1871–1945 increased from 20 percent in the 1946 curriculum, to 33 percent in 1951, and 36 percent in 1988.

From Internationalist to National History

Following the precepts of a materialist historiography, early curricula were internationalist in orientation, and emphasized the role of classes in human development to the exclusion of a history of the nation. However, the shift toward an emphasis of the history of socialism in curricula after the 1960s went hand in hand with a greater emphasis of specifically East German history. This was not only evident in the almost exclusive focus of narratives of post-war history on East Germany and the "socialist world system,"[19] but coverage of earlier historical periods also focused increasingly on locations and individuals associated with East Germany. The lessening of the demonization of Prussia was particularly noteworthy in this respect. These substantive shifts were most pronounced in the latest curricula, although they had already been initiated by changes in the curricula of the late 1960s.

The listing of dates for memorizing offers information about the centrality of the German nation in historical narratives. A shifting proportion of dates drawn from explicitly German historical events summarizes the broader trends toward the increasing emphasis of German history over more general historical developments. The proportion of dates from German history thus shifted from roughly one-half to close to two-thirds of all dates included. Taking this shift as a proxy for the general development in the curricula, later curricula, particularly the last East German curricula of 1988, devoted a much greater proportion of their coverage to German history.

In light of the increased attention given to more recent historical periods in later East German curricula, it could be argued that the increasing attention to German history is merely due to the addition of dates from post-war East German history. However, the difference in the proportion between German dates and GDR dates shows that the increase in attention to the nation was a general one and included an increasing amount of attention paid to all German history, including even that of the Federal Republic.

The increase in attention to national history was a steady, gradual increase with jumps of around 5 percent coming in the curricula of 1954, 1965 to 1970, and 1988. Attention to GDR history, on the other hand, jumped in the late 1960s along with the increase in a focus on post-war history in general. On the whole, dates from earlier, pre-national German history tended to be eliminated, while later dates, more clearly identifiable as German, tended to be added. To take the shift from the mid-1950s to the late 1960s as an example, eight dates from a variety of historical periods were eliminated from the 1954 curriculum, and of the dates added to the curricula of the late 1960s, twenty-five of the forty-six dates were drawn from post-war GDR history. Thus, the memorization dates suggest a trend toward the (re-) nationalization of history teaching in general.

Wissenschaftlichkeit as a Goal of History Instruction

Whereas science only made its debut as an explicit justification and underlying logic of West German history education in the 1970s, Marxist claims for the scientificness of materialism permeated East German discussions from the immediate post-war era on. To quote from the earliest curriculum: "[The] evaluation [of historical developments] must be based on scientific soundness, facticity and truth"[20] (1946: 6). The preamble for the history curriculum for grade six in 1966 stated that history education could fulfill its function primarily by "forming a scientific view of history relying on selected results of Marxist-Leninist historical science and by developing a genuine understanding of history"[21] (1966: 7). As can be seen from the above statements, science not only provided a framework for discussions of historical developments, but also a claim for the superiority of the East German approach to historiography, particularly when contrasted with "bourgeois historiography" as a thinly veiled reference to West German and other capitalist historiographies. Following claims for the scientificness of Marxist historiography, the curricula frequently invoked historical truth and facticity in instructions to teachers: "The supreme law of history education must be to come as close as possible to historical truth"[22] (1946: 4).

East German curricula thus presented narratives as highly rationalized accounts of historical developments which followed the regular laws of materialist interpretations of world history. This highly rationalized account of historical developments was institutionalized in the immediate post-war years, when the big push toward a global rationalization of history curricula was merely beginning. In this regard East German and Soviet bloc history education in general was at the cutting edge of global trends.

Shifts in the Portrayal of Bismarck and the German Empire

The portrayal of the German nation in the late nineteenth century was characterized by two elements in East German curricula: as a necessary and progressive development of bourgeois society and as the culmination of Prussian attempts to gain power over Germany in a united nation-state. The portrayals underwent a development regarding both elements aspects over the course of GDR history. Whereas unification was described mostly in terms of class struggle in the 1950s and as a process of Prussification [*Verpreußung*], later accounts downplayed class relations and portrayed Prussia, and especially Bismarck, in a neutral or even positive light.

The historical narrative of German unification was dominated generally by an account of Bismarck's role in this process. However, beyond his role as the main protagonist of this development, Bismark also served as a villain and as a representative of a despised social class in East German history education. Much was thus made of Bismarck's family background and his associations with various social peers in early curricula, which painted a picture of Bismarck largely drawn from his famous "*Blut und Eisen*" speech to the Prussian parliament. However, later curricula, and especially the 1988 version, portray Bismarck in an increasingly positive light. Not only was Bismarck's character evaluated positively in these later narratives, but the process of unification itself was painted in increasingly positive terms, independent of its economic necessity and of popular support for unification.

Shifts in the portrayal of Bismarck's role in the creation of the late nineteenth century German empire illustrate the materialist focus of East German history education on the one hand, and the turn toward a renewed focus on the nation in the 1970s, on the other hand.

East German Teachers as Transmitters of Soviet Bloc Precepts

As for politics in general, educational policy in East Germany was dominated by the Socialist Unity Party (*SED*). Under the rhetorical guise of "democratic centralism," policy making in the GDR was characterized by authoritarian party rule in all aspects. The Socialist Party had achieved its position of power early on, through the delegation of authority by the Soviet occupation. Through the administrative fiat of the Soviet occupation authorities, East Germany was endowed with an entirely new policy-making regime in education.

Whereas teachers had dominated policy making in the federalist Weimar Republic and through their collaboration with the Nazi regime, power over educational content was handed by the Soviet occupation to central party cadres. This delegation was based on the legitimacy of party rule in opposing fascism and in striving for a socialist society. Given these goals, and the close identification of the pioneer generation of East German leaders with the Soviet Union, party cadres based their policies on the example of the Soviet Union and the Soviet bloc in general. This pioneer generation maintained their monopoly over policy making for the entire existence of the GDR. This monopoly was implemented through the ultimate authority of the party over all decision making. Though intermediate levels of decision making existed in the form of the Academy of Pedagogical Sciences [*Akademie der Pädagogischen Wissenschaften*], for example, access to decision making in such bodies was in turn controlled by the party.

After the death of Stalin and with the emergence of public criticism of Stalin's nationalities policies, the Soviet Union and other state-socialist countries increasingly began to focus on the nation in their rhetoric and policies. As such nationalist discourse was legitimated by the post-Stalin Soviet example throughout the Soviet bloc, the East German leadership followed this example in re-emphasizing particularly national aspects of German history when it faced a number of demographic and economic challenges in the 1970s. Three significant developments in the GDR in the 1970s prompted the nationalist turn: the replacement of Walter Ulbricht at the helm of the party by Erich Honecker; the increased emigration pressure with the thaw in German-German relations initiated by the West German Brandt government; and heightened economic problems caused by labor shortages and slow productivity growth. Particularly, the second and third factors seemed to suggest to the East German leadership that they were facing a lack of an identification of the population with the GDR, which bolstered a desire to emigrate and depressed labor productivity which was already hampered by labor shortages.

The institutionalization of the educational policy-making regime in the immediate post-war years thus focused party cadres on the Soviet Union as a source of their power and of the legitimacy of their actions. As policies on the nation changed in the post-Stalin Soviet bloc, party cadres acted on their interests in maintaining Soviet support and legitimacy by implementing this overall change in the Soviet bloc through a renationalization of portrayals of the nation.

Conclusion

At the outset of this chapter I outlined a general trend in historiography that might influence the portrayal of the nation in history education in Germany: the decline of nation-centered history writing. I also referred to research results of scholars associated with the "world polity" approach, which suggests that history curriculum throughout the world have been increasingly "rationalized" by a shift away from emotional attachments to a primordial nation toward rational accounts of the development of particular nation-states. Based on these parallel trends, I asked whether German policy makers implemented such a rationalization of the portrayal of the nation. I find that transnational trends were implemented in both German states, and argue that the institutional characteristics of post-war educational policy-making regimes account for the implementation of transnational trends at the domestic level, and for differences in the trajectory of this implementation between the East and West Germany. Whereas the East German party leadership looked to the example of the Soviet Union to shift history education toward a greater focus on the nation in the 1970s and 80s, West German teachers championed a shift from an aggrandizing account of German history toward a more social-scientific historiography that focused less on the German nation. Teachers in West Germany thus transmitted a transnational shift that came to them via academic historians with whom teachers identified strongly. While transnational trends can be observed in both East and West Germany, they are different trends with different origins. Elsewhere (Dierkes 2001) I have presented evidence that Japanese history teaching materials are much less influenced by transnational trends and have explained this insulation through an analysis of the institutional characteristics of the educational policy-making regime. This analysis has shown that my model explains the implementation of transnational trends as well as accounting for the blocking of such isomorphic tendencies.

My argument outlines a model for changes in portrayals of national history in educational materials. Although such changes occur in reference to transnational and, indeed, global trends, their implementation at the level of national education policy is dependent on the domestic educational policy-making regime and on the construction of interests of collective actors within that regime. I provide case studies of the mechanisms of the transmission and implementation of global trends in historiography and thus refine world polity arguments about the spread of such trends across the industrialized nations. Both of these contributions offer some predictions for the fate of Europe as a topic of historiography in national curricula of EU member states. Although the evidence is still scarce, my model should be applicable to the creation of a European supranational or "transnational" (Soysal 2000: 130) history curriculum. Since "Europeanization" seems to be on the verge of institutionalization as an "Old World polity" precept, analyses of the implementation of such transnationalizing trends should examine the existence of actors who have come to see these trends to be in their interest. Given the great variety of actors involved in educational policy making in various countries, such interested actors might well differ across Europe. However, without such champions, efforts at a Europeanization of history education are doomed to fail, as East German resistance to global trends may have illustrated.

Appendix: Curricula

Federal Republic of Germany

Note: Where the official date of publication differs from the date indicated for bibliographic reference, I have given the official date in brackets.

Bavaria

Bekanntmachung des Lehrplans für Mittelschulen. Amtsblatt des Bayerischen Staatsministeriums für Unterricht und Kultus, vol. 1950, no. 11 (17 August 1950): 161–68.

Bekanntmachung der Stundentafel und Stoffpläne für die vierstufige Mittelschule in Bayern. Amtsblatt des Bayerischen Staatsministeriums für Unterricht und Kultus, vol. 1961, no. 10 (3 March 1961): 243–55.

Bekanntmachung über die Lehrpläne für die vierklassigen Realschulen in Bayern. Amtsblatt des Bayerischen Staatsministeriums für Unterricht und Kultus, vol. 1969, no. 3 (12 February 1961): 159–71.

Lehrpläne der Realschule—Lehrplan für Geschichte 9. und 10. Jahrgangsstufe. Amtsblatt des Bayerischen Staatsministeriums für Unterricht und Kultus, vol. 1981, Sondernummer 28 (21 December 1981): 1021–35.

Hesse

Einführung der Realschule. Amtsblatt des Hessischen Ministers für Erziehung und Volksbildung, vol. 3 (14 November 1950): 602–607, 623–29.

Bildungspläne für die allgemeinbildenden Schulen im Lande Hessen. Amtsblatt des Hessischen Ministers für Erziehung und Volksbildung, vol.10, Sondernummer 1 (January 1957): 12–16.

Der Hessische Kultusminister. *Rahmenrichtlinien Sekundarstufe I Gesellschaftslehre*. Wiesbaden (1982): 7–52, 88–102.

Northrhine-Westphalia

N. Lübke, *Geschichtsstoffplan für Volks- und Mittelschulen*, Dortmund, 1949.

Richtlinien für die Bildungsarbeit der Realschulen. Beilage zum Amtsblatt des Kultusministeriums (NRW) 3. Jahrgang 1955, Heft 1.

Richtlinien für den Unterricht in der Realschule—Geschichte, Erdkunde und Gemeinschaftskunde. Düsseldorf, 1966.

Kultusminister des Landes Nordrhein-Westfalen. *Empfehlungen für den Unterricht in der Realschule für das Fach Geschichte*, 1973.

Kultusminister des Landes Nordrhein-Westfalen, *Realschule: Richtlinien Geschichte*, Cologne, 1981 [1978].

Kulturministerium des Landes Nordrhein-Westfalen, *Richtlinien und Lehrpläne —Geschichte*, Frechen, 1994 [1993].

German Democratic Republic

Note: All curricula were published under authority of the Deutsche Zentralver-waltung für Volksbildung in der sowjetischen Besatzungszone Deutschlands [German Central Administration of People's Education in the soviet-occupied zone of Germany] or its successor, the Ministerium für Volksbildung der Deutschen Demokratischen Republik [Ministry for People's Education of the German Democratic Republic]. They were published by the Verlag Volk und Wissen, Berlin. I have omitted this redundant information in the listing below. Where it has been noted, I have included the date of promulgation of a curriculum; otherwise its year of publication is listed.

Lehrpläne für die Grund- und Oberschulen in der sowjetischen Besatzungszone Deutschlands: Geschichte (1 July 1946).
Lehrplan für Grundschulen Geschichte 1. bis 8. Schuljahr (1951).
Lehrplan für Grundschulen Geschichte 5. bis 8. Schuljahr (8 August 1954).
Präzisierter Lehrplan für Geschichte: Klasse 5 (30 November 1965).
Präzisierter Lehrplan für Geschichte: Klasse 6 (30 June 1966).
Präzisierter Lehrplan für Geschichte: Klasse 7 (November 1967).
Präzisierter Lehrplan für Geschichte: Klasse 8 (June 1968).
Präzisierter Lehrplan für Geschichte: Klasse 9 (30 June 1969).
Lehrplan für Geschichte: Klasse 10 (June 1970).
Lehrplan für Geschichte: Klasse 10 (1977).
Lehrplan der zehnklassigen allgemeinbildenden polytechnischen Oberschule: Geschichte Klassen 5 bis 10 (1988).

Notes

While collecting the curricula analyzed here, the author was a fellow in the Berlin Program for Advanced German and European Studies. Assistance by the staff of the library of the Georg-Eckert-Institute for International Textbook Research, Braun-schweig, and the Bibliothek für Bildungsgeschichtliche Forschung, Berlin, is gratefully acknowledged. Frank Dobbin, Michèle Lamont, and John Meyer have guided this project and have greatly influenced its orientation. Comments from conference participants at NYU and the EUI contributed many useful suggestions, and Lia Antoniou, David Frank, Daniel Levy, Hanna Schissler, and Yasemin Soysal were particularly generous in offering comments on earlier drafts.

1. See Appendix: Curricula for a list of curricula analyzed. I cite West German curricula only by their state and year of promulgation. All translations are mine. [Insbesondere ist auf das Wort des Dichters in der Deutung des historischen Phänomens nicht zu verzichten.]
2. *Kulturgeschichte* was used in the 1940s and 1950s, not in the sense this term later took on with the paradigm shift of the 1960s, but perhaps more akin to civiliza-tional history.
3. [Bismarcks geniale staatsmännische Fähigkeiten sind zu würdigen, jedoch kann nicht übersehen werden, daß eine Lösung der deutschen Frage den möglichen

Einbezug des Habsburgerreiches auf der Grundlage eines mitteleuropäischen Föderalismus zunichte gemacht hat.]

4. Note that the most recent curriculum (NRW 1994) did not include an assignment of thematic units to particular grades or a chronology that would allow for a judgment of attention to particular episodes.

5. [Der Geschichtsunterricht soll im Schüler die Fähigkeit und Bereitschaft wecken, unwissenschaftliche Identifikation und Indoktrination mit Hilfe der Kenntnis historischer Zusammenhänge kritisch aufzuklären.]

6. [Ideologiekritische Aufgabe.]

7. [Neben der Orientierung am wissenschaftlich bewirkten Erkenntnisfortschritt sollte der Unterricht den Schülern ermöglichen, wissenschaftliche Methoden elementar zu erlernen und sie zu erproben.]

8. [Die wissenschaftlichen Grundlagen für das Fach Geschichte stellt die Geschichtswissenschaft bereit. In den letzten Jahren hat sich das Schwergewicht historischer Forschung zu einer strukturorientierten Geschichtsschreibung hin verschoben.]

9. [Der Geschichtsunterricht muß sich an wissenschaftlichen Paradigmen orientieren. Dabei muß berücksichtigt werden, daß die Geschichtswissenschaft wie alle anderen Wissenschaften durch eine Vielfalt unterschiedlicher Forschungsschwerpunkte und Forschungsperspektiven gekennzeichnet ist, die sich in einem ständigen Wandel befinden.]

10. [Der Geschichtsunterricht soll die Schülerinnen und Schüler zu der Erkenntnis führen, daß Menschen zu allen Zeiten in ihrem Denken und Handeln von der Vergangenheit geprägt wurden und werden.]

11. [3. Wandlungen in der Politik.
    (a) Bismarcks nationale Politik schafft das klein-deutsche Reich
    (b) Bismarcks Innenpolitik nach 1871
    (c) Bismarcks Außenpolitik
    (d) Die Außenpolitik Wilhelms II. schuf neue Spannungen.]

12. Keim (1995) has shown the extent to which many educators were not only compliant in accepting Nazi policies, but were instrumental in setting the stage for the Nazi government and in implementing its policies.

13. I cite from the East German curricula by referring to the year of publication of a cited curriculum. Please refer to the Appendix: Curricula for full citations. All translations are mine.

14. [Mit der Klärung der historischen Begriffe schafft der Geschichtsunterricht die Voraussetzungen zur Lösung seiner wichtigsten Aufgabe, der *Herausarbeitung des inneren Zusammenhangs des geschichtlichen Geschehens.*] (Italics in original.)

15. [Mit zunehmender Beherrschung der Natur erhöht der Mensch die Ergiebigkeit seiner Arbeit. Den Schülern ist zu zeigen, wie diese Entwicklung zur Entstehung des Privateigentums führt und wie die ursprünglich nach Abstammung gebildeten gesellschaftlichen Gruppen sich in Klassen aufzuspalten beginnen.]

16. [Der deutsche Bauernkrieg war der Höhepunkt des Klassenkampfes der Bauern gegen den herrschenden Feudaladel und richtete sich gegen die feudale Ausbeutung und Unterdrückung.]

17. [Geschichtsbilder.]

18. [Die Schüler sind auf dieser Altersstufe nach Maßgabe ihrer geistigen Reife von der bloßen Betrachtung und Aufnahme geschichtlicher Vorgänge und Tatsachen, die im 5. und 6. Schuljahr noch vorherrscht, allmählich an das historische Denken heranzuführen.]

19. [Das sozialistische Weltsystem.]

20. [Diese Beurteilung muß von wissenschaftlicher Gediegenheit, Sachlichkeit und Wahrhaftigkeit getragen sein.]
21. [Seiner Funktion wird der Geschichtsunterricht vor allem dadurch gerecht, daß er an Hand ausgewählter Ergebnisse der marxistisch-leninistischen Geschichtswissenschaft die Grundzüge eines wissenschaftlichen Geschichtsbildes formt und ein echtes Geschichtsverständnis entwickelt.]
22. [Oberstes Gesetz des Geschichtsunterrichts muß es sein, der geschichtlichen Wahrheit so nahe wie möglich zu kommen.]

References

Bude, Heinz. 1998. "Die Erinnerung der Generationen" [The Memory of Generations]. In *Leviathan*, eds. H. König, M. Kohlstruck, and A. Wöll. Special Issue, vol. 18, 69–85.

Conrad, Sebastian. 1999. *Auf der Suche nach der verlorenen Nation Geschichtsschreibung in Westdeutschland und Japan, 1945–1960* [In Search of the Lost Nation – Historiography in West Germany and Japan, 1945–1960], Göttingen: Vandenhoeck und Ruprecht.

Dierkes, Julian. 2001. "Absence, Déclin ou Essor de la Nation: Manuels d'Histoire d'après-guerre au Japon et dans le Deux Allemagnes" [The Absence, Decline or Rise of the Nation: Post-war History Textbooks in Japan and the Germanys], *Geneses*, vol. 44, 30–49.

Erbe, Michael. 1981. "Zur Rezeption der "Annales"-Historie in der Bundesrepublik' [The Reception of 'Annales" [History in the Federal Republic], *Lendemains*, vol. 6, 68–76.

Frank, David John, Suk-Ying Wong, John W. Meyer and Francisco Ramirez. 2000. "What Counts as History: A Cross-National and Longitudinal Study of University Curricula" *Comparative Education Review*, vol. 44, 29–53.

Halbritter, Maria. 1979. *Schulreformpolitik in der britischen Zone von 1945 bis 1949* [School Reform Policies in the British Zone from 1945 to 1949]. Weinheim: Beltz Verlag.

Jaeger, Friedrich and Jörn Rüsen. 1992. *Geschichte des Historismus* [History of Historicism]. Munich: Beck.

Keim, Wolfgang. 1995. *Erziehung unter der Nazi-Diktatur* [Education under the Nazi-Dictatorship]. Darmstadt: Wissenschaftliche Buchgesellschaft.

Kennedy, Paul. 1973. "The Decline of Nationalistic History in the West, 1900–1970." *Journal of Contemporary History*, vol. 8, 77–100.

Lange-Quassowski, Jutta. 1979. *Neuordnung oder Restauration?* [Restructuring or Restoration?]. Opladen: Leske and Budrich.

Levy, Daniel and Natan Sznaider. 2001. *Erinnerung im globalen Zeitalter: Der Holocaust* [Memory in the Global Age: The Holocaust]. Frankfurt: Suhrkamp.

Meyer, John W., John Boli, George Thomas and Francisco Ramirez. 1997. "World-Society and the Nation-State," *American Journal of Sociology*, vol. 103, 144–181.

Rosenzweig, Beate. 1998. *Erziehung zur Demokratie? Amerikanische Besatzungs- und Schulreformpolitik in Deutschland und Japan* [Education Towards Democracy? American Occupation and Educational Policies in Germany and Japan]. Stuttgart: Franz Steiner Verlag.

Ruge-Schatz, Angelika. 1977. *Umerziehung und Schulpolitik in der französischen Besatzungszone 1945–1949* [Re-education and School Policies in the French Zone of Occupation]. Frankfurt: Peter Lang.

Soysal, Yasemin Nuhoğlu. 2000. "Identity and Transnationalization in German School Textbooks." In *Censoring History*, eds. L. Hein and M. Selden. Armonk: M.E. Sharp, 127–49.

Part II

Europe Seen from the Periphery

Chapter 5

❖

Nation and the Other in Greek and Turkish History Textbooks

Vasilia Lilian Antoniou and Yasemin Nuhoğlu Soysal

What could not be achieved by politicians was accomplished by earthquakes that shook both sides of the Aegean Sea in 1999. In the aftermath of the quakes, the Turkish Ministry of Education decided to change history curricula and textbooks that dealt specifically with Turkish-Greek relations, amending their adverse, nationalistic tone. The decision seemed to signal both a thawing of hostilities between the two countries and a step in Turkey's quest to redefine its place within Europe and normalize its relations with Greece. Toward the same end, there are now efforts on both sides of the Aegean to review critically and to propose changes to history textbooks. These attempts are refreshing correctives to the overtly nationalistic content of Turkish education, in which emphasis on national history had, since the 1980s, steadily increased and overshadowed non-national elements. Somewhat earlier, in Greece, after the collapse of the dictatorship in 1974, a new ethos and approach toward history as a school subject similarly arose in bureaucratic circles and among the political elite, modifying some of the nationalistic sentiments apparent in textbooks and curricula. However, it was not until relatively recently that images of Greece and Greekness in relation to depictions of Turkey and Turkishness were altered in Greek school materials. These revisions are indicative of attempts to improve relations between the two countries and reveal Greece's current sense of security in the European Union.

Teaching history is crucial to self-understanding and representations of the modern nation-state. History, as a school subject, narrates both our past and the present. It also locates "us" vis-à-vis similar collectives. While collective belonging is commonly marked by various "banal" cultural symbols, such as the national flag, national anthem, and national currency,[1] it is via the teaching of history that ancestry, heritage, and the victories and calamities of the nation are learned. History education places the national evolution into a neat historical time frame, which dates from time immemorial and continues into the present day, and locates that nation in an internationally recognized geographical space. Hence, history curricula and textbooks have an important role in recounting and envisioning the nation and its evolution, especially in relation to the "other."

In this chapter, our goal is to explore the conceptualization of the nation and its "others" in a comparative manner. Despite conflicting histories, the teaching of history in Turkey and Greece display many similarities, and thus provide productive comparisons. Situated on the margins of Europe, the "true" location of their identity constantly contested, both countries place a strong emphasis on the nation in their history teaching. However, their narration of national history in textbooks exhibits significant differences.

Our analysis suggests that the most salient difference is in the emphasis placed on national time and national territory when conceptualizing nation and identity. While Greek textbooks define national identity primarily in terms of national time, Turkish textbooks give primacy to national territory. This difference, elaborated by references to historical events and the peculiarities of the nation-building process in each country, underlies a number of variations in the depiction of the nation and "others."

In the Turkish case, at one level, there is a seemingly continuous history of the nation: originating with the Turkic tribes of central Asia, the migration to Anatolia and founding of the Ottoman Empire, and finally the creation of the new Republic of Turkey. However, national time proceeds with breaks as the territories of the nation change—from central Asia to the large expanse of the Ottoman Empire, and to the Anatolia of the Turkish Republic. Thus, national territory becomes the defining signifier of nationness, each territory identifying a qualitatively different national past. These different heritages—pagan origins, Muslim Empire, and secular republic—are not necessarily reconciled into one seamless history, remaining more or less discrete in textbooks. When it comes to the history of the republic, the nation proper, the national time begins anew, with a new identity forged around the space represented by the territorial boundaries of the republic. The new national time does not incorporate Islam as a heritage proper, despite Islam's visible position in the most recent textbooks, and thus gives way to an uneasy affiliation with the Ottoman past. The end result is less a synthetic but rather a disjointed national history and identity, with many possible and contested heritages and multiple "others" (Greek, Kurdish, Armenian, Arab), who also covet the same territory as their "own."

Greek national history, on the other hand, strives and succeeds in establishing a national narrative that is continuous in time: beginning with the ancient Greeks, proceeding into Byzantium, and culminating in the construction of the modern Greek nation-state. Despite territorial losses and claims, this chronology remains continuous in the national time frame. The difficult but successful reconciliation of the pagan past with Byzantine Christianity produces a somewhat synthetic national history and identity, referred to as the "Hellenic-Christian tradition."

This tradition is based upon a continuity of culture over time, turning the Greek nation into a cultural community traveling through time. This accommodation between the Hellenic and the Christian world permits that the Greek Orthodox religion becomes a defining characteristic of Greekness. However, the "black period" of Muslim conquest and Ottoman rule, historically represented by the loss and capture of Constantinople by the Ottomans, brings Greek culture to a temporary halt and provides Greece with a persistent Turkish "other" regardless of her location in Europe.

However, the historic positions of both countries vis-à-vis Europe retain a degree of ambiguity.[2] Greece, with its Hellenic past, claims and is accorded the origin story of Europe—the cradle of civilization and democracy—and therefore is considered to be a part of Europe proper. However, its past association with the Eastern Roman Empire, Orthodox Christianity, and Ottoman rule, plus its geographical location, keep Greece in the margins of Europe, tainting her modernity and character with Easternness. Turkey, on the other hand, claims a formal place in Europe, a result of a history of nation-making practiced and expressed as European-style modernization. However, it is located beyond the cultural and political boundaries of European modernity proper. In other words, both Greece and Turkey, located in the margins of Europe—Greece inside but outside, Turkey outside but inside—differentially persist as "others" in or of Europe. Their exercise in nation building remains incomplete and questionable by European standards, a factor that underlies the prevailing emphasis on the symbols and ideals of the nation in curricula and textbooks. Achieving Europeanness demands that, first and foremost, Greece and Turkey realize a proper and unchallenged nationness based on the Western European model.

Recent, albeit reluctant, refutations of nationalism and changes to curricula content illustrate an eagerness in Greece and Turkey to become properly Europeanized. Greece's entry into the European Union in the early 1980s and Turkey's current aspiration to become a more active participant with the final goal of full membership, have stimulated rethinking and debate on curricula and textbooks in both countries. The experience of marginality and the ambiguities of their location have caused them to question their presumed historical positions and roles in Europe. As both countries opened up, there have been attempts to reconsider and change the content of education. This chapter explores the nature and extent of these changes in relation to the teaching of history.

Our focus is on the history curricula and textbooks of lower secondary school education. In Greece, the lower secondary school (gymnasium) comprises grades 7 to 9 (ages 11–14), and constitutes, along with elementary school (grades 1 to 6) and the lyceum (grades 10 to 12), compulsory education. The Ministry for National Education and Religion produces one history textbook for each grade, which, on average, is rewritten every five years, although minor changes are often made on a yearly basis. In Turkey, where lower secondary school comprises grades 6 to 8 (ages 12–15), it was as recent as 1997 that these grades were included in compulsory education. As in Greece, the Ministry of National Education produces textbooks for each grade, with revisions every five years. Since 1997, a number of privately produced textbooks have been published in Turkey. However, strict state-imposed guidelines and the obligatory following of the national curriculum means that they differ only marginally from state-produced textbooks.

Because lower secondary school education in both countries is compulsory, it reflects mass education and, we hope, makes it possible for us to expose the dominant historical narratives taught in schools. Our data come mainly from the most recent history textbooks and curricula; however, we also attempt to illustrate significant changes over time.

Curricula Objectives in Greek and Turkish History Teaching

In Greece, the collapse of the military dictatorship in 1974, and the subsequent period of democratization of the state and society (Diamandouros 1994), heralded a new era for history education.[3] By 1976, the Ministry of Education experienced a significant number of changes: a large number of its personnel were dismissed because of their prior support for the junta; the first national and democratic curriculum for history education became law; and all textbooks that had been in use before 1974 were replaced. Throughout these changes, even in the more recent period, the Greek education system remained centralized with a compulsory, unified history program, with state-produced textbooks the only source material used in the classroom. This has meant that reforms to history education in the post-1974 period have been limited and infrequent. The politicized (ideological) nature of history pedagogy's creation has also hindered the implementation of significant and frequent reforms, especially when compared with educational systems that have a less politicized process for making policies for the teaching of history.

The current objectives of Greek history education are representative of conventional conceptions of history as a school subject and as a method of fostering national sentiments. The post-1974 curricula state that history education has three primary objectives: the cultivation of national sentiments and democratic ideals; the acquisition of historical knowledge and techniques; and the promotion of the nation's historical continuity and its role in the development of global civilization.[4]

The 1986 Greek curriculum, which is currently in use, introduced new pedagogical objectives that signified a change in the ethos and structure of history education without detracting value from the three primary objectives established in the 1976 curriculum. For example, new emphasis was given to peaceful historical periods, while still giving priority to defensive and liberation wars; periods of cultural activity, particularly those of universal significance, were elevated in importance; notions of freedom and justice coexisted with the idea of self-sacrifice for the *patrida*; and history was to be patriotic, not based on a "misguided patriotism," but demonstrating brotherhood among and harmonious relations between peoples.[5]

In Turkey, the 1985 national curriculum, which is also still in use, includes objectives comparable to those in Greek curricula. The primary goals of history education are: teaching students the place of the Turkish nation in world history, illustrating its contribution to humanity, world civilization, and culture; strengthening national feelings, teaching the distinctiveness, energy, and aptitude of the Turkish nation, as well as its appreciation of art and science; communicating these characteristics as a blueprint for behavior; creating a sense of responsibility toward the nation, and elevating it to the level of modern nations in accordance with the directives of Atatürk; and nourishing the value of national independence and democracy, thus cultivating consciousness for protecting the state and national unity, interests and democracy.[6]

These curricular goals reflect continuity with previous national curricula, and by and large replicate the themes advanced in them. Nonetheless, the 1985 curriculum represented a significant departure in Turkish history education.[7] Whereas before 1985 non-national history constituted a significant part of the curriculum, the new curriculum nationalized history teaching along the lines of a new ethos: Turkish-Islamic synthesis. The curricular space devoted to Greek and Roman civilizations and aspects of European history was minimized, freeing space for and adding further emphasis to Turkish-Islamic history. These changes from the 1980s still dominate the Turkish history curriculum.

While the Turkish government decided to overhaul the educational system in 1997 by extending compulsory education to include the lower part of the secondary school, the content of education stayed more or less the same.[8] Despite the existence of private schools and, since 1997, private textbooks, textbook production in Turkey has remained essentially a state activity, and all schools follow a state-produced and unified curriculum (which has been the case since the foundation of the republic). In this, Turkish history education parallels Greek history education, with the state having almost absolute power to design its content and structure. Moreover, in spite of recent attempts, the commanding presence of bureaucratic machinery involved in curriculum development makes reform a slow and unavailing process. Thus, in both Greece and Turkey, undoing curricula appears as an intermittent and a trying venture.

Conceptualizations of the Nation

National narratives frequently describe unitary location and the heritage and culture of the nation(-state) through the notions of time and space. National geographical space signifies the territorial boundaries of the nation, while the

national time frame illustrates its evolution. Both notions validate and legitimate the nation's existence as both a geographical and a cultural entity over
time and in space. Thus, they become salient conceptual tools in creating,
writing, and teaching history.

Greek and Turkish textbooks are replete with examples of how the nation is
conceptualized and defined through the notions of time and space. However,
owing to the two nations' differing historical processes of nation- and state-
making, we observe a different emphasis given to time and space in the writing
of their history textbooks. While the Turkish textbooks stress the notion of
space in conceptualizing and defining their nation, the Greek textbooks highlight the notion of time. This contrast in emphasis reflects the nations'
presumed historical evolution. Greek textbooks present the ancient Greek
world as the early history of the nation, and hence place great importance on
time in subsequent definitions of the nation. This emphasis indirectly panders
to nationalistic ideas of Greek superiority vis-à-vis other national time frames
that do not boast such a distinguished and distant ancestry.[9] By contrast,
emphasis on territory of the nation in Turkish textbooks precludes defining a
continuous Turkish identity, promoting instead the nation's greatest accomplishment and success, that of conqueror. It is perhaps for this reason that
projections of national identity in Turkish textbooks are frequently expressed
with reference to interactions with "others" (Copeaux 2002).

The valorization of national ancestry is very clear in both cases, but with a
different twist. Greek textbooks present their ancestry as the origins of the
modern, civilized European world. This is of particular significance as it is to
the Western European world that the current textbooks aim to locate Greece,
and not in the Balkan world, where Greece, historically, has been one of the
most important actors. The veneration of ancient Greek civilization in textbooks also serves the purpose of displaying the importance of Greek culture
for the European world. The universal importance of this past and its relevance
in locating Greece within the confines of the European world can only be maintained if some sort of continuity over time can be upheld.

Greek textbooks divide the "history of man" into three chronological epochs:
"As we know, the history of man is divided into three periods: ancient history,
medieval history, and modern and contemporary history" (G8 1999: 5). This
chronological approach is not unique to Greek schoolbooks, but is characteristic of those of many other states. What distinguishes Greek schoolbooks is
that they chart the Greek evolution through this historical-chronological time
frame, assuming it to be universally accepted, legitimate, and scientific.
Furthermore, it is through this time frame that they make the claim of linearity in their national evolution.

Claims of linearity promote ideas of continuity and homogeneity over time.
To assert, as the textbooks do, that the "Greek ethnos" has existed since the
ancient Greek period, and has traveled through the Medieval (Byzantine)

period into the modern period gives credibility to such ideas. The national community projected in textbooks appears to be made up of a number of cultural components that have passed through time relatively intact. Hence, the conceptualization of the nation in Greek textbooks is that of a cultural community flowing through time, and originating from the moment the process of civilization begins: "The history of any nation begins from the moment that that people recognizes and uses script" (G7 1998: 7). The ancient Greek period then becomes the early history of the nation in schoolbooks. Its continuity over time places Greece within the European world—testifies to Greece's superior evolution—and minimizes the relevance of the Ottoman period to Greek cultural and intellectual development:

> The Greeks maintained their customs and traditions [from ancient and Byzantine times], as well as creating new ones. They organized their life significantly differently from those that enslaved them [the Ottomans]. It is through this method that they differentiated themselves, and maintained their national consciousness. (G6 1996: 59)

> The year 1453, when the Turks conquered Constantinople, represents the end of the political life of Byzantium. However, its cultural life continued. After the decline of the Byzantine State, Hellenism in its new form (the neo-Hellenic) continued its traditions. It preserved the precious inheritance, namely the unification of the ancient Greek world with the Christian spirit that Byzantium had created, and found the strength not only to preserve but also to flourish and continue. (G8 1999: 340)

> At a time when the Catholic Church was confronting the acute crisis of the Reformation and the Renaissance movement, wise Greeks, usually monks or clerics, kept alive the intellectual and national tradition of the Nation or tried to spread Greek intellectual culture to other Orthodox countries. (G9 1999: 118)

Continuity in national evolution is thus sustained, despite the fact that there is a qualitative difference between ancient Greece's pagan nature, and the Christian Middle Ages and Christian present. This difference exposes a notable contradiction in schoolbooks (and in Greek historiography more generally), representing a rupture in an otherwise seamless and synthetic evolution: "In the beginning, Christianity and Hellenism came into conflict because they represented two different worlds" (G8 1999: 91).

Byzantium—the original sponsor and distributor of Orthodox Christianity across Europe—becomes significant to modern European civilization and the conceptualizations of contemporary Greek identity in that it allows textbooks to transcend this rupture, and hence maintain the meta-narrative:

> Slowly, however, they [Hellenism and Christianity] came nearer as a result of the important role played by the Fathers of the Church [the Patriarchs]. They had studied the ancient Greek works, and understood their value. Hence, with the passing of time, the different components [which made up the two different worlds] united and created the distinctive and unique appearance of Byzantium, that is, its simultaneous Hellenic and Christian character. (G8 1999: 91)

Indeed, it is the accommodation between the two cultures (periods) that promotes a teleological understanding of the historical process, in which the era of the modern Greek nation-state represents both the culmination and the desired state of Greek evolution.

In contrast to the cultural continuity of the nation in Greek textbooks, the Turkish national time frame appears somewhat disjointed. The sense of continuity appears primarily through the idea of conquering new territories. The Turkish nation starts in the "steppes of central Asia," and triumphs in Anatolia. The central Asian origins of Turkish culture and identity are celebrated in the great character and military successes of the Ottoman *Beys* who conquered the Middle East and Anatolia. As the sixth grade history book claims, Turks contributed to the prospering of the Middle Eastern and Aegean civilizations through a wave of migrations and conquests:

> Turks from Central Asia migrated to various parts of the world, and helped the natives who still lived in the Paleolithic Age to move into the Neolithic Age. They learned from the Turks how to cultivate the earth, and how to work metals. In these new countries, the Turks made further advances, building big cities and founding strong states. Important centers of civilization were thus created in Mesopotamia, in Anatolia, in Syria and around the Aegean Sea. (T6a 1991: 25, cited in Millas 1991: 16)

In Turkish textbooks, national evolution is often represented by invasion and conquest of other lands, the rise and fall of Turkish dynasties, and the consecutive building of the state. The structure of the textbook follows the historical periods identified with the governing family, clan, and dynasty, and the subsequent states they founded. Central Asia remains the "first motherland of Turks" but not the focus of a cultural/national identity. The "glory" of the Turkish nation stems from her military achievements and successful state experiences. Cultural continuity is only presented in assumed characteristics (such as the ability to rule, competence in warfare, and fairness), military achievements, and statesmanship of the leaders, but not in collective cultural representations. This can be seen in both the sixth and seventh grade textbooks:

> Our ancestors, Bumin Kagan and Istemi Kagan, formed and protected the state and the customs of the Turkish nation. They had enemies all around. But the Kagans were knowledgeable and brave. They managed to take all the other nations under their sovereignty. (*Orhun* inscriptions, T6b 1996: 16)

> Atilla is the unforgettable Turkish Emperor for Europeans (T6b 1996: 30).

> Sultan Mehmet II is the best example of the greatness and of the humane approach of the Turkish nation, as he allowed the non-Muslim inhabitants of Istanbul to keep their religion and traditions. (T7a 1991: 19, cited in Millas 1991: 18)

Thus, Turkish identity is conceptualized as one that embraces the space of the state (it is a state/political identity as oppose to a cultural identity), resulting in an emphasis on the great military leaders who helped actualize this political identity.

These examples clearly illustrate that Greek and Turkish textbooks conceptualize the nation in ways that are distinctly different. In Greek textbooks, culture is supremely important in describing the nation, with its value, traditions, and customs drawn from its presumed continuity over time. While space is important (for example, "places of memory" such as Constantinople, and the current boundaries of the Greek state),[10] temporal cultural continuity is given precedence. This is perhaps associated with the changing nature of national geographic space over time. The current Greek nation-state may share the same space as that of the ancient Greek world, but Greece's assumed role as the bearer and sustainer of the culture of antiquity, through Byzantium and into modern times, is deemed more significant. This cultural continuity over time argues that Greek culture (and the modern Greek nation-state) claims a formal and legitimate place within Europe. The ancient and Byzantine heritages of Greece support the assertions that Greece is both the "mother of Europe" and unique among the European nations.

In Turkish textbooks, however, it is the space of the nation-state that defines the nation and identity.[11] Turkish identity is closely connected to territory, and to those leaders that have helped actualize the territory. This emphasis on territory is the principle reason why past leaders of the state, their military successes, and the supposed inestimable civilizing role they play in subjugated realms, enjoy a central position in textbooks. Although culture plays an important role in textbooks, it is treated in a rather schizophrenic manner. Turkish textbooks simultaneously embrace and dispute cultural influences upon Turkish identity (for example, the Arabic civilization and the Ottoman period) as well as downplaying, at least until the 1980s, the Islamic heritage. After the 1980s, the focus in textbooks is on the Turkish Islamic states and their successes. The efforts of each sultan to build mosques and schools [*medrese*] in the newly conquered lands are mentioned in the chapters on "Art" and "Civilization" in schoolbooks. Respect for religion, not only Islam but also Christianity and Judaism, is also represented as a characteristic of Turkish rulers. Despite these achievements, the main cultural continuity appears via the language: "When the Islamic state was flourishing, Arabic became widespread in the invaded territories. But because Turkish is a strong language, Turks managed to maintain their national consciousness, even after converting to Islam" (T7b 1996: 55). Hence, Turkish identity is conceptualized as one that embraces the space and the language of the modern nation-state. It is essentially a state/political identity based on the successful creation of a political unit within sovereign borders, as opposed to a cultural identity that displays elements of continuity over time. Independence and protection of the motherland (referring now to the current boundaries of the Turkish state) become the dominant national virtues. In this sense, Turkey also claims a proper and rightful place in Europe. The creation of a secular state based principally on a civic conception of membership demonstrates the modernizing (European) values that characterize modern projections of the nation and identity.

While the manner in which the Turkish and Greek national narratives define and describe their respective nations and identities are markedly different, both narratives substantiate (both symbolically and historically) claims for full membership in Europe: Greece via its ancient and Medieval heritages, Turkey via its more recent state-building actions.

Conceptualizations of the "Other"

In Turkish textbooks, the problematic relationship between the Turkish Republic and the Ottoman Empire is peculiarly amplified in the presentations of the "other." Given the Ottoman Empire's contentious history with eastern and European empires, at different historical points, a number of states (China, Iran, Austria-Hungary, Russia, France) have appeared as the nation's "other." This is different from Greece, where a clear sense of otherness is bestowed upon the Turks and, less so, upon the Roman Catholic West. The Greek nation-state was a direct outcome of independence from the Ottoman Empire, so it is understandable that the Ottoman, but in particular the Turkish elements of the Ottoman, represents the "other" of the Greek nation. What is perplexing is that, once we move to the Turkish Republic's history, the Ottoman also becomes the Turkish national "other," as the Turkish Republic's own history can only be written as a clean break with the Ottoman Empire and what it represents. At the end of the First World War, the defeatist Ottoman leaders and the Empire became the "enemy" to fight against.[12] Intensifying the appearance of cultural discontinuity in the evolution of Turkish identity is the fact that the history of the Turkish Republic is taught separately (in the eighth grade) from Ottoman history (in the sixth and seventh grades). This topical—and seemingly technical—organization of the way history is presented frames the overly narrated histories of leaders and states with proper beginnings and ends.[13]

The commonality in the portrayal of the Ottoman Empire as the Greek and the Turkish nation-states' "other" within the context of the modernity of nation-stateness is most striking. Nevertheless, the manner in which this historical period and this "other" are conceptualized and presented differs greatly in the textbooks of the two countries. This difference is most visible in the amount of textbook space given to the Ottoman period. In Turkish textbooks, grades six and seven deal exclusively with Ottoman history. Evidently, the Ottoman period makes up an important, albeit confused, part of Turkish national history. The Ottoman past represents the ancestry of the Turkish nation yet, paradoxically, its demise represents the birth of a new nation. It is for this reason that the Ottoman period occupies such a large proportion of, yet appears to play such an unclear role in, Turkish history textbooks. In contrast, Greek textbooks, although according the Ottoman historical period with significantly less textbook space than their Turkish counterparts, bestow a very precise role to this historical period. In the eighth grade textbook, only two sections are dedicated to the Ottomans: the conquering of Constantinople, and the creation of the Ottoman state. This takes up about 3 percent of the total textbook. In the ninth grade textbook, the space given to the Ottoman period is marginally more, with an entire chapter dedicated to life under Ottoman rule and another chapter focusing on the process of liberation. However, all references to the Ottoman period relate to the experience of the Ottoman occupation of Greece.

The Ottoman period of history represents the "black period" of Greek history and, consequently, the Ottoman Turk is accorded with the role of the "other" in Greek textbooks. While the period of Ottoman rule, which lasted over four-hundred years, is not neglected, it is conceptualized as a significant period in the "History of Greece," but not in the "History of Greeks." This distinction represents this "other" as having minimally influenced the Greeks; indeed, it is suggested that its presence only helped further to unite Greeks:

> The Greeks never believed that the Turkish conquest [of Greece] also ended the life of Hellenism. There is further proof that shows that the Tourkokratia [Ottoman rule] coincides with the reshaping of Hellenism. During the darkness of slavery, with tremendous tenacity, the neo-Hellenic consciousness was united and, in 1821, they took the reactionaries in Europe by surprise [with their liberation struggle against Ottoman rule]. (G8 1999: 347)

In Greek schoolbooks the Ottoman "other," then, represents a threat to the Greek nation, which is further amplified in the sections that deal with Ottoman interactions with Greeks:

> One of the most tragic forms of Islamification was "pedomazoma" [child-capturing], which began a century before occupation under Sultan Mourat II. Pedomazoma was based upon the strict selection of children and adolescents with highly developed physical and intellectual abilities, and their subsequent inclusion into the military of the huge Turkish [Ottoman] state. This practice, which continued until the early 18th century, meant that the enslaved [Greeks] were denied the most vital part of the population, and resulted in enormous dangers for Hellenism. (G9 1999: 105)

In Greek schoolbooks, the Ottoman occupation is presented as a period of darkness and fear for Greece, and is attributed, perhaps more significantly, with removing Greece from the path of Western European development, tainting the modern Greeks with Easternness. Allocating responsibility for modern Greek underdevelopment to an external "other," as opposed to internal developments and circumstances, sustains the projection of an Ottoman Turkish "other" in educational materials, and legitimates claims of the Europeanness of Greece.

The exchange of populations between Greece and Turkey in the 1920s, and the 1974 invasion of Cyprus by Turkey provide Greek schoolbooks with the rationale for maintaining images of a Turkish "other," albeit of a more modern form: "In July 1974, a coup d'etat organized against the President of the Cypriot Republic, Archbishop Makarios, by the [Greek] junta failed. Turkey, as a 'protectorate power,' took advantage of the circumstances and invaded the island (20th July 1974) with great military strength, capturing and retaining 40% of Cypriot land" (G9 1999: 374). These more recent historical interactions between Turkey and Greece and their inclusion in educational materials project a historically permanent generic Turkish "other" in the Greek national narrative. This "other" continues to be presented as a mighty military force, whose civilizational and ethical values are questionable. "Turkish" behavior is presented as aggressive toward Greeks and other Greek-speaking peoples—their "innocent" victims—depicting two "nations" that, throughout history and into the present, have had tense relations with one another.

Greek textbooks, however, do not single out the Ottoman/Turk as the only "other." The Roman Catholic West also enters in this role into the historical narrative of the Greeks. This Roman Catholic "other" is not historically permanent, as is the case with the Ottoman/Turk: it is a temporary "other" associated with a specific historical period. Hence, it is conceptualized and presented as the "other" only in specific contexts, namely, when discussing the Crusades and the division between the two Christian churches:

> The idea for the [fourth] Crusade came from Pope Innocente III, his aim being to attack the Muslims in Egypt, who after the death of Saladdin were engaged in civil war. From there, according to his calculations, he believed it would be easy to liberate Palestine. Simultaneously, the Venetians, who were thinking about their own economic gains, convinced the Pope to incorporate their aims, namely to both loot and attack Byzantium. Pope Innocente believed that this was the perfect moment to capture the Eastern Church, and bring it back under Roman Catholic control. (G8 1999: 265)

The Crusades result in a strangely united Greek and Turkish point of view, creating a common temporary "other" in Western Europe. The Crusades were launched not only against the Orthodox Church but also against Islam. More importantly, they were launched against Constantinople (Istanbul). The Turkish textbook states: "The Crusaders, under Peter the Hermit, ravaged every place they passed through and did the worst they could do to the people... . They ruined Istanbul and plundered monuments and burned part of the city" (T6b 1996: 86). In Turkish textbooks the terms "Crusader Christians" and "Europeans" are used interchangeably. Here, through a common Easternness, Greek and Turkish textbooks converge. In the narratives of desolation and destruction, the Crusaders, as the western "other," close the national distance between the Greeks and the Turks. Constantinople/Istanbul, the "Great City" in both national narratives, connects the diverging paths of the national histories, and renders visible the shared legacies and spaces.

The conceptualization of the Roman Catholic West as a temporary and context-specific "other" is more pronounced in recent Greek history textbooks. Previous textbooks, particularly those used in elementary schooling, presented the Roman Catholic West as a more prominent "other" (Antoniou 2004). The presentation of the Roman Catholic West as the "other" is clearly a result of the importance attributed to the Orthodox Christian tradition as a defining national characteristic. Although Orthodoxy remains one of the defining components of Greek national identity, the changing relations with Western Europe (as a result of European Union membership) have altered the projections and connotations associated with this Western "other."

When analyzing the images of the "other" in Greek and Turkish textbooks, both similarities and differences appear. As mentioned previously, the most striking similarity emerges in the form of the common Ottoman "other." However, the degree to which that "other" is in fact a part of the dominant "us" is where Greek and Turkish textbooks diverge. To disregard the Ottoman period of history in Turkish textbooks is akin to disregarding the early history and beginnings of the nation, yet to assimilate it with the modern secular political/state identity is far too difficult. Coming to terms with one's own history, as with Turkey, makes reappraising and reevaluating that history all the more difficult.

The differences between the textbooks can be seen in the number of "others" displayed. While Greek textbooks have two dominant "others" (of which only one, the Ottoman Empire, is permanent), Turkish textbooks have numerous, and always temporary, "others;" the result of a secular identity that is defined by territory. Any grouping, within or without, that threatens or covets national space is automatically conceptualized as an "other." Thus, over time, Chinese, Arabs, Europeans, Russians, Greeks, and Armenians all appear as "others":

> The Chinese, who could not compete militarily with the Hun Empire, resorted to internal measures. They sent Chinese princesses. They married [Turkish] leaders and created hostilities among Turkish states. (T6b 1996: 15)

> Romen Diyojen, a Byzantine Emperor, was bothered by the Turkish invasions into Anatolia, and wanted to stop them.... His main aim was to prevent Turkish settlement in Anatolia. (T6c 1999: 68)

> Our compatriots living here [in Greece] have some problems because of the attitudes of the Greek Government. Some obstacles have been created in economic, cultural and social spheres in the areas where Turks live. They have been forced to migrate, and their territories have been nationalized, their national consciousness eroded. (T7c 1999: 156)

> The main reason for the emergence of the Armenian problem is the policy of [other] states, which wanted to divide the Ottoman state. It was not even started by the Armenians. (T8 1999: 39)

The images associated with the "other" have been those most subject to change in recent schoolbooks. In Greece, these revisions to history textbooks can be deemed to be part and parcel of the post-1974 process of Europeanization. The entry of Greece into the European Union helped alter the images associated with Western Europe in Greek history schoolbooks. Becoming a fully-fledged member of the European Union also opened up the Greek educational establishment to significant global pedagogical trends, such as cultural history, women's history, and history-from-below. These have undoubtedly limited the amount of space that can be dedicated to the presentation of the history of the nation in relation to "others." The Balkan Crises of the late 1980s and early 1990s, and the consequent marginalization of the area from the West, have similarly stimulated a debate on how regional history appears in Greek textbooks. While a long way from being presented in a neutral manner, these moves have shifted the focus to the south-east Balkan Peninsula and have led to the omission of direct negative references, even when discussing the Greeks' dominant "other," the Turk.

In Turkish textbooks, a similar change can also be seen. In 1993, the Turkish UNESCO committee made revisions to history textbooks, with the aim of integrating into them an international perspective and universal values, and presenting the national history along with world history (in line with UNESCO's general recommendations). These revisions were also motivated by a desire to cease teaching history as solely a narrative of wars and military struggles, and to illustrate and emphasize social, cultural and intellectual developments. The sections in current textbooks on daily life in villages, cities and the palace aim to reflect the diversity of the Ottoman state.[14] Despite all the changes introduced into textbooks, the main character of the Turkish historical narrative seems to remain intact.

Conclusion

Recently, both Greek and Turkish governments have shown a commitment to amend and reappraise history textbooks and curricula. This commitment has generated a great deal of interest and debate, both in educational spheres and in academia. The desire to revise and the process of amending history textbooks actually began before Greece became a member of the European Union. Under the auspices of UNESCO, officials and educators from both countries were brought together to begin work on improving history textbooks. These efforts have continued until today, and as Europe became an official reference point, with Greece's actual and Turkey's potential membership, they have intensified. The relatively marginal status of both countries vis-à-vis Europe has generated local intellectual debate on the validity of the historical assumptions and approaches that underlie history education in both countries, as has a global trend toward teaching a more humanist world history.[15] In addition, the aspirations for "proper European" status have opened the way for a more productive relationship between the two countries, which has already resulted in the incorporation and implementation of some significant textbook changes. The Greek Government's decision not to blockade Turkey's entrance into the EU may represent the most telling gesture, heralding a new phase in the writing of history in Turkey and Greece. No doubt the realization of a sensible history education not rooted in national bias will require strong political will on both sides, and will take more than a rapprochement between the two countries. Nevertheless, it seems that the road to reform and improvement has been opened.

Notes

Data and arguments presented in this chapter draw upon Vasilia L. Antoniou's Ph.D. (2004), and Yasemin Nuhoğlu Soysal's ESRC project "Rethinking Nation-state Identities in the New Europe." The project has received further funding from the Fuller Bequest Fund, the University of Essex, the British Academy, and the Leverhulme Trust. We are grateful to Ayca Ergun for her invaluable assistance in locating and collecting data for the Turkish case. Lia Antoniou would like to express thanks to Gella Varnava-Skouras and Laura Mamakos for their assistance with the Greek case.

1. For "banal nationalism" see Billig (1995).
2. For the ambiguous place of Greece and Turkey in Europe see Herzfeld (1986, 1987, 1992) and L. Soysal (1992).
3. Despite the major pedagogical change that 1974 ushered, the curricula produced in the post-1974 period display continuities with their pre-1974 predecessors.
4. See Greek National Curriculum for History (1976: 1), and Greek National Curriculum for History (1986: 1–2).
5. See Greek National Curriculum for History (1986: 3–4).
6. See Turkish National Curriculum for History (1985: 365–88).
7. This was the first curriculum introduced after the 1980 military coup d'état, which demonstrated a particular zeal in targeting progressive intellectuals and educational institutions.
8. In 1999, the government introduced yet another change. The social sciences replaced history and geography teaching in the elementary and lower secondary school curricula. The effect of this change on textbook content and topical emphasis remains to be seen.
9. As Lowenthal (1996) noted, ideas of being first are often associated with ideas of being best.
10. National space often has cultural connotations associated with it. For example, Constantinople has an important place in the Greek national narrative; its symbolic significance emanates from its past Hellenic and Christian nature. While such a presentation speaks of culture, it indirectly claims that space as Greek.
11. Like Greek historiography, Turkish historiography also attempts to offer a temporal understanding of national evolution, though this is less pronounced in recent historiography and textbooks. The 1930s Kemalist "History Thesis" was based on the principle of proving the ancientness of Turks and their culture, attempting to debunk the "Greek miracle" and citing the Turkish origins of ancient Ionian civilization. See Copeaux (2002: 398–401).

12. Symbolically, in textbooks there is no reference to the empire until the narration of the history of Turkish Republic. Until that point, the term Ottoman state is used.
13. As we noted before, after the introduction of the 1985 curriculum, there has been a visible change in the textbooks, with a pronounced emphasis on the Ottoman legacy and its Islamic cultural content. Still, however, they do not resolve the cultural discontinuity in Turkish identity's evolution.
14. See Koullapis (1994) for a more detailed analysis of these changes.
15. In the mid-1990s, the History Foundation in Turkey organized a series of international symposiums, with the goal of including new approaches into textbooks (such as humanist and world history), as well as reevaluating Greek and Turkish textbooks in light of these new approaches. Similarly, in Greece, the Pedagogical Institute (a branch of the Ministry of Education made up of academics who consult on educational matters) has organized and funded numerous research projects, with the aim of improving the manner in which Turkey is portrayed in schoolbooks.

References

Antoniou, Vasilia L. 2004. "Does History Matter? Temporal and Spatial Projections of the Nation and Identity in Post-1974 Greek History School Books." Ph.D. diss. European University Institute.

Billig, Michael. 1995. *Banal Nationalism*. London: Sage.

Copeaux, Étienne. 2002. "Otherness in the Turkish Historical Discourse: General Considerations." In *Clio in the Balkans: The Politics of History Education*, ed. C. Koulouri. Thassaloniki: CDSEE, 397–406.

Diamandouros, Paschalis Nikiforos. 1994. "Cultural Dualism and Political Change in Post-Authoritarian Greece." Working Paper, no. 50, Madrid: Juan March Institute.

G6. Greek Elementary History Textbook (6th Grade). 1996. *Sta Neotera Chronia* [In Modern Times]. Athens: Organismos Ekthoseos Didaktikon Biblion.

G7. Greek Gymnasium History Textbook (7th Grade). 1998. *Istoria ton Archaion Chronon os to 30 p.x.* [History of the Ancient Years until 30BC], Athens: Organismos Ekthoseos Didaktikon Biblion.

G8. Greek Gymnasium History Textbook (8th Grade). 1999. *Istoria - Romaiki kai Byzantini* [History – Roman and Byzantine]. Athens: Organismos Ekthoseos Didaktikon Biblion.

G9. Greek Gymnasium History Textbook (9th Grade). 1999. *Istoria - Neoteri kai Sychroni* [History - Modern and Contemporary]. Athens: Organismos Ekthoseos Didaktikon Biblion.

Herzfeld, Michael. 1986. *Ours Once More: Folklore, Ideology, and the Making of Modern Greece*. New York: Pella Publishing Company.

———— 1987. *Anthropology Through the Looking-Glass: Critical Ethnography in the Margins of Europe*. Cambridge: Cambridge University Press.

———— 1992. *The Social Production of Indifference: Exploring the Symbolic Roots of Western Bureaucracy*. Oxford: Berg Publishers.

Koullapis, Lory Gregory. 1994. "Türkiye'de tarih ders Kitapları ve UNESCO' nun önerileri" [History Textbooks in Turkey and the Recommendations of UNESCO]. In *Tarih Öğretimi ve Ders Kitapları* [History Education and Textbooks], ed. S. Özbaran. Istanbul: History Foundation, 273–82.

Lowenthal, David. 1996. *The Heritage Crusade and the Spoils of History*. London: The Free Press.

Millas, Herkul. 1991. "History Textbooks in Greece and Turkey." *History Workshop Journal* 21, no. 2: 16–18.

National Curriculum for History (Athens). 1976. Athens: National Ministry for Education and Religion.

National Curriculum for History (Athens). 1986. Athens: National Ministry for Education and Religion.

National Curriculum for History (Ankara). 1985. Ankara: Ministry for National Education.

Soysal, Levent. 1992. "Greece and Turkey: Reflections on Ethnography in the Margins of Europe," Unpublished paper. Harvard University.

T6a. Turkish Secondary School History Textbook (6th Grade). 1991. *Milli Tarih I* [National History I]. Ankara: Ministry of Education.

T6b. Turkish Secondary School History Textbook (6th Grade). 1996. *Milli Tarih I* [National History I]. Ankara: Ministry of Education.

T6c. Turkish Secondary School History-Geography-Civic Textbook (6th Grade). 1999. *Sosyal Bilgiler 6* [Social Knowledge 6]. Ankara: Ministry of Education.

T7a. Turkish Secondary School History Textbook (7th Grade). 1991. *Milli Tarih II* [National History II]. Ankara: Ministry of Education.

T7b. Turkish Secondary School History Textbook (7th Grade). 1996. *Milli Tarih II* [National History II]. Ankara: Ministry of Education.

T7c. Turkish Secondary School History-Geography-Civic Textbook (7th Grade). 1999. *Sosyal Bilgiler 7* [Social Knowledge 7]. Ankara: Ministry of Education.

T8. Turkish Secondary School History Textbook (8th Grade). 1999. *Türkiye Cumhuriyeti İnkilap Tarihi ve Atatürkçülük VIII* [History of the Turkish Revolution of the Turkish Republic and Kemalism VIII]. Ankara: Ministry of Education.

Chapter 6

❖

"Europe" in Bulgarian Conceptions of Nationhood

Tim Pilbrow

A sense of belonging to Europe is central to the way Bulgarians conceptualize their national identity. However, a constant theme in the public discourse on national identity since the fall of state socialism in 1989 has been the need to move closer to Europe, to become more European. This bespeaks a certain ambivalence in Bulgarians' sense of their relationship to Europe, and my intention here is to explore how this ambivalent understanding in fact gets reproduced itself as a central element in Bulgarian conceptions of national identity. Of particular interest in this regard is the contrast between how Bulgaria's relationship to Europe is portrayed through school history teaching, and how this relationship is portrayed in other forms of public discourse in Bulgaria.[1]

Whereas the school history curriculum stresses the organic, indelible ties binding Bulgaria to Europe, in the public sphere more generally Bulgarian claims to a European identity are treated with considerable irony and cynicism. Where official history meets with other discourses on national identity in the public sphere, I suggest, there emerges a national ideology that incorporates and reproduces the ambiguities surrounding Bulgaria's place in Europe. The school curriculum's mission to assert a solid, organic tie to Europe is but one side of a larger public discourse on identity in which the certitude of such ties is called into question. This ambivalence and ambiguity over Bulgaria's "Europeanness," I argue, is a central component of Bulgarian national ideology. I use the term "ideology" here in the sense of the ideational frameworks through which people understand their national identity in relation to their broader social experience, rather than as an imposed worldview. Explicit and imposed ideological programs (such as those projected through official histories or school curricula) are but one side of a broader field of discourse in which ideologies take shape. However influential explicit ideological programs may be, they do not as such predetermine the shape of national ideology as it emerges in the public sphere.

"Europe" and "Europeanness" have long been central referents in the ideology of national identity in Bulgaria, yet as is the case for all symbols, what exactly they reference is the object of negotiation and dispute. While all Bulgarians would agree as to the centrality of Europe and Europeanness to their own sense of national identity, these symbols are construed differently by different social agents. My aim here is to unravel something of the dynamics of the relationship of the nation to the symbolic and institutional spaces of Europe in post-state-socialist Bulgarian conceptions of nationhood. Examining the way Europe is used in the fashioning of national ideologies in Bulgaria prompts a reconceptualization of national identity away from a consensus model toward a model in which identity can be seen to coalesce around ambivalence and conflict regarding central symbols.

My point of departure is the unfolding of the public discourse of national identity in Bulgaria during the mid 1990s at the key site occupied by the secondary school history classroom.[2] My research involved long-term observation of history classes in a number of secondary schools in Sofia, Bulgaria during 1995 and 1996, as well as considerable informal interaction with history teachers outside of the classroom. "Working up" from grounded and delimited field research to a discussion of national culture and identity demands that we regard the nation as a community of interest, or, more accurately, a community of cross-cutting and competing interests. The interests of any particularly positioned members of that community are, from such a perspective, of considerable importance to our building up of a picture of that whole. This approach follows the logic of much contemporary ethnographic research in its insistence on portraying the texture of localized or particularized identities as a means to grasping the dynamics of their broader social and cultural context. Much recent anthropological research into the cultures of large-scale societies (cities, states, nations) has as a consequence been grounded in research on geographically localized communities. As Herzfeld (1997: 91) writes, "a remote village, while not in any analytically useful sense typical of an entire country, may nonetheless serve to draw out some of the latter's more distinctive self-typifications."[3] However, anthropologists and other social scientists have become increasingly interested in how people's social networks and identities transcend geographical locality.[4] Within the nation-state, institutional settings provide a useful means to defining a community of interest and thereby grounding the analysis of national culture.

The school history classroom is such an institutionally defined setting, and one where, moreover, a variety of communities of interest come to bear (for example, teachers, pupils, school administrators, the education ministry, academic historians, parents) and one where the transmission and reproduction of conceptions of national identity are explicitly foregrounded. While formal educational settings and processes are but one component of much broader processes of social and cultural reproduction, their role in the transmission of the values and ideologies of the nation-state is important. As such, formal educational settings may be regarded as important venues for gaining perspective on the broader public sphere. Moreover, in a period of rapid social, political, and economic change, such as that following the fall of state socialism in Eastern Europe (that is, since1989), the self-conscious efforts of the educational establishment to define and impart a new value system (ideology) in keeping with the post-state-socialist transition toward pluralist democracy and free market capitalism, grants formal educational processes a highly visible and specific role in the production and reproduction of the citizenry.

Conceptions of Europe: School Curriculum and Ironic Self-representations

Early on in my field research in Bulgaria (from 1995 to 1996) I was struck by the differences between the way history and national identity were presented in school history classes and the way they were represented in other media of general public discourse. Whereas in the print, talk and visual media a deep-seated ambivalence surrounding Bulgaria's status vis-à-vis Europe was often dwelt upon, the school history curriculum and textbooks, as well as classroom discussions, dealt largely with claims to an indelible, organic, and long-standing European identity. These claims are based upon the understanding of a direct line of descent from the strength and splendor of the mediaeval Bulgarian Empire via processes of modernization and democratization parallel to and (in part) deriving from those in Western Europe, as well as the geographical certainty of Bulgaria's location in Europe (albeit at Europe's south-eastern margin) and linguistic and cultural affinities. In this reading, membership in Europe is claimed by historical right through demonstration of an unbroken cultural tradition within the geographical space of Europe. Bulgaria's modern history is marked by the progressively successful struggle to assert that right, and gain rightful recognition as a European nation-state from its rebirth as an incipient ethnic nation in the late eighteenth century. The previous 500 years of Ottoman domination, in this reading, left a legacy of economic stagnation and cultural stasis, but Bulgaria's progress in catching up—and proving her intrinsic European identity—is undeniable, and fuller incorporation into Europe is merely a matter of course.

Official history as reflected in the school history curriculum and in classroom practice is nevertheless but one reading of history. Europe and Europeanness are potent symbols, and can as easily be used to challenge as to support the claims of official history. If Europeanness is considered an ideal to be lived up to, rather than as an aspect of cultural heritage, then claims to European identity can be measured in terms of performance, and Bulgarian culture can be represented as at odds with European norms and values. Such interpretations are not uncommon in everyday humor, as well as to some extent in national literature, and in the broader public discourse on national identity in Bulgaria.

Europe as a Symbolic and Institutional Space

Moreover, if Europe forms a broad symbolic space within and against which Bulgarian national identity is produced, Bulgarians' experience of Europe as an institutional and geopolitical space is decidedly ambivalent. In 1995, when ten member states of the European Union put into place a unitary visa system, whereby foreign visitors would need a visa only for the country of their initial port of entry and could move among these states freely (the so-called Schengen visa system), Bulgaria was placed on the list of countries whose nationals would require a separate visa for each country visited.[5] While this did not in fact alter the status quo, Bulgarians were unanimous in interpreting this as a slight—as the reconfirmation of an exclusive Western Europe at a time when there was so much talk about opening up the European union, eventually to include the Central and Eastern European countries. Travel to Western Europe thus continued to involve considerable bureaucratic tedium and the indignities that so often attend visa applications for any country. Bulgarians were upset that they were held to the same standards as citizens of non-European, Third World countries, and that even citizens of some Third World countries (for instance, India) were spared these indignities.

If Bulgarians sensed such bureaucratic and institutional barriers separating them from full participation in the community of European nations—to which they felt a right based on historical and cultural considerations—they were not unaware also of a certain cultural distance separating them from what they considered to be Europe proper. As one newspaper columnist put it:

> Europe is a dream. A videoclip. You see yourself in France, you move on to Holland, by the well-lit roads you know you are in Belgium, a moment later you are in Germany, you hear Mozart and ask yourself, are you still in Germany or in Austria, when a grain of sand gets in your eye, you wake up and realize that you are in Slovakia, hey brother, there's a problem, says the customs agent, who blackmails you into giving him 100 marks, no problem, says the agent, as you approach Hungary you get sand in your other eye, your eyes start to water, hey brother, there's a problem—your clothes aren't the right size for the Hungarian customs officer, but that's no problem, brother—your shoes fit him just fine, above the sand like graveside crosses stand the spires of cathedrals, but even these marks of civilization gradually disappear, the sand has buried the border with Romania, but some uniformed scorpion explains that Romania—that's him, and that you have to take your shirt off in Romania, you wish you could fly, but you crawl across the desert towards Bulgaria. (Kulekov 1995: 11)

This excerpt is from a short piece, entitled "The Road from Europe," published in a popular Bulgarian daily newspaper (*24 Chasa* [24 Hours]) in mid 1995: a cynical portrait, but the point is clear. As the Bulgarian traveler returns from (Western) Europe, a place where seemingly he feels comfortable, he is rudely awakened to the realities of life in Eastern Europe—things begin to appear less and less "European." He suffers humiliations brought on by a combination of economic stagnation and the abuse of power and position. The Bulgaria to which he returns, the author continues, has been sucked dry by corruption and crime—a mere shell of what it was (or should be). Visiting (Western) Europe is uplifting: returning to Bulgaria is humiliating, disenchanting. The Bulgarian feels an affinity with the real Europe until the rude reminder that between Bulgaria and Europe lies a buffer of "not-quite-Europeanness." There still remains the sense that there is some essential unity, affinity, but this is spoiled by others, those who have ransacked Bulgaria from greed, and those in Bulgaria and the rest of Eastern and Central Europe who help produce and reproduce this image of a quaintly backward, if not corrupt and dangerous East. The encroaching sands of the Orient[6] represent cultural impoverishment (from a Eurocentric standpoint). The author of the piece decries particularly the (seemingly widespread) descent to the values of the ubiquitous petty trader[7]—speculation and fraud[8]—which run counter to European cultural values.

There is more than a hint in this short piece that the Bulgarian (or at least *this* Bulgarian, the columnist) is somehow above this, for he at least feels this as humiliation, as somewhat out of kilter with what should be; he feels a certain fulfilment in visiting Western Europe and knows deep down that there is something of this "European" in his soul. While presenting a case for Bulgaria's failure to meet European standards of conduct, the author nevertheless hints at an underlying identity. Indeed, he seems to be suggesting that it is not so much that Bulgaria's culture falls short of a European standard as that Bulgarians fail to hold to their true European identity and heritage. The ambiguity deriving from this dual experience of being European yet experiencing exclusion from full participation in the community of European nations is, I suggest, a central element in Bulgarian national ideology.

Irony in Literary Portrayals of the National Self

Such ironic portraits of Bulgaria's ambivalent status in relation to Europe are fairly common in the print and broadcast media in Bulgaria, as well as more generally in Bulgarian humor and literature—the *bai Ganyu* [Uncle Ganyu] stories,[9] Aleko Konstantinov's 1895 literary classic, are perhaps the most poignant (and hilarious) portrayals of the clash of Bulgarian and European sensibilities. In a series of vignettes, bai Ganyu, a stereotypical small town or village Bulgarian, is depicted making cultural gaffes in various European settings. The narrator of each tale, on the other hand, is always a Bulgarian student who is painstakingly attempting to "pass" as a member of the host society, but is always caught in an embarrassing position when bai Ganyu blunders in. One can, of course, read the bai Ganyu stories in a number of ways[10]—Konstantinov is having a dig at the educated, cosmopolitan Bulgarian as much as at the archetypical folksy, rural Bulgarian. He is also making fun of "European" sensibilities. In one vignette (Konstantinov 1992: 42–63), bai Ganyu visits Prague and, needing a place to stay, turns up at the doorstep of the Czech historian Konstantin Jireček, author of the first major academic history of Bulgaria (in 1876), who had resided for some years in Bulgaria and had even held the post of Minister of Education for two years (1881 and 1882)—itself a fascinating example of the way European models were imported in the incipient Bulgarian national state. Ganyu seeks Jireček's hospitality, playing on the fact that they both had resided in Sofia, and that Jireček is, after all, a friend of Bulgaria. Czech conventions of hospitality, however, are, to Ganyu's dismay, not as developed as those of Bulgarians—Jireček condescends to give him lunch, then has him taken to a cafe frequented by Bulgarian students. He ends up staying with a Bulgarian student, who is boarding with a middle-class Czech family. In one scene, Ganyu, arriving back at his hosts' home hungry, is shocked to see the cook about to poach a fish. He grabs it out of her hand, douses it with salt, improvises a grill on the stove, and fills the house with the aroma of grilled fish and smoke, rescuing the Czechs from the culinary disaster they were about to commit. Embarrassingly, the student becomes caught in the middle, having told his hosts that Ganyu was a relative who had become a millionaire in the renowned Bulgarian rose-oil trade. His ability to pass as a denizen of Central Europe is compromised by Ganyu's antics as an exotic "other." At the same time, Konstantinov (the author) is clearly having a dig at the cultural proclivities of Central Europeans who lack the warmth and hospitality that Bulgarians take for granted. The image of bai Ganyu resonates still, as a column by Kalojanov (1995) from the Socialist Party daily, *Duma*, shows: "[w]e've come a long way now, but we still haven't caught up with the Europeans... . The future is before us. We are moving towards Europe with the good old image of bay Ganyo, brought up-to-date and prettified by these our glorious heroes" (here indicating those Bulgarian leaders who make the rounds of Europe seeking support for Bulgaria's bid to join NATO, the EC and other bodies).

Recognition of such cultural distance occurs also at a more mundane level. One day in a class I was observing at an elite secondary school in Sofia, the teacher took some time at the end of a class to discuss arrangements for a forthcoming study tour to a Western European destination. As part of this she lectured the students on how and how not to behave in Europe: not to drop litter on the streets; not to draw attention to themselves by getting overly excited about the range and quality of goods in the shops; not to pick up things they weren't intending to buy or spend too long merely browsing in shops, and so on. In an aside to me later, the teacher explained that she wanted to avoid embarrassing situations, because as Europeans they should comport themselves like Europeans and not cause others to view them as uncivilized.

History Teaching in Context

I present three illustrations—the newspaper column, the bai Ganyu stories, and the teacher's lecture on how to behave as Europeans—in order to introduce something of the context within and against which history is written, taught, and read in contemporary Bulgaria. These illustrations play on a performative understanding of Europeanness—there are behaviors and cultural practices that mark one as European or call a claim to Europeanness into question. Alongside such performative understandings of Europeanness there exists, as I mentioned earlier, a sense that there are indelible, organic ties that place Bulgaria squarely within the European orbit. For instance, the official history curriculum of the Bulgarian Ministry of Education for the year 1995/96 outlines as an express aim of primary and secondary history education "the formation of national historical consciousness and national pride ... through outlining phenomena, processes and events that demonstrate the inseparability of Bulgaria from European cultural values, the values of European civilization" (MONT 1995: 10).

Such aims are further woven into the curriculum descriptions for particular grades so that demonstrating the Europeanness of Bulgarian culture and history occupies a prominent position for both Bulgarian and world history. Explicit references in school history textbooks to the Europeanness of Bulgarian cultural identity are used sparingly, but suffice to set the tone for the narrative development of the Bulgarian nation as a part of Europe. For instance, in a textbook for the tenth and eleventh grades (spanning the entirety of Bulgarian history until the dawn of the state-socialist period), European models are explicitly drawn upon to validate Bulgarian culture and history:

> The history of the majority of European peoples [*narodi*] shows that they arose during the Middle Ages out of the long-term interaction of several different ethnic groups. The formation of the Bulgarian ethnic group [*narodnost*] is no exception. It is the natural result of the merging of three foundational ethnic components—Thracians, Slavs and Bulgars.[11] (Bakalov et al. 1993: 167)

Similarly: "The Bulgarian economy (of the fifteenth to seventeenth centuries) was typically European in form"(Bakalov et al. 1993: 195). One of two authorized fifth-grade textbooks from 1995 (Ivanova et al. 1994: 6) begins with a review chapter on the Mediaeval Bulgarian Empire: "The state in which we live today is *the oldest Slavic state in Europe*. It was founded over thirteen centuries ago" (when the Bulgars reached the mouth of the Danube river and overcame the Byzantines, who were forced to recognize a new state in the Balkans) (emphasis mine). Once the parameters have been set in this fashion, all subsequent description can be read as affirming the Europeanness of Bulgarian culture through time.

Along these lines, the role of Christianity in achieving a unified ethnic identity is stressed, as is its role in preserving this identity throughout the long period of Ottoman rule. The fact that during the Middle Ages Bulgaria had for some time an autocephalous church is taken as proving Bulgaria's strength as a major Mediaeval European power on a par with Byzantium and the Frankish Empire—and, by extension, as validating its rightful place in Europe today. Moreover, the existence for over 1,100 years of a vernacular-based written language, presaging such developments elsewhere in Europe,[12] is also stressed as a factor behind Bulgarians claims for both national and European status.

Another key source of validation for Bulgarian claims to nationhood and Europeanness is provided by travelogues written by Western Europeans passing through the Balkans at various times (particularly during the National Revival Period of the late eighteenth and nineteenth centuries), which remark upon the European character and plight of the Christian population of the Ottoman lands. Textbooks and historical readers were replete with excerpts from such travelogues. Similarly, mediaeval chronicles that mention Bulgaria and Bulgarians are a source of validation of Bulgaria's early existence in Europe. On several occasions, teachers made explicit use of such materials in class. In one tenth-grade class on the restoration of the Bulgarian Empire in A.D. 1185 after one hundred years of Byzantine rule, the teacher brought up the fact that certain Romanian historians considered the leaders of the Bulgarian uprising to have been Vlachs—that is, romanized Dacian herders.[13] This would, in effect, undercut the legitimacy of Bulgarian claims to the continuity of Bulgarian hegemony over territories along the present Bulgarian—Romanian border. The teacher asked the students instead to read an excerpt from a Byzantine chronicler—on the basis that if the Byzantines, who were not favorably disposed to Bulgaria, referred to these leaders as aristocratic Bulgarians, the case was closed.[14] This was part of a longer discussion on the need to show—like other European nations—an unbroken cultural and ethnic presence from the original mixing of Bulgars, Slavs and Thracians (which, the students were unanimous, was a peaceful process), through the Middle Ages and to the present. This is a central theme in the presentation of Mediaeval Bulgarian history, and a key element in the way nationhood is conceptualized in Bulgarian national ideologies. Breaks in the continuity of the Bulgarian state—after succumbing to Byzantine rule in the eleventh and twelfth centuries and Ottoman rule from the fourteenth to the nineteenth centuries—could be rendered immaterial if an unbroken cultural and linguistic tradition and ethnic presence could be proven. Thus, if the Byzantine chronicler could still identify Bulgarians as actors on the political stage, even after 150 years of Byzantine rule, the resilience of Bulgarian culture and the legitimacy of the Bulgarian claim to statehood would be attested.

The Meaning of Europe

If such textual references and motifs serve to establish the presence of a Bulgarian ethno-national group—squarely situated in Europe (by analogy with the Frankish and Byzantine empires and the processes of nation formation in the rest of Europe)—what exactly is meant by "European" is not always so explicit. In classes on world history, the development of European cultural and political forms is a dominant theme—as is Bulgaria's relationship to such processes, particularly the parallels between the Bulgarian National Revival of the eighteenth and nineteenth centuries and the Western European Renaissance. Aside from these more specific understandings of "European" as denoting particular cultural, political and institutional forms, Bulgarians use "European" in a variety of positively valorized meanings: progressive, modern, civilized, chic, non-oriental (see Buchanan 1995; Smollett 1993).

Reference to Europe is pervasive also in discussions of life under the Ottoman yoke. Here the references are negative: as several historians said to me, history stood still for five-hundred years; connections with the rest of Europe and European culture were largely broken. Under state socialism, moreover, official history had bracketed the Ottoman period as an unimportant, static period in the development of the Bulgarian nation, a period of economic and cultural stasis outside the march of human progress. It is only more recently that serious investigation by Bulgarian historians into the progressive development of Bulgarian culture through this period has begun.[15] One exception to this is the treatment of the period of the Bulgarian National Revival, which took place over the last century or so of Ottoman rule. This is treated as a separate period and has always been prominent in Bulgarian history. Paralleling and drawing from the ideas and models of the Western European Renaissance, Bulgarians began in this period the process of resituating themselves as a European nation, vying for support from the various European powers who were vying among themselves for control of the declining Ottoman Empire. A further aspect of the treatment of the Ottoman period more generally is the implicit definition of Europeanness (and Bulgarianness) as the antithesis of that which is Ottoman, Oriental, Turkish, Islamic. This has led to the marginalization within Bulgarian polity of those minorities (especially Turks and gypsies) who epitomize that which is un-European. Like attitudes to Europe, attitudes to the Turkish influence on Bulgarian culture are often conflicted and ambivalent.[16]

As can be seen, Europe figures prominently in the "imagining" of the Bulgarian nation, as a positively valorized locus of identity, as a powerful geopolitical and institutional space to which fuller membership is desired, and as a mirror against which Bulgarians measure their aspirations and failings, and represent themselves and their current situation to themselves. The narrativization of official historical tradition in textbooks serves to instill within the current generation of pupils a sense of commonality with Europe as an integral component of Bulgarian national identity. This it achieves through rendering as unmediated fact—a general property of narrative, to paraphrase White (1973, 1987; see also Barthes 1972)—the factors upon which claims to European identity are based. Thus, Bulgaria is situated within the symbolic space of Europe. However, this vision is at odds with present-day experience of the exclusivity of Europe as an institutional space. Official history and the school history curriculum are largely silent on this count. It is in other media, genres of writing, and public discourse that attempts at resolving this dilemma are most apparent. Irony abounds in such attempts (as in the newspaper article cited above), in stark contrast to the straightforward literalism of the official historical account as represented in school textbooks and classroom discussion.

An examination of how both Europe and the nation are "imagined" through historical narrative elucidates further the processes of identity construction involved. Europe is imagined, or idealized, as a grouping of homogeneous nations with clear-cut and hermetic boundaries (ideally linguistic and cultural) between them. Separate nations are defined through similarity (what they have in common as nations in terms of overall social and political organization) and contrast (what distinguishes a particular group). Ethnic minorities feature in Bulgarian history only as a result of transgressions against the ideal principle of the nation: for example, when Bulgarians have been under foreign domination and when their lands have been split among neighboring countries (as they have several times since liberation from the Ottoman Empire was achieved in 1878). The present-day existence of ethnic minorities within Bulgaria is a sore point for many ethnic Bulgarians: their existence, as much as the existence of Bulgarian minorities in neighboring states, alludes to the incompleteness of the Bulgarian nation and a falling-short of the imagined European national ideal. Although this ideal is in fact far from the realities of current European experience, nevertheless, it is largely consistent with how the nation is *imagined* elsewhere in Europe and the West, namely as ethnically homogeneous. Indeed, the principle of national self-determination (along ethnic lines) remains a potent force among the international community, and particularly so in regard to the restructuring states of Eastern and Central Europe and the former Soviet Union (see Roeder 1999); it is the use of violent means to achieve ethnic homogeneity that is held in disregard.[17] The Bulgarian case, I believe, highlights a more general European ambivalence as to the nature of the nation, and invites a more rigorous analysis of the production of national identity in Europe.

What we see in the Bulgarian discourse of national identity is a continual appeal to European values that are portrayed as "objective" and as lying outside of the nation, however much their meaning is produced within the national discourse. There is appeal also to outside "European" institutions (such as the EC, NATO,[18] the Council of Europe, and others), and to relationships with particular European states. Yet this is no simple nesting of the national identity within ever-broadening categories; rather, there are a variety of cross-cutting supranational and international contexts (see Buchanan 1995; Gupta and Ferguson 1992) that impinge upon the way the nation, both as abstract concept and as grounded locus of social and cultural life, is "imagined." While the institutional/structural boundaries of Europe are more rigid, the symbolic space of Europe is ambiguous and loosely defined. Europe is a shifting category—now broadly encompassing, now more narrowly Western. Bulgarians can, after all, speak of living in Europe and yet also of traveling to Europe. In this respect they tap into a marginalizing or even orientalizing discourse wherein they acknowledge and rationalize at some level their marginality to Europe.[19] Yet they are able to subvert this through irony, as well as through their insistence on inclusion in European initiatives.

Ideological Transmission

If both Bulgaria and the Europe it would bind itself to are, as my discussion above indicates, shifting categories, how does this bode for the reproduction of the symbols and values of the nation? As we have seen, the secondary school history curriculum is attuned more to the delineation of what appear as unambiguous organic links between Bulgaria and Europe. However, the virtual silence in the textbooks as to the dilemma posed by present experience already bespeaks ambivalence and ambiguity. Moreover, it defines the school history classroom as a site at which such ambivalence is bracketed.

Reigning theories of the nation (for example, Anderson 1991; Gellner 1983; Hobsbawm 1990) as well as much anthropological literature on Eastern Europe (for example, Verdery 1991) assume a neat and straightforward carry over from elite constructions of ideologies to public opinion. I have sought to describe, for the Bulgarian case, how in fact top-down ideological programs are only part of the picture. There can be no straightforward carry over because ideology is not transmitted in a vacuum, but rather emerges through discourse. If the Bulgarian history curriculum is regarded as representing an ideological program, it becomes readily apparent that whatever is intended in that program is encountered by pupils (and mediated by teachers) with reference to the broader public sphere, in which different assessments of Bulgaria's position and other, nonlinear (for example, ironic) modes of discourse also prevail. In this sense the school classroom, like any particular site in the public sphere, must be seen as a window onto a broader field of public discourse, rather than as a clearly demarcated and controlled setting. The field of symbols and the range of available meanings are outside the control of the teacher or the educational institution. Although, as I have illustrated, it is a particular understanding of Bulgarian history that is transmitted through the school history classroom, this vision of history, however much it is presented and considered as authoritative, is not the only vision of history that the pupils come in contact with.

The practice of history teaching in Bulgaria is currently in flux as systemic changes are slowly instituted. While the curriculum carries some authority, it now represents merely one perspective among several. Academic historians disagree over the interpretation of symbols central to the national identity. The news and current affairs media represent a wide range of interests, and citizens are in the position of having to situate their own perspectives against this field of possibilities. The curriculum's situating of Bulgaria as inseparable from the "values of European civilization" (MONT 1995: 10) allows a range of responses, from a casting of European identity in terms of inherited cultural traits to an open embracing of free-market democracy. Across the spectrum of public opinion there is a binding sense that recognition of their Europeanness (and greater integration into the institutional webs that define Europe) is what Bulgarians desire above all from the rest of Europe. However, this leaves much room for debate and divisive conflict as to the means to achieving this aim, which scarcely hides a deep-seated ambivalence regarding Bulgaria's true position vis-à-vis Europe and the nature of nationhood. While political groupings tend toward particular poles in the interpretation of what constitutes Europeanness—with socialists emphasizing the organic ties, and free-market democrats a performative model necessitating radical change (Smollett 1993)—there are no watertight boundaries, and Bulgarians of all hues flit from pole to pole as the occasion requires.

Conclusion: Irony and Identity in Bulgarian National Ideology

As I have shown, irony is a prevalent means of representing the ambivalent position Bulgaria occupies in relation to Europe. Nevertheless, it is at the juxtaposition of the unequivocal organic sense of belonging with the questioning and ironic stance that Bulgarian national ideology takes shape. Official history and ironic self-portraits are conceived within a symbolic field they both occupy, and against the daily experience of life in a still-divided Europe.[20] More to the point, it seems to be central to Bulgarians' sense of national identity that there is a lack of fit between their sense of heritage and belonging as a European nation, and their perceptions of Europe as a divided place. Irony and self-caricature are a means of rationalizing this lack of fit without entirely accepting it. Without the sense of unequivocal belonging, there would be no call for irony. The use of irony, moreover, highlights and questions the lack of fit, and can be seen as an assertion (however indirect) of an underlying positive identity. As Herzfeld (1997) intimates, it is a prerogative of the native to recognize and comment upon the embarrassing and negative aspects of his/her culture: "National identity comprises a generous measure of embarrassment together with all the idealized virtues. It is this rueful self-recognition, this inward acknowledgment of cultural intimacy, that all the top-down accounts of the nation-state miss" (Herzfeld 1997: 6). The centrality of irony as a mode of discourse in the negotiation of post-socialist identities is attested not only in the more or less explicit discourse on identity such as I have described here: ironies abound in a variety of other arenas of life. The pronounced ironies and contradictions of everyday life during the state-socialist period and the early post-state-socialist transition are captured well with Creed's (1998: 5) terms "conflicting complementarity" and "domesticated socialism": the socialist state had to accommodate itself to the myriad coping mechanisms ordinary people devised to alleviate their conditions in an ever-changing spiral of economic reforms. This certainly fed the ironic bent in much humor. It also was a factor in the demise of the state-socialist project, leaving a legacy of complex economic problems—and ways of talking about them. Creed (1999: 240) describes also the ironies inherent in the political alignments of Bulgarian villagers in the post-state-socialist period, for whom socialism can become a "vehicle of protest in a supposedly postsocialist context."

The use of irony in self-representations, then, enables certain aspects of national identity to be expressed, but always runs the risk of actually upsetting some members of the national community. Like any joke, irony can be played along with or reacted against (see Basso 1979), and thus serves to highlight aspects of the culture (such as the relationship to Europe) about which there is no general consensus but about which people feel strongly. As James Clifford suggests, irony can be conceived as "an ideology of order, or perhaps of acceptable disorder.... 'predicaments of irony' can be tolerated and managed ... but only by not questioning some horizon of order, some ultimate sense that things are ultimately translatable or will come out all right in the end" (2001: 256). I suggest that in the Bulgarian case, national ideology encompasses the ambivalent meanings of certain key national symbols (such as Europeanness) and the lack of consensus over their interpretation. Unequivocal assertions of historical right and ironic self-representations are both used strategically by those who seek to influence public opinion. Neither the ideological undertones of official history nor the ironic questioning of them prevails, but rather it is out of the struggle over defining national identity that there emerges a national ideology, that at a deeper level would seem to bind Bulgarians together as a people whose identity is constituted through this struggle.

Notes

1. Field research in Bulgaria (1995–96) was supported by the Wenner-Gren Foundation for Anthropological Research and the Open Society Foundation. This chapter draws on and elaborates further several themes explored in my doctoral dissertation (Pilbrow 2001).
2. Bulgaria had during this period a government controlled by the Bulgarian Socialist Party (in power 1994–97).
3. For a discussion of the importance of regional spheres of social and cultural action to the analysis of national cultures see Lomnitz-Adler (1992).
4. For instance, the burgeoning literature on transnationalism, and the concern within the urban studies field with communities of interest.
5. This was later expanded to include other EU countries (excepting Great Britain and Ireland), as well as Iceland and Norway, which are not members of the EU. Bulgaria was finally removed from this list in April 2001.
6. The imagery of the sand as signifying the Orient was suggested by Gerald Creed (personal communication).
7. For a cogent discussion of petty trading in Bulgaria see Konstantinov (1996) and Konstantinov et al. (1998).
8. Native cunning (which underlies fraud and speculation) is often celebrated and aspired to in Bulgarian folkore and popular culture, if hesitantly acknowledged by intellectuals as a particularly Bulgarian (rural/peasant) trait.
9. Two Bulgarian forms exist: Ganyu and Ganyo (with variant transliterations: Ganiu or Ganio). "Bai" is an archaic address term, which I have glossed as "uncle."
10. For an interesting survey of Bulgarian interpretations of bai Ganyu and the cultural assumptions that underlie them, see Daskalov (2001).
11. *Narod* = nation, people, (akin to German *Volk*); *narodnost* = nationality, ethnicity, ethno-national group.
12. Deletant (1996) provides a discussion of similar strategies of legitimation in Romania.
13. Dacians being proto-Romanians.
14. The text chosen, Nicetas Acominatos (Choniates) (1978), was in fact somewhat ambiguous on this point in that it also used the term "Vlach," though was prefaced with the explanation that at that period, the Byzantines referred to Bulgarians as "Vlachs" but meant Bulgarians. Unpacking this hermeneutic tradition is beyond the scope of this chapter. Seemingly, the Romanian historians were playing on the potential ambiguity of reference here, while the Bulgarian hermeneutic tradition emphasizes the spirit of the reference, which presumably is supported by comparative textual research.
15. Interestingly, many would now bracket the state-socialist period for similar reasons.
16. See Buchanan (1996) for a cogent discussion of changing attitudes to the Turkish influence on Bulgarian folk music and folk-derived music.
17. Hence the ambivalence with which the breakup of Yugoslavia was met, particularly in the case of the Bosnian war. The aggressive pursuit of "ethnic cleansing" was condemned, but the complexity of the ethnic mixing in Socialist Yugoslavia was also used as an argument for its artificiality and as a rationalization for its coming apart at the seams. The de facto partition of Bosnia into ethnic zones thus finds a certain resonance in the West.
18. Although NATO is not purely European, the same argument seems to apply here. Moreover, the extranational aspects to Bulgarian national identity construction are, of course, not limited to the European sphere. Smollett (1993) describes the attraction of America in the initial post-state-socialist period.

19. For a cogent analysis of orientalist discourses on and in the Balkans, see Todorova (1997) and Bakić-Hayden and Hayden (1992).
20. In this regard, the un-ironic stance of the school history curriculum—its bracketing of irony and of the experience of Europe in the present as an institutional space—may itself be regarded as a form of irony.

References

Acominatos, Nicetas (Choniates). 1978. "*Izbuhvane i hod na vŭstanieto na bratyata Petŭr i Asen*" [The Outbreak and Development of the Uprising of the Brothers Petŭr and Asen]. In *Hristomatiya po istoriya na Bŭlgariya*, vol. 2. Sofia: Izdatelstvo "nauka i izkustvo."

Anderson, Benedict. 1991. *Imagined Communities: Reflections on the Origin and Spread of Nationalism*, 2nd ed. London: Verso.

Bakalov, Georgi, Petŭr Angelov, Tsvetana Georgieva, Dimitŭr Canev, Bobi Bobev, and Stoycho Grŭncharov. 1993. *Istoriya na Bŭlgariya. Za gimnazialnata stepen na obshtoobrazovatelnite i profesionalnite uchilishta* [Bulgarian History. For the Upper-Secondary Level of General and Professional Schools]. Sofia: Bulvest 2000.

Bakić-Hayden, M. and R.M. Hayden. 1992. "Orientalist Variations on the Theme 'Balkans': Symbolic Geography in Recent Yugoslav Cultural Politics." *Slavic Review,* vol. 51, no. 1, 1–15.

Barthes, Roland. 1972. "Myth Today." In *Mythologies*. A. Lavers, trans., New York: Hill and Wang, 109–59.

Basso, Keith. 1979. *Portraits of "The Whiteman": Linguistic Play and Cultural Symbols among the Western Apache*. Cambridge: Cambridge University Press.

Buchanan, Donna A. 1995. "Metaphors of Power, Metaphors of Truth: The Politics of Music Professionalism in Bulgarian Folk Orchestras." *Ethnomusicology,* vol. 39, no. 3, 381–416.

——— 1996. "Wedding Musicians, Political Transition, and National Consciousness in Bulgaria." In *Retuning Culture: Musical Changes in Central and Eastern Europe.* ed. Mark Slobin. Durham, NC: Duke University Press.

Clifford, James. 2001. "The Last Discussant." In *Irony in Action: Anthropology, Practice, and the Moral Imagination.* eds. James W. Ferndandez and Mary Taylor Huber. Chicago: University of Chicago Press, 253–59.

Creed, Gerald W. 1998. *Domesticating Revolution: From Socialist Reform to Ambivalent Transition in a Bulgarian Village.* University Park, PA: Pennsylvania State University Press.

——— 1999. "Deconstructing Socialism in Bulgaria." In *Uncertain Transition: Ethnographies of Change in the Postsocialist World.* eds. Michael Burawoy and Katherine Verdery. Lanham, Maryland: Rowman and Littlefield, 223–43.

Daskalov, Roumen. 2001. "Modern Bulgarian Society and Culture through the Mirror of Bai Ganio." *Slavic Review,* vol. 60, no. 3, 530–49.

Deletant, Dennis. 1996. "The Debate between Tradition and Modernity in the Shaping of a Romanian Identity." In *The Literature of Nationalism: Essays on East European Identity.* ed. R. Pynsent. New York: St. Martin's Press.

Gellner, Ernest. 1983. *Nations and Nationalism.* Ithaca: Cornell University Press.

Gupta, Akhil and James Ferguson. 1992. "Beyond 'Culture': Space, Identity, and the Politics of Difference." *Cultural Anthropology,* vol. 7, no. 1, 6–23.

Herzfeld, Michael. 1997. *Cultural Intimacy: Social Poetics in the Nation-State*. New York: Routledge.

Hobsbawm, Eric J. 1990. *Nations and Nationalism since 1780: Programme, Myth, Reality*. Cambridge: Cambridge University Press.

Ivanova, Svetlana, Keta Mircheva, Aleksandŭr Antonov, Evgeniya Davidova and Darina Bilyarska. 1994. *Istoriya na Bŭlgariya. Za peti klas na obshtoobrazovatelnite uchilishta* [Bulgarian History. For the Fifth Grade of General Educational Schools]. Sofia: Bulvest 2000.

Kaloyanov, Georgi. 1995. "*Kŭm Evropa s dobriya star imidzh na bai Ganyo*" [Toward Europe with the Good Old Image of bai Ganyo]. *Duma*, no. 267 (13 November), 7.

Konstantinov, Aleko. 1992 [1895]. *Bai Ganyu*. Veliko Tŭrnovo: Slovo.

Konstantinov, Yulian. 1996. "Patterns of Reinterpretation: Trader-Tourism in the Balkans (Bulgaria) as a Picaresque Metaphorical Enactment of Post-Totalitarianism." *American Ethnologist* 23, no. 4, 762–82.

Konstantinov, Yulian, Gideon Kressel and Trond Thuen. 1998. "Outclassed by Former Outcasts: Petty Trading in Varna." *American Ethnologist,* vol. 25, no. 4, 729–45.

Kulekov, Ivan. 1995. "*Pŭtyat ot Evropa*" [The Road from Europe]. *24 Chasa*, no. 236 (30 August), 11.

Lomnitz-Adler, Claudio. 1992. *Exits from the Labyrinth: Culture and Ideology in the Mexican National Space*. Berkeley: University of California Press.

MONT (Ministerstvo na obrazovanieto, naukata i tehnologiite [Ministry of Education, Science and Technology]). 1995. *UKAZANIE za organizirane na obuchenieto po ISTORIYA v srednite obshtoobrazovatelni i profesionalni uchilishta prez uchebnata 1995/96 godina* (INSTRUCTIONS for the organisation of HISTORY education in general and professional secondary schools during the 1995/96 academic year). Sofia: MONT.

Pilbrow, Tim. 2001. "Negotiating the Past for a Present in Transition: Secondary-School History and the Production of National Identity in Bulgaria." (Ph.D. diss., New York University).

Roeder, Philip G. 1999. "The Revolution of 1989: Postcommunism and the Social Sciences." *Slavic Review,* vol. 58, no. 4, 743–55.

Smollett, Eleanor. 1993. "America the Beautiful: Made in Bulgaria." *Anthropology Today,* vol. 9, no. 2, 9–13.

Todorova, Maria. 1997. *Imagining the Balkans*. New York: Oxford University Press.

Verdery, Katherine. 1991. *National Ideology under Socialism: Identity and Cultural Politics in Ceausescu's Romania*. Berkeley: University of California Press.

White, Hayden. 1973. *Metahistory: The Historical Imagination in Nineteenth-Century Europe*. Baltimore: Johns Hopkins University Press.

——— 1987. The Content of the Form: Narrative Discourse and Historical Representation. Baltimore: Johns Hopkins University Press.

Chapter 7

❖ ─────────

Learning about Europe and the World: Schools, Teachers, and Textbooks in Russia after 1991

Robert Maier

Since Russia's national history began to be written in the nineteenth century, there has been a separation of Russia's own history and the history of the world outside Russia. The latter was rarely characterized as "world history," since this would have marginalized Russia's "own" history, the "history of the fatherland" [otechestvennaia istoriia]. The alternative classification "istoriia zarubezhnykh stran"—conversely—expressed the priorities the other way around: taken literally, the world merely consists of "countries located behind the border."[1] During Soviet times, this terminology was obligatory. Moscow was considered to be the center of the world by the Bolshevik rulers, and the history of the Soviet Union represented the "real" start of history, beginning with the October Revolution of 1917. Any human history prior to this was considered a type of "prehistory" and the history of previously ruling cultures was a history that was "fading away." The outcome was twofold: on the one hand, Russian and Soviet schools did not provide a place for a coherent examination of world history; on the other hand, in considering the world from the Russian or Soviet viewpoint, one is confronted with a more or less arbitrary gathering of various countries' histories that we regularly encounter when scouring the index tables of textbooks—England, Germany, the U.S.A., France, and Italy, as well as China. Depending on the epoch, the order of the countries that are being named, might be changing.

I want to show that contemporary writing of history textbooks continues to be confronted by these two premises, which have a longstanding tradition in Russia. When I say "confronted," I mean this in a positive, scientific sense of the word: when one "confronts" in the scientific community it means that foundations are being discussed and challenged.

In general, it is incomprehensible that a country, whose longitudes span almost half of the earth's circumference and is located in two continents while touching a third, does not provide a more globally-oriented history education. In addition to the geographical factor that should push globally-oriented education, there are also cultural and ethnic factors to consider. There are almost one-hundred different ethnic groups living in Russia who, in turn, belong to different cultural traditions. The limitations of history education cannot be due to a lack of scientific foundations: traditionally, ethnography, the study of oriental culture, and Asian studies have existed in Russia on a sophisticated level since the nineteenth century. There has always existed pressure against a purely Western intellectual orientation within the Russian political elite. This became apparent in a classical fashion within the philosophical and political currents of Slavophilism and Eurasianism. To this day, this attitude is nurtured by intellectual and political circles that adhere to *kul'turologiia*. *Kul'turologiia* is not only a discipline of study at universities, but also a school subject. It attempts to construct a post-communist identity in Russia, which entails an intellectual view of the world, set against the materialistic approach of communist times. In the context of this theory, Russia is being understood as an independent organism, as a special type of civilization, juxtaposed against the "West" (see Scherer 2003).

The fact that these favorable conditions gave rise to neither worldliness nor to an inclination to interpret history and its education more broadly and globally can, in turn, be attributed to the fact that the carriers of universal thoughts and cosmopolitan ideas in nineteenth century Russia were identified as Westerners. Their fixation on (Western) Europe prevented them from recognizing, and even more so from overcoming, the narrow-mindedness imposed by the virulent ways of thinking and the value systems that were prevalent within Western and Central Europe. Eurocentrism, therefore, became a stronghold that was even more steadfast and pronounced in Russia than in the places from which it originated.[2] Europe was and continues to be a synonym for a pronounced cultural status in Russia. In almost no country other than Russia are terms such as "uncivilized" and "barbaric" so strongly associated with Asia. Uncultured behavior is frequently labeled "Aziachestvo" (a slander for Asian).

In Russia, as early as the reign of Peter I, a feeling of backwardness gave the scientific paradigm of the West an iconic status. The Russian historiography that emerged from that situation was, until way into the twentieth century, little more than historical research on Western Europe (see Hecker 1983: 37). The scientific grounding of history began, as in the West, under the premises of nation building and was subsequently accompanied by a narrowing of viewpoints and a reduction of approaches that dealt with universal problems. One could go so far as to view Marxism as the highpoint of an uncritical adoption of Western historical ideology.

The problems mentioned so far are magnified in the field of textbook historiography. Hence, it is not surprising that history textbooks in Russia were and continue to be highly affirmative in terms of their content and conservative in terms of their conception. New ideas prevail only slowly. Textbook content

usually orients itself around the opinions and experiences of the older generations. The idea of a textbook that is ahead of public opinion is hardly
conceivable. On the contrary, until the end of the Soviet era ideas were maintained and disseminated which had their origins in the nineteenth century. The
notion that historical development follows certain "laws," carried to its extreme
in Marxism—Leninism and "historial materialism," appears to be ineradicable
even today. The *a priori* positive valuation of territorial expansion is a common
thread in Russian textbook writing (see Shevyrev 1995: 399). The intellectual
vacuum following the collapse of a communist world view resulted in the
reassessment by some authors of the period prior to the Bolshevik era. This led
to another intellectual "loan" stemming from the nineteenth century; a time
when the study of occidental cultures was flourishing.

I do not imply that there has been no progress in Russia's textbook historiography. On the contrary, a dynamic textbook market developed after 1991 (see
Maier 1999; Kaplan et al. 1999). In addition, one should consider the ability of
most of the authors to step beyond a hermetically closed worldview and to
provide new, challenging answers to old historical questions—a huge intellectual task. My criticism is more concerned with the fact that the fundamental
questions have basically remained the same. Historical questions continue to
be fixated on political history and are attached to national interest. More recent
approaches and questions of mass psychology, gender studies, microhistory,
history "from below," and an approach that promotes a view of "one world"
have hardly been incorporated into historical narratives.

It is probably true that almost no other country has instrumentalized and
regulated history education as much as the Soviet Union. The legitimatization
of the dominant political ideology was formed on the basis of history. History
teachers had a high degree of responsibility educating loyal Soviet citizens. In
doing so, they were able to gain enormous prestige. Studying history implied
being subjected to rigorous selection criteria, because most students who
studied history were supposed to take an official position in the Communist
Party. Training to become a history teacher took one year longer than teacher
training for any other subject. The content of history books or, to be more
precise, the content of *the* history book provided for each grade, was ultimately
decided by the politburo. Even the formulation of sentences was predetermined. A student's ability to repeat the contents verbatim was considered the
greatest achievement of educational quality. Teachers had to take into consideration that controlling authorities listened in on what was going on in the
classroom. Classrooms in many places were equipped technically to do so.

Nonetheless, one should not gain the impression that all history teachers in
communist Russia were functionally delivering the dominant ideology. Some
fought against the regime's demands, and it is their reports about classroom
practice that provide fascinating insights into the potentially subversive actions
of the "small fish in the big pond," that is the regular citizen in a totalitarian

system. One such report is provided by the teacher Maksim Khloponin (1995), who summarizes his dilemma: "One could not teach the way it was commanded – it was impossible, but one could not teach the way one thought best, because it was not allowed. What remained was the daily maneuvering at work between giving the students the incentive to think on the one hand and disguising one's own, secret protest to a certain degree on the other."

Since the fall of communism, the pedagogical framework in Russia has dramatically changed. The elimination of ideological constraints, however, did not automatically lead to a better history education. I will outline the forces that have enabled the status quo to be overcome whilst also facilitating a new orientation in history education and the writing of textbooks—against all odds.

Reforming History Teaching

One important factor was the change in the political climate. In 1991, the first post-Communist Minister of Education, E. Dneprov, who supported a radical-liberal political direction, was resolutely determined to dissolve the Soviet educational paradigm. The school system was fundamentally restructured, new types of schools with their own educational programs were established under the umbrella of diversification. Schools were granted a significant amount of autonomy and independence while private initiatives were permitted and promoted. Historical education was now to be based upon the values of a democratic society. The stated goal of education was no longer to produce a convinced young Leninist; instead, it was the creation of a citizen who could function in an open society. This can be inferred from many documents, ranging from the 1993 Educational Bill on curricular guidelines, to ministerial announcements (see Tiulaeva 1995).

Particularly noteworthy are the efforts by the Russian Federation's Ministry of Education to develop a historically based identity for the different nationalities and regions within Russia; an initiative that was to be reflected in history lessons and textbooks. These efforts are remarkable because the ministry resisted the temptation to centralize once again the education system. With the support of the Ministry of Education, textbooks and teaching materials were created for many different regions of the Russian Federation.[3] Since 1997, the financing of textbooks is the responsibility of the regions. It remains to be seen how far the renewed centralization efforts under Putin's regime will again curtail this cultural autonomy of the regions.

Another factor that contributed greatly to the diversification of teaching materials was the creation of a competitive textbook market. Next to the state-owned publishing house *Prosveshchenie,* which continues to dominate the market, there is the large private publisher *Drofa,* in addition to numerous smaller textbook publishers, whose headquarters are not necessarily found in

Moscow. During the period of Perestroika, several young, enterprising researchers from Moscow State University gathered at the internationally known MIROS-Institute (Moskovskii Institut Razvitiia Obrazovatel'nykh Sistem [Moscow Institute for developing educational systems]) which has its own publishing house.

The activities of Russian publishers are quite noteworthy—something implicitly related to the good income prospects if a book is included in the ministry's recommended textbook list. When this occurs, the circulation can easily reach into the millions. Pirated copies are a big problem, and hence it is not a coincidence that directors of textbook publishing houses are targeted by the Mafia. Some even have been killed.

However, it is not exclusively financial considerations that motivate publishers' actions. For some, the sociopolitical commitment is significant. Alexander M. Abramov, the former director of the MIROS-Institute, initiated a campaign in which he implored the public to be aware of the grave consequences that the neglect of education would have under current politics (Abramov 1996: 6). Sponsorship is also significant: for example, publishing *Zapriatannaia istoriia tatar* [The Renounced History of the Tartars], with a circulation of 180,000, was, according to the preface, only possible with the generous support of two Tartan businessmen, who dedicated the book to the students of Tatarstan (see Imamov 1994). The aims of the sponsors—characterized by local patriotism and national awareness—are unambiguously expressed in the book's content. Among other things it is stated: "Today we lead a just and holy war to establish the independent Republic of Tatarstan, which is free of Moscow's dictate and looting" (Imamov 1994: 6).

Some educational initiatives also come from organizations such as the Russian Holocaust Center. Since 1995, the center has published materials for schools, teachers' manuals, and didactically prepared compilations of sources (Altman et al. 2001). The gap filled by these texts becomes apparent when one examines a 1993 textbook on modern history by V.K. Furaev (1993). In a chapter on "The Effects of the Second World War," one reads the statement: "The extent of the Nazi crimes against humanity far exceeded the evils inflicted during the Inquisitions of the Middle Ages. Out of 18 million Europeans that were in concentration camps, Hitler's followers killed over 11 million" (1993: 35) The actual Holocaust, however, was simply ignored in these summary statements. A study from 1997 finds that "it is unfortunate that Russia's schools have so far failed to address the Holocaust when teaching modern history"(Poltorak and Klokova 1997: 37)

Another essential stimulus was the demand by teachers for better history textbooks. As early as 1988 teachers had begun to make demands for the creation of completely new textbooks, and some teachers and young historians took the initiative and began to write textbooks. These activities were encouraged by competitions. About one-thousand manuscripts were submitted when the Ministry of Education organized a textbook competition for the Soros Foundation. (The "Open Society", founded by George Soros has been very active to promote democracy and cultural activities in Eastern Europe after 1989.) There are some other striking examples of the self-generated initiative of teachers. In the city of Taishet in the Irkutsk area existed a group of *Memorial* (an institution with the aim of critically work through the past, founded during Perestroika). This group in Taishet researched the relicts of the Soviet concentration camp system, the GULAG. Excavations were undertaken, witnesses were interviewed, and contact with former inmates was made (Seleznev 1993: 172–3).

The break with a pedagogically authoritarian educational philosophy and the egalitarian visions from Soviet times, solidified as a result of social-stratification processes. Based on the demands of upper middle-class parents performance-based school structures were created, which demonstrably and not without certain social-Darwinist undertones set themselves apart from mass education institutions. The innovative strength of these educational institutions, which are mostly prestigious high schools, is quite substantial, given their sophisticated infrastructure, motivated teaching staff, and dynamic school principles. On one hand, the social-humanistic educational ideology of these schools contributes to the dismantling of authoritarian ways of thinking. On the other hand, this ideology is keener to build a social consensus than the radical-democratic movement. It intends to integrate the Russian humanistic educational traditions of the nineteenth century—an influence considered always to have been latently present, even during Soviet times—well into the present in order to foster a new feeling of community.

The rebuttal of collectivism, as evident in government documents and the way in which education is reformed, has led to an almost euphoric emphasis on individual personality. That schools should exist primarily for students and not as a forum in which government objectives are carried out was the "great discovery" made by educators after the Soviet era. Postulating that the focus of schools is on the individual student may not guarantee that didactic concepts of a student-oriented education will endure, but it does inevitably imply that teaching and textbooks will have to undergo scrutiny based on the expectations of students. Students, for the first time, will become an authority that has an influence on teaching and teaching content. As students are living in a free information society and their quest for knowledge is no longer arbitrarily limited, they will surely be able to live up to this task.

Textbook construction also began to become a matter of public debate in the media. As a result textbook authors are no longer defenseless when it comes to fighting political pressures. Authors and publishers can defend themselves against politically motivated attempts to influence textbook content, but are also held accountable by the public. One example of this tendency is the debate about the book *Noveishaia istoriia. XX vek* [Recent History: The Twentieth

Century] by Aleksandr Kreder (1995). In 1997, the Duma of the Voronezh region recommended that teachers no longer use this book in the classroom. According to the newspaper *Rossiiskaia Gazeta,* members of the Voronesh Duma were infuriated because the textbook was originally published with the financial help of a non-Russian organisation, the Soros Foundation. In addition, they considered the dignity of the "fatherland's" history and culture to be undermined by the book. They objected to the "liberal approach" taken in the depiction of twentieth century history such as, for example, the way in which the book implied that the Soviet Union carried considerable (co-) responsibility for the outbreak of the Second World War. The newspaper reported Kreder's position and arguments that a democratic Russia would benefit from detaching itself from Soviet traditions and that "students should immediately, irreversibly and for all times adopt the values and realities of the present while taking a critical stance toward the past" (Litvintsev 1997: 3).

Subsequently, the newspaper created a forum in which readers could give their views and suggestions on how textbooks could be incorporated into the process of educational reform. Aleksei Vodianskii, from the Russian Ministry of Education, reported that the Russian Veterans' Organization was vehemently objecting to Kreder's portrayal, saying that the battle of Stalingrad was not properly described and that the October Revolution was not praised enough. In response, the ministry is said to have pointed out that different interpretations of historical events were desirable in a pluralistic society. At the same time, Vodianskii pointed out that "classical patriotic textbooks always followed the same pattern in Russia: everything that Russia does is good. Whoever criticizes the government, the authorities, or the regime is criticizing the Fatherland. All Russian textbooks were put together in this relatively straightforward patriotic spirit. The protection of the state, no matter in what condition it was, was considered a patriotic duty"(1997: 3) Vodianskii praised Kreder's (1995) book for not following this pattern. He stressed that other countries also have an ability to develop a critical attitude when it comes to national self-portrayal in their textbooks. This should be considered an entirely normal process. (1997: 3). Another contribution to the readers' forum, by Jurii Poliakov (1997: 3), considered Kreder's book an attempt to portray the history of the fatherland as a "series of monstrous crimes." In his view, the outrageous situation—namely, that the state financed and propagated an "anti-state ideology" with its textbook politics—had ensued. Andrei Kuraev, a deacon, alarmed by "strange views on Russia" amongst graduates, whose causes he attributes to textbooks, echoes this view: "It is the business of scientists and academics to argue about whose conception of Russia's history is correct, but state schools do not have the right to educate children in an anti-state and anti-national fashion" (Kuraev 1997: 3) It is remarkable that the only support Kreder received in this forum came from Vodianskii, a representative of the Ministry of Education. Not only Kreder's book was affected by the censorship efforts in the Voronezh region:

the local Duma distributed a blacklist to all schools, which listed fifteen other textbooks as well as Kreder's (Maslikova 1997: 2).

The fact that so many textbooks have caused discomfort in communist and nationalistic ranks signals that textbook authors are attempting to express new viewpoints and are avoiding catering to old or new clichés. When irritated contemporaries discover that one fact can easily lead to an array of contradictory, sometimes even mutually exclusive, statements and that "a complete chaos of interpretations and assessments" has become commonplace, not only in the writing of history but also in the classroom (Maslikova 1997: 2), it only emphasizes how much has changed since the times of prescribed unified opinions. Authors are also moving in different directions when it comes to the theoretical foundations of textbooks. Some use modernization theory, which views humanity as on a steady path of social and economic progress, others favor a "civilizational approach." In terms of the theory of totalitarianism there are proponents and opponents. Some authors are committed to being objective in their depiction of history, avoiding emotional expressions, while others are not afraid to include their opinions. The most crucial differences between authors occur in their assessments of the prerevolutionary period, the October Revolution, the Civil War, and the 1920s and 1930s. The differences start to disappear with the "Great Fatherland War."[4] Most authors agree on the condemnation of the Soviet invasions of Hungary and the Czech Republic as well as the intervention in Afghanistan. Among textbook authors there is no lack of radical positioning, with some questioning the role of the classical textbook as a classroom guide. Iurii Troickii, for instance, advocated that textbooks be entirely replaced by compilations of sources and exercise booklets. That way, he argues, students could actively participate in the selection of sources and avoid being caught up in the structural problems of textbooks based on political and ideological premises.[5] These deliberations fit well into the discourse that has taken place in Western textbook historiography and history didactics in recent years.

All in all, it is obvious that Russian society is opening up to Western influences. What in the 1990s were contacts and encounters exclusively among well-known scholars in the historical profession are now permeating the lower levels of education. Popular pedagogical Russian journals, for example *Prepodavanie istorii v shkole* [History Teaching in School], now allow contributions by Western history educators signifying that Russia wants to participate in international discussions.

This brings us to another innovational factor in the textbook sector: outside influences. Shortly after the collapse of communism, the Soros Foundation initiated a comprehensive program aimed at the creation of new history and social studies textbooks in Russia. The outcome was the creation of about twenty textbooks which, even though they did not have a high print volume, were of great importance to textbook authors as an experimental initiative.[6]

The Council of Europe is also involved in improving the conceptualization of history textbooks. Under the Council of Europe's initiative, a series of international textbook conferences has taken place in Russia during the last few years. The European umbrella organization for history teacher associations, EURO-CLIO, is also active in Russia.[7] The textbooks that EUROCLIO has put out are made up almost exclusively of didactically arranged source materials. However, given these books' radical and innovative conception, they will find it difficult to assert themselves against traditional wishes of many teachers for authoritative study guides. Since modern Western standards are realized in an exemplary fashion by the Russian authors of these books, one could, despite the obstacles, expect these new books to energize the Russian debate over new didactical paradigms in history teaching. Thus teachers can familiarize themselves with how these principles work in practice.

Within this context, the German-Russian textbook conferences organized by the MIROS Institute, the history faculty of the Moscow State University and the Georg Eckert Institute for International Textbook Research should also be mentioned. One of these conferences dealt with the "Treatment of the Socialist Past in Textbooks"; another, in Wolgograd in September 2001, dealt with the post-war period.[8] In all these encounters it was confirmed that integrating international "know-how" into the current Russian situation and making Western experiences constructive for Russian users can only occur if Russians themselves are actively seeking, reflecting on, and expanding on suggestions. It is not superimposition that promises success but joint projects such as these.

Forces of Retardation in History Education

The democratization of history education in Russia is still in its infancy and has to fight against resistance and setbacks. Democratic education cannot be prescribed or installed ad hoc and those who suggest that it can be implemented immediately by decree are possibly still thinking in terms of Bolshevist-type categories of feasibility. Even excellent textbooks that might be written would not "function" unless they are applied in proper environments. The principle that democratic norms depend upon democratic awareness continues to be an unassailable truth. New educational goals that aim for a civil society have to be supported by a corresponding political culture. Institutional reforms are otherwise in danger of merely creating modern facades.

One example of this is the development of the Russian rule of law: in terms of basic rights the country possesses probably the most modern constitution in the world; it is the implementation of the rule of law that is sadly lacking. The reason for this is that very few in the legal profession, let alone the citizens, are conscious of what it really means to have a state based on the rule of law.

Democracy depends upon courageous acts and civil courage. Within a democratic discourse, teachers must dare openly to criticize authorities, they must be able to speak out against traditional opinions, they must have the courage to experiment, they must be prepared to resist political pressures, and they must have their own viewpoints and be able to defend them. All this is much easier to facilitate if teachers can rely on the implementation of a rule of law and are protected from arbitrariness. At this point, I am sceptical of teachers' powers to defend themselves against the measures of higher-ranking authorities using the judicial system in Russia. Karl Eckstein (1998), an expert on the Russian judicial system, hit the nail on the head when he wrote: "Here, at the lower administrative levels, ranging from school regulations to the regulation of municipal fees, the majority of constitutional violations is to be expected." According to Eckstein, there is an almost frantic obsession with rules at this level, resulting in a "mass-production" of regulations "without any legal expert familiar with the constitution ever examining these regulations first." The daily relevance of basic rights is minimized under these conditions, while the temptation courageously to implement them is greatly reduced. But if teachers cannot and do not display civil courage, students certainly will not do so either.

A significant handicap for implementing modern democratic standards in education is the material shortage in education sector. The supply of textbooks continues to be inadequate and often books are outdated. The German newspaper *Frankfurter Rundschau* published an article in 1995 titled "The Rich Are Going to Private Schools, the General Public Crams in Demolished Houses" (Ostermann 1995). This tendency has increased rather than decreased in the last few years. Because of the poor salaries teachers are paid, the young tend to avoid the teaching profession even though they are the ones who could break through the old crust. Women who are both working and supporting their families make up the majority of teachers. Many teachers have a second job, which means that their commitment to classroom reform can only be limited. People, teachers as well as students, whose lives are marked by economic hardship are inclined to look for the uplifting and idyllic in history.

The fact that Russia has an aging teacher population makes it harder to overcome rigid mental structures and hinders the ability to overcome longstanding mental images. The former Russian Minister of Education, Evgenii Tkachenko, admitted in an interview that "our older teachers cannot manage this new system. Thirty-five per cent of them have worked in schools for more than 20 years, so it is very difficult for them to change" (Baker 1994). One has to assume that authoritarian behavior is still dominant. In 1997, Vladimir Batsyn, Deputy-Minister of Education, pointed out in an essay that people seemingly have an incurable habit of immediately dividing everything in a Manichean-Bolshevik manner into "good" and "bad," into "ours" and "not ours," and into "black" and "white." The result is a constant readiness for conflict and an insufficient inner readiness for tolerance. This also is true for teachers. Batsyn points out that communist agitation focused for decades on what are now essential terms, such as "democracy," "human rights," and "a culture of peace"—especially in history courses. Deeply rooted Soviet prejudices with regard to these principles are extremely unyielding. (Batsyn 1997: 18–9). That many teachers lack an independent, self-sufficient approach to their work should not come as a surprise, given the fact that they have been used to taking orders and functioning as transmission agents throughout their careers. In 1994, Elena Lenskaia, the head of the Department for Curricular Development within the Russian Ministry of Education, admitted that "there is still one single view instead of pluralism. Teachers do not know what pluralism and diversity mean in the classroom, how you address different children and how you get them to ask different questions rather than having one answer" (Baker 1994).

The responsibilities of a history teacher change in a democratic environment. The question of effectively conveying information becomes secondary, while issues concerned with how to ask questions which, in turn, imply specific methods and teaching styles, move to the forefront of classroom practice. Teachers who have been accustomed to predetermined content, values, and judgments will find it difficult to take on responsibility for new educational goals and new ways in which information can be presented in the classroom. We know from the German experience after 1989 that only a small number of teachers in East Germany considered the new situation to be a welcome opportunity. The majority of teachers reacted in an uneasy and anxious manner toward the new freedoms. The German example also destroys any illusions one might have about a new understanding of the role of teachers or about the persistence of intended behavioral changes. After working in the area of continuing education for teachers for five years at the Brandenburg Ministry of Culture, Hilda Rohmer-Stänner summed up the issue: "During classroom visits, we observe that the new content—if [any] at all—is mainly conveyed using old methods and that diversity of perspectives, the ability to discuss issues, and the ability to form critical judgements rarely surface" (Rohmer-Stänner 1996: 72).

In light of this, what can be expected of Russian teachers in terms of classroom performance should be adjusted. The conditions under which they work are far less fortunate than those of teachers in East Germany. Expertise in historiography is missing, since historical research also has to free itself from the chains of Marxism-Leninism. Developments in history didactics are still in their early stages in Russia. Continuing education programs for teachers suffer from a lack of materials and dynamic, experienced personnel. Even the easiest path, making didactic-methodological literature available to history teachers, is difficult. The mandatory salary bonus for teacher journal subscriptions has not been paid in years. A teacher's salary, ranging from approximately $30 per month for young and inexperienced teachers in rural areas to $140 for highly qualified teachers in Moscow, does not allow for such additional expenditures. Given this state of affairs, the conclusion drawn by two observers in 1995 regarding the advancement of modern pedagogical methods very likely still holds today: "The basic authoritarian nature with which students are treated has frequently changed very little while unproductive teaching methods continue to prevail"(Barabanov and Baranov 1996: 78). Within this context, Barabanov and Baranov also mention the traditional "glorification of teachers as knowledge bearers," which blocks the transfer of Western teaching methods with its much more student-oriented teaching methods. How strong the old ways still are and how few new beginnings are sought in this area becomes immediately apparent when considering the recommended literature for continuing education programs. The author of an essay on various forms of teaching published in the journal *Teaching History in Schools* recommended a total of eleven readings in 1998, of which only two were from the post-Soviet era, international references were not mentioned (Klimenko 1998).

The political pressure on textbook authors remains significant and also comes from within the teaching profession. Especially discernible is the duty to be uncritically "patriotic," a concept that would be violated if a book were funded by foreign sources. What is not even conceivable, according to the majority of the Russian Parliament, is the involvement of a person who is not a citizen of the Russian Federation in the writing of a textbook. It was concluded in a decision by the Duma on June, 9 1995: "The participation of foreigners and foreign firms in the determination of the content of Russian textbooks is inadmissible" (Egorov 1995). The chairman of the Committee on Education of the Voronezh Duma took the stance that the way in which the textbook by Aleksandr Kreder portrayed history was intended to "suffocate the development of national awareness and honor amongst children at its core and instill in them a feeling of humiliation, inferiority and an 'inner crouching' toward anything foreign" (Surkov 1997: 3). The battle lines in this confrontation, according to the newspaper *Rossiiskaia Gazeta*, were drawn between the author and the Ministry of Education on the one hand and the Voronezh Duma, a group of teachers, academics, and local politicians, on the other (Litvintsev 1997: 3). From a Western viewpoint it is surprising that historians can be persuaded to try and ban colleagues with different views from the textbook métier. Collegiality should prevent them from doing so. What becomes most apparent from such behavior, however, is that the principle of scientific freedom is not assigned a high enough priority. Who should defend the principle of academic freedom in the first place if not the historians themselves?

Considerable parts of the old pedagogical Soviet intelligence continue to occupy important positions and are strengthening antireform sentiments. Many have proven their inability to restructure their thinking and intellectually to confront the new situation. They cling nostalgically onto the past instead of exploring new paths. Because their hopes for a return to neo-authoritarianism and the reinstitutionalization of classroom practices did not materialize, their switch toward nationally conservative, patriotic attitudes happened all the more swiftly. In claiming its "own special path" that Russia supposedly is taking, Western models are discarded and sometimes demonized while liberal thoughts are attacked. The catastrophic consequences of the social transformations taking place in Russia at present form the basis on which such agitation proliferates. The financial difficulties facing education, the socially selective access to higher education, and the loss of quality in general education are attributed to the new democratic regime. In hindsight, the conditions under the Soviets are positively evaluated.

The versatile Russian textbook landscape should not conceal the fact that textbooks continue to be marked by many characteristics which, on the one hand, may be associated with Soviet tradition and, on the other hand, with the transformational nature of the current generation of textbooks. Professors rather than teachers continue to be the authors of widely used textbooks. Everyday history, especially the kind that is based on youth-specific topics, continues to be a neglected area, while gender history is unknown. A disproportionate amount of attention is paid to the terminology with which historians work. Instead of developing a pragmatic, instrumental relationship with terminology, it is treated, disputed or accepted as a belief system. Theoretical models are usually classified as "right" or "wrong." Instead, textbook authors should learn to use these models as tools to help pupils grasp history. Instead of being "right" or "wrong," theoretical models have a certain scope, they have strengths and weaknesses that should be addressed in textbooks and discussed in the classroom. Because many of these issues have been neglected, some teachers assert that not much has changed in textbook construction and that all that happened is a change in ideology.

During the initial years following the collapse of communism it was understandable that given the hunger for a new portrayal of history, many authors developed their own premises and just started to write. Now, however, is the time to undertake more serious didactical theory development. The traditional gap between academic historians, who cannot divorce themselves from the past and continue to write encyclopedia-like teaching materials, and the methodologists, who just want to optimize the infamous "Nuremberg Funnel" (a metaphor for inserting huge amounts of facts into students' heads), can only be bridged by historians who have focused on history didactics as an autonomous discipline. Those in the educational profession greet euphorically every success in this area. S. Smirnov in his 1996 study on new textbooks wrote: "The first hurdle has already been overcome: University lecturers have learned to write good textbooks in collaboration with real teachers."[9] What I find remarkable in this context are the approaches by the Novosibirsk Laboratory for Experimental Education in Schools and Universities, whose director is Iurii Troitskii. These approaches are innovative in terms of their emphasis on source-oriented, investigative learning, perhaps because their results are rather controversial (Troitskii 1994; Umbrashko 1996). Up to this point the authors' texts still dominate Russian textbook historiography. Sources are usually nothing but illustrations for the main narratives. If this relation is reversed, an approach can really be innovative, thus enabling the author's text to play a supportive role in the development of and familiarization with the material.

The change in history didactic paradigms in West Germany during the 1970s showed that the break with textbooks that have a traditional and conventional educational mission is a highly explosive political endeavour. The likelihood of success is directly correlated with whether strong forces can be mobilized in the political arena. The West German teachers' associations were given a central task in this context. This type of potential for innovation has so far been missing in Russia. Teacher Union representatives have a marginal influence at best and furthermore are concerned only with the material situation of teachers. History teacher associations were only founded recently in some cities (for example, Moscow, Chabarovsk, and Novgorod), and the hope is that one day they will be in a position to consolidate reform initiatives and effectively represent them toward new audiences.

One institution that was able to reestablish itself in an impressive fashion was the Russian Orthodox Church. This, in principle, should be welcomed, but the separation between the church and the state should not be endangered and xenophobic, reactionary opinions such as those found in the letter by the deacon Andrei Kuraev, quoted before (Kuraev 1997), should not gain considerable influence on educational content. Causes for concern exist. Recently, a textbook on *The Russian Orthodox Culture* written by A. Borodina was printed by the Moscow publishing house Pokrov. In this book the secular history of Russia is portrayed as a series of miracles, where the basic assumptions of Enlightenment are thrown overboard. Surprisingly, the Ministry of Education gave the book its blessing. The Civil Movement for Human Rights, filed a lawsuit with Moscow's public prosecutor against the book in June 2002, based on its belief that the book advocates ethnic and religious frictions (see Holm 2002: 34).

Russia continues to search for a new identity. This search should not be left to the politicians or other elites. Classroom discussions about history and society as well as critical questions being asked by the younger generation should play a central role in solving identity issues. In order to encourage these discussions, good textbooks are needed. It cannot be emphasized enough that amongst current Russian government representatives there exists a deep skepticism toward the traditional textbook based on prescientific, indiscriminate consensus and traditional self-confidence. The skepticism is rooted in an experience of the past, where consensus proved to be fictitious and history education had no bearing on the attitudes of people and no lasting influence on their thoughts and actions. This was compellingly expressed by the former Deputy-Minister of Education, Vladimir S. Batsyn, who, at a time when he was still influenced by the war in Chechnia, pointed

out that even though the separatist leader Dzhokhar Dudaev and his counterpart, the Russian general Konstantin Pulikovskii, may have studied from
the same history textbook, they obviously took away very different lessons.[10]

Europe and the World in Russian Textbooks

Russia's search for an identity is essentially related to the question of how Russia
defines itself vis-à-vis Europe and the world. This is why this final section of
the chapter will consider some contemporary works by Russian textbook
authors more closely. I consider all to be representative of the various directions that can be taken by "intellectual processing" of the identity problem. The
historical picture of Europe and the world that emerges from these textbooks
can be considered a snapshot of the quest for a new identity.

The first book, *The World in the twentieth Century* (Soroko-Tsiupa 1996),
sketches a world without Russia. This connects to the previously mentioned
concept of "countries located behind the border." While the author explains that
Russian history is a separate subject, this book nevertheless suggests that world
history can be conceived without Russia. The organization of the book is
predictably chronological; the narrative in each epoch is organized according
to "continents." However, Europe and North America are considered one entity,
Australia is missing entirely, Asia and Africa are grouped together, South and
Central America stand for the American continent. Within this structure, chapters dealing with the world wars and their consequences are integrated as focal
points. Thus, war ties together the individual histories of countries.

The term "Europe" is central in Soroko-Tsiupa's textbook. For the author,
Europe was the center of the world at the beginning of the twentieth century.
It appears that he considers the Western European model of economic and
social development transferable to the rest of the world and a precursor toward
global civilization. The history of the twentieth century is, in essence, interpreted as an effort by the "rest of the world" to catch up with the Western
European level (Soroko-Tsiupa 1996: 5).

The absence of Australia testifies to the fact that the world is viewed primarily from a perspective of political power, or in other words, in terms of
relevance to one's own country. The mention of Africa in the chapter heading
is mostly an unfulfilled promise: the subsequent paragraphs make no mention
of this continent. One of the seventeen chapters that does not fit with the
general pattern of the book is dedicated to science, technology, literature, and
art. A slightly exaggerated description would be that this chapter is more of a
"hit-parade" of nations. For example, in the two pages on science and technology one encounters twenty-four references to nationalities. The main
account of the atomic physicist Enrico Fermi is that he is an Italian who
emigrated to the United States.

The chapters on continents are subdivided into an array of stories about individual countries, frequently dealing only with the "most important" countries. In Europe these are Germany, England and France. Eastern and Central Europe, the Balkans, Scandinavia, and the Iberian Peninsula are generally mentioned only in connection with wars. The author singles out China, India, and Japan with respect to Asia, and assigns Mexico, Cuba, and Chile the main role when it comes to describe Latin America. Ideas on modernization theory that still contain Marxist elements in combination with the "white man's" perspective block any important insights into Third World societies. In the chapters on Latin America, for example, ethnic conflicts are not acknowledged or are simply entirely overshadowed by social conflicts. Indigenous movements figure as peasant rebellions. The coexistence of various ethnic societies is overlooked. "Latin American" is introduced as a unique combination of Native American, Negroid, and European elements. Stereotypical descriptions prevail: "Latin Americans distinguish themselves through a particular temperament often found amongst people of the South; a tendency to express themselves in a lively and emotional manner" (Soroko-Tsiupa 1996: 58).

While the book by Soroko-Tsiupa has a historicist approach and is based on modernization theories, the two volume *New History* (Iudovskaia et al. 1998) follows a civilizational approach. Therefore the authors more easily avoid the compulsion of dragging historical processes before a judge of alleged progressiveness and to have them evaluated accordingly. As a result, Iudovskai et al.'s descriptions of non-Western civilizations are written empathetically. They state decidedly, "Each of these civilizations has its own culture, its own morale." But is it enough to learn about the customs and traditions of other cultures and peoples? The questions the authors pose to students in an almost suggestive manner are at least capable of making stereotypes a topic for discussion; for example: "Can Eastern civilization be associated with terms such as rigidity, stagnation, and arbitrariness?"(Iudovskaia, et al. vol. II 1998: 234). In the opinion of the authors it is nevertheless the achievements of European civilization that ascend to the center of universal human values. This implies a superiority of European civilization in comparison to the so-called "traditional societies" of Asian and African countries.

Seemingly entirely different, yet astonishingly similar, is the approach by Rodriges (1998) in his work *Recent History of the Foreign World*. Here, Russia is described as a natural part of the West; that is, part of those countries that had the say in the "eurocentric [*sic*] world of the twentieth century."[11] The book boasts that it is the first textbook that comprehensively describes the recent history of the countries of the East. In addition, Africa and Latin America are dealt with at length. I do not know of any other textbook that lays out as many facts about Third World countries. The events, so the author claims, are illuminated from the viewpoint of the people living there. However, what the author does is to convey a one-sided viewpoint that feeds off the traditions of

Soviet anti-imperialism. Favorite topics are the Cuban Revolution as well as Chile during Salvador Alende's rule. In this way, the book fails to do justice to the history of any other groups except white men; women do not come into view at all. Ironically, the filter of perception through which Rodriges looks is a specific variant of Western ideology.

A textbook at the opposite end of the spectrum is the volume *History of Western Civilization* (Khachaturian 1999) for tenth and eleventh grades, which can be attributed to a *kul'turologiia*-approach. This book covers early history up to the beginning of the twentieth century. The aim of this textbook, according to the preface, is "to convey an image of the underlying laws of and direction taken by the process of Western civilization" to the students (Khachaturian 1999: 7). Once again it can be seen that parting with the laws of history is a difficult undertaking. It is noteworthy that almost half of the volume is devoted to the East. If one counts Russia as part of the East, it would be substantially more. Australia, Africa, and the Americas before colonization are missing almost entirely.[12] At one point it is noted that no states really existed there or that these were at a relatively low developmental stage. By the same logic, not a single sentence makes the problems stemming from the clashes between indigenous and the West European cultures a topic of discussion. This in itself is very telling. In her analysis, Jutta Scherrer (2003: 129) has attested the following to the protagonists of *kul'turologiia*: "The image of a foreign culture is not painted for its own sake and to better understand that which is foreign, but is used for the portrayal of one's own culture. It functions merely as a mirror." In order to assign a prominent place, perhaps even a mission, to Russia in the East-West paradigm, the neglected cultures simply become irrelevant.

Egypt is counted as an Eastern civilization and removed from its African heritage. The portrayal of the ancient Greek civilization is the same as in traditional Western historiography. Critical questions broaching the "Europeanization" of Greece casting doubts on its "northernization," are not raised, and African and especially Egyptian influences on ancient Greek history are nowhere to be found. Only the East is held in high esteem. Khachaturian considers the key to a favorable development of humankind to be a combination of the achievements of the East and the strengths of Western civilization. According to her, the West does not have a monopoly on the principles of free elections, democracy or civil society. These principles, according to Khachaturian, correspond to deeply rooted needs of human nature and were easily accepted by representatives of other cultures. Western civilization, however, is said to display a striking weakness in the application of these principles, which lead to a tragic escalation of the problems humanity faced at the end of the twentieth century: It is a tendency to divide radically and construct opposing principles and subsequently weigh them, thus creating "winners" and "losers," that characterizes Western Civilization. An equilibrium is missing. One side always dominates the other: humans rule nature, the individual stands above society, innovation within a culture displaces tradition. There is only one solution: "In order to solve the global problems, Western science, technology, vigor, and energy are necessary, yet the thousands of years of Eastern experience that tie humanity into a cosmic rhythm and prevent it from destroying nature and more are just as necessary"(Khachaturian 1996: 78). We find the same argument here that the Russian philosopher Kireevskii (cited in Goerdt 1995), propagated one-and-a-half centuries ago in his book *On the Character of the Enlightenment of Europe and its Relationship to the Enlightenment of Russia*. According to Kireevskii, Russia's strength was based on its "wholly mystical experience" and should be brought together and dialectically joined with the "worldly ratio" that comprised Europe's strength in order to determine the "historical future of the world"(Goerdt 1995, 266: 291). While Russia still appears as the antipole to "Europe" in Kireevskii's writing, Khachaturian envisions the great cultures of Asia preventing the fatal downfall of the West.

This critical attitude toward the West is not unique to Khachaturian. Buganov and Zyrianov (1995: 9–11) write in their introduction to the *History of Russia:* "Unfortunately it is also true that Russians from neighbouring countries not only received the good and the useful but also many things that are destructive, especially in terms of the spiritual life in the West." Such views position one's own country. Sakharov and Buganov launch their textbook with the following thought:

> In each significant historical era of Russia, in each abrupt turn of its fate, decisive spirits questioned the historical choice of the country: Which path should one take, who should Russia turn to for orientation, where and with whom can salvation be expected? We will continue to pass these questions onto future generations. Not without reason is Russia considered the only Eurasian country in the world, a peculiar bridge between worlds on which two world civilizations meet. (Sakharov and Buganov 1997: 7–8)

The fact that this enormous landmass contains a multitude of ethnicities, according to Sakharov and Buganov, produces outcomes that positively distinguish Russia from Western Europe: "Within this multinational atmosphere, nationalism – in contrast to the countries of Western Europe – was never quite proliferated and, given the social and economic bonds between people of different nationalities, oftentimes was even entirely forced into the background" (1997: 12). The textbook by Buganov and Zyrianov (1995:7) also observes that widespread "traditions of mutual tolerance, respect and understanding toward one another" amongst Russian people are "a specific trait of Russia in comparison to many West European countries."

The criticism of the West can serve two different purposes: on the one hand, it can be a result of distancing oneself from the Enlightenment and, on the other hand, it can be used to express anticapitalist or anti-Marxist elements. Its compensatory function in each case is instantly recognizable and enables an externalization of responsibility for the adverse social and economic conditions in Russia. Alternatively, in its capacity as a propagation mechanism of a uniquely Russian trait, it extends the traditional Russian messianism, lays claim on a moral superiority, and keeps hopes of again reaching imperial greatness.

That it is possible to distance oneself from Europe without becoming suspect of the (just mentioned) super-power chauvinism is proven by the new textbook by Zagladin (2000) *Recent History of the World Outside of Russia*. In explaining his approach, Zagladin criticizes the overall trend in Russian textbooks of paying too much attention to Europe and North America. He claims that his book differs from others in the sense that the key events of the twentieth century center around the collapse of colonialism, the modernization of previously underdeveloped countries in Asia, Latin America, and partially in Africa, as well as their introduction to industrial civilization. In following this approach, the book claims to avoid the "flawed view" that these developments are merely "an appropriation of the achievements of Western civilizations (or of the Soviet variant of socialism) and an overcoming of underdevelopment or barbarianism." The book should rather be understood as an attempt to "synthesize national cultural traditions with the achievements of European science and technology" (Zagladin 2000: 51–52). Zagladin also distances himself from the traditionally prevalent understanding of history as a mere sum of events that have occurred in different countries. He contrasts this with an "understanding of causes for this or that event as well as their interconnectedness" as a general learning objective. His topics are never constrained by the scope of national histories, but rather, deal with border transcending issues and problems. In correspondence with the model of civilization laid out by him, he takes (in addition to the U.S.A., Japan, China, and India) Western Europe, Eastern Europe, Latin America, the states of the Arabic-Islamic world, and those of southern Africa as cohesive and historically influential cultural spheres.

Zagladin thus sets a new direction for Russian textbook historiography. This is taken even one step further by Panteleev and Savateev's (1999) textbook *The World in Present Times* in the sense that it eliminates the separation of Russian and non-Russian history. The five main chapters of the book are: Global problems of Humankind; The Developed Countries of the West; The Soviet Union and Eastern Europe; The Countries of Asia, Africa and Latin America after the Second World War; and Philosophical Problems of Humankind Today. For the first time, a Russian history textbook incorporates political science, sociology, and cultural studies in an interdisciplinary fashion. The comparison of political structures in various types of societies; the connection between modern and premodern times; ecological problems; the effects of the scientific-technological revolution, etc. can be examined and discussed in much greater analytical detail this way. The authors want to convey "an encompassing picture of our current era to the students, in which humankind is joined by thousands of visible and invisible threads, where changes in one area such as ideology have automatic effects on other areas such as politics, social relationships and even the economy (and vice versa)"(Savateev 2000: 69).

The curricular leeway of an integrated approach, as demonstrated by Panteleev and Savateev, does not take hold in practice until students have reached advanced grades. The Russian curriculum provides a chronological voyage through Russian and non-Russian history for grades 5–9 and 10–11 respectively, which is characterized by an enormously dense number of facts. The number of lessons devoted to the history of the "fatherland" is one-third more than non-Russian history. Although an integrated instruction in both curricula is, theoretically, always possible; however, the best-case scenario is that it may happen in practice during grades ten and eleven, when students develop their specific profile and additional interdisciplinary courses in the area of social studies are added to the curriculum.

Panteleev and Savateev's book manages to build a bridge to social studies textbooks, which it resembles in many areas. This can only be advantageous for Russian history textbooks. For years Western observers have noted with surprise that the interesting discussions about history are taking place in social studies textbooks. While the emancipation of the subject history from a "learning subject" to that of a "thinking subject" is only progressing slowly, profound historical excursions that allow an in-depth, controversial discussion of contemporary topics could be found in Russian social studies textbooks years ago. In these, questions about the role of personality in history, about historical truth, the meaning of ideologies, thoughts on progress and totalitarianism, the opposition of Western civilization and premodern society, the role of the nation, Russian identity, and "one world" are vented (Bogoliubov 1992; Bogoliubov 1996; Lazebnikova 2000; Mukhaev 1997; Mushinskii 1998; Poliakov 1992; Zagladin 1994).

Conclusion

In Russia, the fracturing of communist certainties has lead to more liberal and pluralistic approaches in the construction of school history textbooks. This process is characterized by the growth of private publishing companies and by academics and teachers revisiting traditional conceptions of Russian history and Russia's place in the world in a way that questions traditional core narratives that have been dominant politically and ideologically for a long time. Associations and social groups influence history education and the content of school textbooks. Being part of developing a civil society and by establishing international cooperation, a greater openness toward international influences can be observed. Additionally, the state was interested in a paradigm change in historical education and initially supported the attempt of nationalities and regions to develop their own identities.

However, this process has not been without its problems. Textbook writing went from communist doctrines to what might be described as a nationalist ideology, which threatens to keep Russia in an isolated spot internationally. Mostly, the same people are in charge, and even if the agenda has changed, the writing of textbooks in the new Russia remains full of political and ideological tensions and contradictions. Pedagogically, Russian teachers as a rule do not possess the knowledge, skills or experience to develop more investigative approaches to the study of the past. Teachers are mostly from the older generation and support conservative attitudes. Reforms are not helped by the enduring economic hardship. These factors considerably limit pedagogical development.

In new textbooks, Russia's view of its place in the world remains confused. Russia is caught between at least two traditions. The textbooks do not really provide a framework from which to integrate fully Russia's past into a comprehensive view of the world. Russia became smaller as the Soviet Union crumbled. Especially, now Russian population hubs in the Asian part of Russia frequently border on Southern neighbors that are in a process of culturally reidentifying with "Asia." The regions of East Siberia and the far east of Russia are becoming increasingly aware of their direct proximity to China, Korea, and Japan. The West Siberian region is confronted with strong Central Asian influences. This goes hand in hand with the realization that the regions' development opportunities are based on an open exchange with these neighboring countries. A merely Eurocentric history education as it prevails at present would be an obstacle to these processes. In the future, Russia must reevaluate its view of history if it wants to play a role in the future history of the world.

Notes

This chapter was translated from the German by Esther Conrad.
1. A systematic overview of the terminology used in these subsets of Soviet and pre-Soviets times is provided by Hans Hecker (1983).
2. Ultimately, Slavophilism also fits in this category because it defines itself especially through a negative differentiation from (Western) European ways of thinking.
3. I will only name a few of the numerous publications: Andreianov at al. 1996; Anisimov et al. 2002; Krugov 2002; Larin et al. 1998; Miftakhov at al. 1995; Rogachev et al. 2000; Sabirzianov and Gumer 1995; Sechenikova et Kolozhvari 1998; Selivanov 2000; Shamski et al 1995; Sinicyna 1995; Vinogradov et al. 2001; Vysokov et al. 1995; Zavalishin 1999; Zverev et al. 1999–2001.
4. For an elaborate discussion see Golubev (1999: 103–13).
5. Under Troickii's initiative a series of exercise booklets for history has already been issued (see Golubev 1999: 112).
6. Soros invested U.S. $ 2,5 million in this project (see Smith 1997).
7. The last book published is Saplina at al. 2000.
8. Materials were published in German and Russian: Keghel and Maier (1999) and Chernev (2002).

9. S. Smirnov in his review of the two textbooks on medieval history in Russia by Katsva and Iurganov, and Boitsev and Shukurov respectively (see Smirnov 1996: 2). In this article, teachers are encouraged to use both books simultaneously and to vary them freely in the classroom.

10 V.S. Batsyn during the Seminar on Textbooks by the Council of Europe held in Suzdal, 12–14 December 1996.

11. See Rodriges, vol. I (1998) 5). Eurocentrism is apparently not considered a problem in the writing of history but rather an objective attribute of actual history.

12. Such a fixation on the "East" can lead to a complete change of geographic coordinates in which history is perceived. In a Ukrainian textbook we find the following statement when it comes to colonialism, which is usually conceived as a problem of the industrialized north toward the underdeveloped south: "The contradictions between the advanced West and the East that remained underdeveloped industrially, became one of the burning questions of humanity in the first half of the 20th century" (Berdichevski and Ladychenko 2002: 6).

References

Abramov, Aleksandr M. 1996. "Prosushchestvuet li kultura v Rossii do 2005 goda?" [Will Culture Survive in Russia until 2005?]. *Uchitelskaia Gazeta,* no. 6.

Altman, Ilia A. Alla E. Gerber, and David I. Poltorak, 2001. *Istoriia Kholokosta na territorii SSSR* [History of the Holocaust on the Territory of USSR]. Moskva: Fond "Kholokost."

Andreianov, A.A. et al. 1996. *Istoriia i kul'tura Mariiskogo naroda"* [History and Culture of the Mari]. Joshkar-Ola: Mariiskoe Kn. Izdat.

Anisimov, A.L. et al. 2002. Istoriia dalnego vostoka. Epokha srednevekovia (V – pervaia polovina XVII veka) [History of the Far East. Middle Ages from the Fifth Century until the First Half of the Seventeenth Century]. Khabarovsk: Chastnaia kollektsiia.

Baker, Mike. 1994. "… to the steppes" (Education 10–11), *Guardian,* 7 September, Education 1994.

Barabanov, Vladimir V. and Piotr A. Baranov. 1996. "Geschichte als Lehrfach im heutigen Bildungssystem Rußlands." *Beiträge zur Historischen Sozialkunde,* vol. 26, no. 2. Geschichtsunterricht in Zentral- und Osteuropa.

Batsyn, V.K. 1997. "O reforme istoricheskogo i obshchestvovedcheskogo obrazovaniia v sovremennoi rossiiskoi shkole." [About the Reform of the Historical and Patriotic Education at Russian Schools]. *Prepodavanie istorii v shkole* [History Teaching at School], no. 8.

Berdichevski, I.M. and Tatiana V. Ladychenko. 2002. *Vsemirnaia istoriia (dlia 10 klassa)* [World History (for 10th grade)]. Zaporozhe: Premier.

Bogoliubov, L.N. et al., 1996. *Chelovek i obshchestvo. 10–11 klassy* [The Individual and Society. Tenth to Eleventh Grade]. Moskva: Prosveshchenie.

Bogoliubov, L.N. and A.I. Lazebnikova. 1992. *Osnovy sovremennoi tsivilizatsii* [Foundations of Modern Civilization]. Moskva: Izd. Aktsionernogo obshchestva Biuro Dendi.

Buganov, Viktor I. and Pavel N. Zyrianov. 1995. *Istoriia Rossii, konec XVII – XIX* [History of Russia from the End of the Seventeenth to the Nineteenth Century]. Moskva: Prosveshchenie.

Chernev, Igor. ed. 2002. *Vozrozhdenie iz ruin: vozpominaniia, mifi i tabu v prepodovanii istorii poslevoennogo vremeni v Rossii i Germanii* [Risen from the Ruins: Memories, Myths, and Tabus of Postwar History in Russia and Germany].Volgograd: VAGS.

Eckstein, Karl. 1998. "Russlands steiniger Weg zum Rechtsstaat." *Neue Zürcher Zeitung*, 14–15 February.

Egorov, Vladimir. 1995. "Uchebniki - 95, 96, 97, 98, 99, 100…" [Textbooks – 95, 96, 97, 98, 99, 100 …]. *Pervoe Sentiabria* [1st of September], no. 166.

Furaev, Viktor K. 1993. *Noveishaia istoriia 1939–1992* [Contemporary History 1939–1992]. Moskva: Prosveshchenie.

Goerdt, Wilhelm. 1995. *Russische Philosophie.* 2nd ed. Freiburg, München: Alber.

Golubev, Aleksandr V. 1999. "Das Bild der sowjetischen Vergangenheit in den russländischen Schulbüchern der letzten Jahre." In *Auf den Kehrichthaufen der Geschichte? Der Umgang mit der sozialistischen Vergangenheit,* ed. by Isabelle de Keghel and Robert Maier. Hannover: Hahn.

Hecker, Hans. 1983. *Russische Universalgeschichtsschreibung. Von den "Vierziger Jahren" des 19. Jahrhunderts bis zur sowjetischen "Weltgeschichte" (1955–1965).* München: Oldenburg.

Holm, Kerstin. 2002. "Rüstzeug für die Armen im Geiste. Starker Konsens, schwacher Protest: Neue Religionslehrbücher für russische Schulen." *Frankfurter Allgemeine Zeitung*, no. 197/35 (26 August).

Imamov, Vachit. 1994. *Zapriatannaia istoriia tatar* [The Renounced History of the Tartars]. Nabereshnye Chelny: Gazetno-knizhnoe izdatelstvo "KAMAZ."

Iudovskaia, Anna I., Piotr A. Baranov, and L.M. Vaniushkina. 1998. *Novaia Istoriia 1500–1800,* [New History 1500–1800] vol. 1. Moskva: Prosveshchenie.

——— 1998. *Novaia Istoriia 1800–1918,* [New History 1800–1918] vol. 2. Moskva: Prosveshchenie.

Kaplan, Vera, Pinchas Agmon, and Liubov Ermolaeva, eds. 1999. *The Teaching of History in Contemporary Russia. Trends and Perspectives.* Tel Aviv: University of Tel Aviv.

Keghel, Isabelle de, and Robert Maier, eds. 1999. *Auf den Kehrichthaufen der Geschichte? Der Umgang mit der sozialistischen Vergangenheit.* Hannover: Hahn.

Khachaturian, V.M. 1996. "Istoriia mirovoj tsivilizatsii" [History of World Civilization] (preprint) *Prepodovanie istorii v shkole* [History Teaching at School], no. 3.

——— 1999. *Istoriia mirovoj tsivilizatsii* [History of Western Civilization]. Moskva: Dom Drofa.

Khloponin, Maksim S. 1995. "'Wie ich mich durch die letzten Jahre schlug.' Ein Geschichtslehrer aus der russischen Provinz blickt auf das vergangene Jahrzehnt zurück." *International Textbook Research*, vol. 17, no. 4, 451–59.

Klimenko, A.V. 1998. "Lektsii i seminary v prepodovanii istorii i prava." [Lessons and Seminars in Teaching History and Law]. *Prepodavanie istorii v shkole* [History Teaching at School], no. 3.

Kreder, Aleksandr A. 1995. *Noveishaia istoriia. XX vek* [Recent History. Twentieth Century] Moskva: Tsentr gumanitarnogo obrazovaniia.

Krugov, Aleksei I. 2002. *Kenigsbergskaia tetrad* [Königsberg Work Sheet], vol. I. Kaliningrad: Biznes-Kontakt.

Kuraev, Andrei. 1997. "Urok istorii." [History Lesson]. *Rossiiskaia Gazeta*, (12 November).

Larin, V.L. et al. 1998. *Istoriia rossiiskogo Primor'ia* [History of the Primorsk Area]. Vladivostok: Dal'nauka.

Lazebnikova, Anna I. and Maksim I. Brandt. 2000. *Uroki obshchestvoznaniia v 11 klasse, metodicheskoe posobie po kursu "Chelovek i obshchestvo."* [Lessons in Civics for the Eleventh Grade, Methodical Materials for the Course "Man and Society"]. Moskva: Drofa.

Litvintsev, Gennadii. 1997. "Chinovniki derutsia – u shkolnikov chuby treshchat" [The Bureaucrats Argue—The Pupils Have to Stick it out]. *Rossiiskaia Gazeta* (5 November).

Maier, Robert. 1999. "Kräfte der Demokratisierung in Russland am Beispiel von Geschichtsunterricht und Schulbuchschreibung." In *Russland und Deutschland auf dem Weg zum antitotalitären Konsens,* ed. Ludger Kühnhardt and Alexander Tschubarjan, Baden-Baden: Nomos: 169–86.

Maslikova, Tatiana. 1997. "Patriotizm po Sorosy i Surkovu"[Patriotism in the Way of Soros and Surkov]. *Rossiiskaia Gazeta* (19 November).

Miftakhov, Zufar Z. and Diliara S. Mukhamadeeva. 1995. *Istoriia Tatarstana i tatarskogo naroda. Tom I. Uchebnik dlia srednich obshcheobrazovatelnych shkol, gimnazii i litseev* [The History of Tartastan and the Tartars]. Kazan: Magarif.

Mukhaev R.T. 1997. *Politologiia. 10–11 klassy* [Politology. Tenth to Eleventh Grade]. Moskva: Drofa.

Mushinskii, V.O. 1998. *Azbuka politiki. 10–11 klassy* [Primer for Politics. 10–11th grade]. Moskva: Mezhdunarodnoe otnoshenie, Tsentr gumanitarnogo obrazovaniia.

Ostermann, Dietmar. 1995. "Die Reichen gehen ins Lyzeum, das gemeine Volk paukt im Abrisshaus." *Frankfurter Rundschau* (27 September).

Panteleev, M.M. and A.D. Savateev. 1999. *Sovremennyi mir. Uchebnoe posobie dlia XI klassa srednikh uchebnykh zavedenii* [The Contemporary World]. Moskva: MIROS.

Poliakov, Iurii. 1997. "Urok istorii" [History Lesson]. *Rossiiskaia Gazeta* (12 November).

Poliakova, V.L. and N.I. Eliasberg. 1992. *Gumanisticheskie tsennosti evropeiskich tsivilizatsii i problemy sovremennogo mira. Posobie dlia uchashchikhsia 10 klassa.* [Humanistic Values of the European Civilization and the Problems of Today's World. Materials for Pupils of the 10th Grade]. Moskva MORF.

Poltorak, David and G. Klokova. 1997. "Ob izuchenii kholokosta" [Teaching the Holocaust]. *Prepodovanie istorii v shkole* [History Teaching at School]. no. 7.

Rodriges, Aleksandr M. 1998. *Noveishaia istoriia zarubezhnikh stran (chast 1 i chast 2)* [Recent History of the Foreign World]. Moskva: Vlados.

Rogachev, M.B. et al. 2000. *Istoriia Respubliki Komi* [The History of the Komi Republic]. Moscow: DIK.

Rohmer-Stänner, Hilda. 1996. "Erfahrungen beim Aufbau der Lehrerfortbildung im Fach Geschichte in den neuen Bundesländern am Beispiel des Landes Brandenburg." *Beiträge zur Historischen Sozialkunde,* vol. 26, no. 2. Geschichtsunterricht in Zentral- und Osteuropa, 71–75.

Sabirzianov, Gumer S. 1995. *Narody srednego Povolzh'ia i Iuzhnogo Urala v panorame vekov* [The Peoples of the Middle Wolga and the Southern Ural Throughout the Centuries]. Kazan: Magarif.

Sakharov, Andrei N. and Viktor I. Buganov. 1997. *Istoriia Rossii s drevneishikh vremen do konca XVII veka* [History of Russia from Ancient Times to the End of the Seventeenth Century]. Moskva: Prosveshchenie.

Saplina, E., V. Sorokin and I. Ukolova. 2000. *Trudnye puti k demokratii* [The Difficult Paths to Democracy]. Moskva: MIROS.

Savateev, A.D. 2000. "Novoe uchebnoe posobie po istorii XX veka" [New Teaching Aids for the History of the Twentieth Century]. *Prepodovanie istorii v shkole* [Teaching History at School], no. 3.

Scherrer, Jutta. 2003. *Kulturologie. Russland auf der Suche nach einer zivilisatorischen Identität.* Göttingen: Wallstein.

Sechenikova, Liudmila F. and Inga A. Kolozhvari. 1998. *Velikii Novgorod i ia* [Greater Novgorod and I]. A Student Workbook. Fifth to Nineth Grade]. Moskva: Prosveshchenie.

Seleznev, E.S. 1993. [Letter to the Editor.] *Voprosy Istorii,* no. 1.

Selivanov, A.M. 2000. *Istoriia Iaroslavskogo kraia s drevneishykh vremen do kontsa 20-kh gg. XX veka.*[History of the Iaroslav Region from Ancient Times to the End of the 1920s]. Iaroslavl: Iaroslavskii gosudarstvennyi universitet.

Shamski, Sultan and Iskander Izmailov. 1995. *Volzhskaia Bulgariia v rasskazach dlia detei.* [Wolga-Bulgaria in Stories for Children]. Kazan: Slovo.

Shevyrev, Alexander. 1995. "Das Bild Russlands in heutigen russischen Geschicht-slehrbüchern." *International Textbook Research,* vol. 17, no. 4, 397–424.

Sinicyna, Klara R. 1995. *Istoriia Tatarstana i tatarskogo naroda. Tom II. Uchebnik dlia srednich obshcheobrazovatel'nych shkol, gimnazii i litseev.* [The History of Tartastan and the Tartars]. Kazan: Magarif.

Smirnov, S. 1996. "Vozmozhen li dialog uchebnikov?" [Is a Textbook Dialogue Possible?]. *Pervoe Sentiabria,* no. 59, (1 June).

Smith, Michael. 1997. "Soros to help Russia wipe Marxist slate clean." *Sunday Times* (Business section) (5 January).

Soroko-Tsiupa, Oleg. 1996. *Mir v XX veke* [The World in the Twentieth Century]. Moskva: Prosveshchenie.

Surkov, Ivan. 1997. "Urok istorii" [History Lesson]. *Rossiiskaia Gazeta* (12 November).

Tiulaeva, Tamara I. 1995. "Die Reform der historischen und sozialkundlichen Bildung an russischen Schulen." *International Textbook Research,* vol. 17, no. 4, 387–95.

Troitskii, Iuri L. 1994. "Novaia technologiia istoricheskogo obrazovaniia." [New Technology in History Education]. *Pervoe Sentiabria,* no. 45, Istoriia - prilozhenie k gazete.

Umbrashko, K.B. 1996. "Razvitie tvorcheskogo myshleniia na urokach istorii." [The Development of Creative Thinking in History Lessons]. *Prepodavanie istorii v shkole,* no. 2.

Vinogradov, Nikolai B., Georgii N. Chagin and Vladimir A. Shkerin. 2001. *Istoriia Urala s drevneishykh vremen do kontsa XVIII veka* [History of the Ural from Ancient Times to the End of the Eighteenth Century]. Ekaterinburg: Dom uchitelia.

Vodianskii, Aleksei. 1997. "Urok istorii." [History Lesson].*Rossiiskaia Gazeta* (November 12).

Vysokov, M.S. et al. 1995. *Istoriia Sakhalinskoi oblasti s drevneishich vremen do nashich dnei* [The History of the Sakhalin Region from the Early Ages to Now]. Iuzhno-Sakhalinsk: Sakhalinskii tsentr dokumentatsii noveishei istorii.

Zagladin, N.V. 2000. "Postroenie kursa zarubezhnoi istorii XX veka v osnovnoi shkole." [Conception of a Course in Foreign History of the 20th Century for Comprehensive Schools]. *Prepodovanie istorii v shkole,* no. 5.

——— 2000. *Noveishaia istoriia zarubezhnikh stran. XX vek, (dlia 9 klassa)* [Recent History of the World Outside Russia]. Moskva: Russkoe Slovo.

Zagladin, N.V. et al. 1994. *Mirovoe politicheskoe razvitie: vek XX, posobie dlia prepoda-vatelei.* Moskva: AO Aspekt Press.

Zavalishin, A.I. 1999. *Istoriia dalnego vostoka Rossii v novoe i noveishee vremia* [History of the Far East of Russia in Recent and Current Times]. Khabarovsk: Chastnaia kollektsiia.

Zverev, V.A., A.S. Zuev, and F.S. Kuznetsova. 1999–2001. *Istoriia Sibiri* [History of Siberia], 3 vols. Novosibirsk: Infolio-Press.

Chapter 8

❖

Europe in Spanish Textbooks: a Vague Image in the Space of Memory

Miguel A. Pereyra and Antonio Luzón

> "Bad! Bad! What? Does he not—go back?"
> Yes! But you misunderstand him
> when you complain about it.
> He goes back like every one who is about to make a great spring.
> Friedrich Nietzsche, *Beyond Good and Evil.*
> *Prelude to a Philosophy of the Future*

Europe as a Learning Process

For some time now, it has been held that the citizens of Europe should become aware of their transnational identity as Europeans, for the unity of the "Old Continent" is gradually drawing closer. The idea of oneness becomes more rhetorically relevant and transcendental given the multiplicity, variety, and indeed, complexity of the economic, political, social, and cultural conditions that are gradually and compellingly gaining strength. The obstacles are evident, and this new dimension of "European citizenship" has its skeptics. However, as it is frequently stated, we run the danger of considering European integration after the Second World War as an isolated and fragmentary phenomenon, focused exclusively on an economy-driven process aimed at meeting the challenges of being the leading world trade center. Obviously, this reductionist view does not take into account the great transformations that have shaped an innovative unitary project, endowed with the creation of a certain European identity—at least theoretically—which was first called the European Community and later became the European Union (EU). Still, it is interesting and at the same time ironic to note the lack of historic concretions to corroborate the development of a collective will regarding the construction of Europe. In fact, it is still nothing more than a conglomerate upheld by a certain sense of optimism, a far cry from that collective mentality furnishing a renovated identity that would set aside local identities and submit them to a supranational community—the Europe of nation states with their regions—based on socialization processes through cooperation and solidarity.

Leaving aside this utopian or idealistic image of Europe, featuring solidarity and cooperation, the creation of "European awareness" not just in the political sense but also in the educational dimension, is becoming a predictable necessity. This is due to the expectation that, "the more institutionally integrated the EU with its distinctive institutions and sovereign governing principles, the greater the likelihood of a shared identity and culture which is discernible at the level of individual citizens and can expectedly replace or at least undermine national identities" (Soysal 2002: 59). Therefore, there is a need for a collective mentality that may bring Europeans closer to that macro-reality, not envisaged as an illusion. The proposal for "transforming Europe into an idea of a nation," quoting the Spanish philosopher José Ortega y Gasset, is not exclusively political and economic, but also cultural and educational: it is more about the nature of the learning process than its outcome, as stated recently by Jürgen Habermas (see Therborn 2002: 15).

The requirement of a "European education," which is at times a recurrent expression, and its more recent version, a "European model of education" (see Nóvoa 2002), allude to a somewhat vague and contradictory concept of unity, given that within the European educational context, utter diversity prevails. However, within the context of this varied European mosaic, it would seem appropriate to ask what images of Europe the different countries have now, when it is already a central reference in the teaching of each national history. At the same time, we need to query the role played by pedagogical discourses in each individual country in shaping attitudes toward becoming more tolerant and democratic citizens. This local approach is essential for exploring the vague and imprecise contours of the European dimension of education, and especially for social participation in the construction of Europe.

Official knowledge, by and large based on the content of school textbooks, reflects a set of political, economic, and cultural interactions legitimating a specific view of knowledge and culture organized and systematized by each country, hence its relevance. For this reason, and given a context increasingly projected toward European integration, as well as the collateral influence of different aspects such as tourism, language learning, and professional and academic mobility, our intention is to analyse the image of Europe in Spain through the official curriculum. We shall carry out a review of school textbooks that determine how the pupils—the potential European citizens—are informed. Our focus is on social science subjects, and particularly history since history is an essential ingredient in the formation of identity. Indeed, narratives about the past serve as a kind of "cultural tool" in "mediated action" that creates and recreates identity (Wertsch 1997).[1]

Europe: an Imagined Community or an Idealized Reality

The Europeanization of Spain is not a recent discourse. It was a historic constant throughout the twentieth century and was darkened by periods of regression such as the Franco regime. We can clearly find it in 1898, when the political and social formations had to confront the loss of the last colonies of the Spanish Empire, during the monarchical restoration. As an ideological orientation, the so-called *Regeneracionismo* introduced a reformism that was mainly positivist with historicist and traditionalist bases, and also a utopian view. All this was present in the paradigmatic regenerationism of the Spanish historian and reformer Joaquín Costa. His project for the Europeanization of Spain *Reconstrucción y europeización de España* [Reconstruction and Europeanization of Spain] is a good example (Costa 1903). He saw education as an axis to structure and modernize an obsolete country suffering a deep identity crisis. Although with a certain ambivalence, the intellectuals of the Spanish "Generation of 98"—a literary and cultural movement in the first two decades of the twentieth century—strove to find a positive and modern image of Spain that could once and for all do away with its inquisitorial, primitive, romantic, premodern and, in short, anti-European image.

A negative view of anything Spanish impregnated the image of a modern, rationalist and learned Europe where science and democracy prevailed. Spain was the antithesis of modernity, and a dividing line was traced which would only be overcome in the late twentieth century. The look towards Europe—symbolized as "the other self"—is due to the creation of a collective myth in the Spanish imagination which pushed toward nationalization and aimed at overcoming the decline of Spanish identity and the feeling of decadence of the Spanish Empire. The modernizing figure symbolized by José Ortega y Gasset in his statement, "Spain is the problem, Europe is the solution," took shape as the search of an accelerated Westernization to cast away the figures of backwardness and Africanization, which were more typical of different times. Such attempts were not successful. The myths of historic exception and the resurgence of the stereotypes of the past confirm their failure (Lamo de Espinosa 2001).

The romantic image that eventually normalized and legitimized the regime of Franco (1939–1975) with a pro-government and monotonous discourse about the construction of a standardized, European, and modern Spain contrasted with the narrative of failure. It is sufficient to mention the widespread view of Spain as a spiritual pool of Europe, or the inconsistent and ambiguous Spanish self-image. In the face of a historic iconography of permanent exception, the exemplary democratic transition brought back historic memory. Spain awoke from its collective amnesia, and a repeatedly procrastinated process of modernizing Spain began, and culminated with Spain's integration into the European Union as a full member in 1986. With European integration, the vague boundaries of Spanish identity, which had been symbolized by difference and supported by a narrative of failure, began to fade. Spain started to seek a recognizable identity that would erase once and for all the dividing line marked by the Pyrenees.[2] The institutionalization of European citizenship was included as a right in the Treaty of the European Union (Amsterdam, 1997). It is clearly the greatest effort made so far to close ties between European institutions and the citizens. The aim is to make Europeans feel the joint construction of Europe as something that affects them beyond economic and administrative regulations and has to do with their rights and duties, that is, with their identity. It is therefore possible to wonder if this new defining framework of Spanish reality can serve as a basis to ascertain mimetically in advance whether the knowledge about Europe that has been and is currently taught in the Spanish curriculum is sufficient, adequate, and meets the new pro-European expectations. We wish to find out if the above is true or if, instead, the prevailing feature is the introduction of certain topics just because it is obligatory to include knowledge about Europe and pro-European attitudes in the curriculum of member states.[3]

From Knowledge to an Understanding of European Reality

If we understand Europe as a supranational entity that currently bears the name of European Union, the proper teachings that must be provided by schools can be synthesized around two parameters (Mencía de la Fuente 1996: 35): (1) The raison d'être and behavior of the EU as a supranational legal and political body; and (2) the geographic, social, political, cultural, and historic reality of the countries that make up the European Union.

The most appropriate form of knowledge refers to formal education, which is systematized through the curriculum and revolves around issues of social content, mainly through subjects such as geography and history. This does not exclude other alternative formulas and education modalities such as nonformal and nonsystematic education or extracurricular activities. We are referring here to the way the image of Europe is organized in the most homogenizing teaching means, mainly textbooks. In Spain, unlike in France, there is currently no specific subject with a civic content. Such contents are organized in a crosscutting way across the different subjects and included in the syllabuses of other areas or disciplines. The study of the most relevant meanings and images of the European Union in the curriculum has to be done by looking at the subjects whose content or object of study includes issues related to the European Union, be they geographic, historic or cultural.

We intend to show how Europe was portrayed by Spanish primary and secondary education textbooks in the twentieth century, especially during the Franco dictatorship and the democratic transition. We shall also analyze the current meaning and relevance of Europe, within the Europeanization—Europeanism binomial, and as a consequence of the juxtaposition between "Europe as a concept" and "Europe as a reality" in the meaning of Spain's full participation in the European project. Images are projected through textbooks. This does not only apply to the transmission of specific knowledge, but also to the development of integrating attitudes loaded with symbolism that contribute to legitimizing the new situation.

A Vague Image of Europe in the Textbooks of the First Half of the Twentieth Century

In 1997, Societas pro Investigatione Comparata Adhesa Educationi (SPICAE) [International Group for Researching Comparative History of Education in South Europe] organized a conference on "the image and idea of Europe in textbooks between 1900 and 1945."[4] Several participants investigated the ways that Europe was shaped by the different national cultures before the unification process started. According to Agustín Escolano (2000), the image of Europe found in Spanish textbooks from the late nineteenth century and the first-half of the twentieth century revolved around five spheres: a space, a setting inhabited by different peoples or national formations, economic relations, political relations and, finally, national cultures versus European civilization. Escolano finds that the territorial image of Europe is diverse, given its imprecise eastern borders. Yet, there is harmony as regards the physical elements of which Europe consists.

Catalina Albacete (2000) argues, on the contrary, that the prevailing image of Europe in geography textbooks from the first third of the twentieth century is mainly descriptive and stems from a centuries-old tradition of the discipline, because Europe is the continent that is studied the most and allowed a greater space in books. Most textbooks are structured as a dialogue in which the students are asked: "What is Europe? It is the less vast, but the most civilized of all and the most advanced in science, arts and industry. It is the smallest and the best of the five parts of the world, which confirms that a great soul fits in a small body. It is the continent that is blessed the most by the best geographic conditions on the globe. It is the most populated, richest and most civilized part" (Albacete 2000: 285).[5]

It was not usual to mention political matters but rather simply to list the countries Europe consisted of. The most outstanding features of the main European states were highlighted. England was the most admired country: "It is the first country in the world for its economic value, its intense trade and because it is the first colonial power in the world" (Albacete 2000: 287). France was pictured as "the most educated of the Latin peoples" and Paris was seen as "the most famous and beautiful city in Europe." Italy stood out for its wealth in monuments, history, and art. Rome was considered outstanding because of its link with Christianity, because it was the residence of the Pope. Germany and

Russia followed in importance. Given the link of geography with colonialism, it was common practice in textbooks to list the European colonies in the different continents.

According to Albacete (2000) the most prominent feature of the geography textbooks of that time was their view of the world, which revolved around Eurocentrism and nationalism and merged with other subjects such as History. European civilization became the leading cultural pattern in the early twentieth century. The pride of being European, the superiority of the white race, Europe's economic development, military superiority, and degree of civilization were the traits that defined the European collective imagination of the times. Yet, in spite of the common geographic and historic heritage, a paradox was patent, and a centripetal force arose. It was based on nationalism and the praise of one's own country above the other nations, and was a source of conflicts and confrontations between peoples and nations.

The duality mentioned above also applies to history textbooks. There were positions in favor of Europeanization, versus others that defended extreme nationalism. The romantic passion of patriotism and the strength and weight of national interests prevailed over the fragile pro-European ideas (Escolano 2000). Thus, European virtues, which were supposedly superior, were not considered relevant because they were not really Spanish. Therefore, the efforts to transform and modernize Spain were not only considered useless but also immoral and unpatriotic (Boyd 1997). The texts present the two historic cycles that Europe was immersed in during the first third of the twentieth century— the period prior to the First World War and the period that followed—as a consequence of the dismemberment of the Austro-Hungarian Empire. In the light of the disaster of the First World War, the Spanish conservative right wing insisted upon the breakdown of "European values" and aimed at making Spanish ideals universal at the same time. These images and the categorical statement by the school teacher Félix Martí Alpera, who said in 1904 that "the State and the City Councils must make schools more European" (Delgado 2000: 310), contrast with the few or nonexistent references to Europe in history teacher training questionnaires. According to Delgado (2000), out of the five teacher training curriculums of the first-half of the twentieth century, the ones drawn up in 1914 and 1931 (during the Second Republic), were not exactly pro-European. They presented a very vague image of Europe although there is no evidence that they were anti-European either. Europe was not understood as a territorial and political whole, or even as a cultural whole. More specifically, "In teacher training questionnaires and syllabuses there is no presence of Europe; there are states and nations that form it with whom friendship relations are established only sporadically, or against whom conquests, invasions or control ambitions are usually planned" (Delgado 2000: 311).

In short, in the Spanish imagination, Europe meant modernity and progress, new frames of reference and stimuli of different intensity. These traits and profiles were reflected by textbooks in the first half of the twentieth century, albeit with vagueness and imprecision, and often in duality with national sentiments. The attempt to combine "tradition corrected by reason" (Pérez Garzón 2000: 104) was frustrated by the Franco dictatorship, which returned to the dogma of traditionalism and national Catholic fundamentalism.

Europe Erased from Memory

It was not long before the reaction against the Republican educational structure took place. The weight and importance of education as an indoctrinating bastion of the new regime was crucial for the triumph of the nationalist side, led by Franco. Therefore, the change of tone in education began in the midst of the civil war. The first legislative reforms began in 1938, with the reform of *Bachillerato* [secondary education], not compulsory at that time. Schools became the ideological seed of the new authoritarian and fundamentalist atmosphere advocated by the national forces. Their approach was clearly patriotic and aimed at the salvation of Spain. Catholic education took over, and thus began the condemnation of secularism and of the humanistic and democratic principles praised by the republican school. A rigid moral doctrine was imposed. It aimed at "exerting an influence on the conservation and promotion of social discipline since [i.e., from] youth," as stated in a provision of the newly created body in charge of culture and education, Comisión de Cultura y Enseñanza [Commission of Culture and Education] (Cámara Villar 1984: 70). Intolerance, one-sidedness, and exclusion became the new coordinates of the educational map, whose objective was to dismantle the product of the work done by the republicans. The purification process not only affected the teaching staff but also the content of textbooks and manuals, which fell under the supervision of the Catholic Church.

The new history syllabi for primary education were shaped and established following the slogan "Spain, One, Great and Free" and others related to Hispanism. The core of History syllabuses consisted of references to the so-called Imperialist Renaissance in texts and biographies about the deeds of Spain in America and the Spanish Golden Age. The idea and prominent role of Spain as the savior of Christianity eclipsed the image of Europe. It was a historic and at the same time teleological image of Europe, where history had been twisted and manipulated to show Spain as a spiritual nation and the savior of Europe. In short, as mentioned by Clara Revuelta (2000: 337), there was a projection of "an image of Europe as an entity that Spain saves and frees—or at least attempts to do so—from malignant forces (the Muslim invasion, Protestantism, the Turks, communism)." The new regime used history as an argument to instill the main dogmas of fundamentalist Catholic thought. Martínez Tórtola (1996: 37) maintains that, "the doctrinaire role of History was a peculiar feature of the reform of *Bachillerato* which had no precedent in other reforms." The book

Manual de Historia de España [Handbook of Spanish History], for example, was published by an anonymous author in 1939, under the auspices of the newly created Instituto de España (Cereceda 1943). The book shows the overwhelming extent that history was used to the benefit of the prevailing conception of national Catholicism—a brand of extreme right-wing ideology–once the civil war was over: "In no other region of Europe do men live in such high lands. Castile is the balcony or terrace of Europe, since in the times of the great Spanish monarchy it was said that the throne of Spain was the one closest to God" (*Manual de Historia de España: Segundo grado* [Handbook of Spanish History: second level], quoted in Carreras 1995: 211).

The use of History is clear in the syllabuses of the new *Bachillerato*. History was present in each of the seven courses it was structured in. The subjects geography and universal history were only taught in the third and fourth years of *Bachillerato*. As mentioned above, it was common practice to use certain topics in an ideological and instrumental way, and always to refer to Spain as a model. The romanization process and the influence of Rome on Hispania were considered to be positive because they created awareness about Hispanic unity. Not surprisingly, the contribution of Hispania to the Roman culture was also mentioned with a certain triumphalism.

When the shaping of nationalities was dealt with, "the moral purity of the Spanish nationality, a faithful follower of the catholic spirit of medieval Christendom" was asserted. The English revolution of the seventeenth century was discredited because of its "hypocritically puritan and tyrannically Catholic nature" (Martínez Tórtola 1996: 45). The reasons for the independence of the Spanish colonies in America during the eighteenth century were manipulated and labeled as "Masonic and encyclopedist influences." In the History of Culture syllabus for the fourth year, Italian fascism was defended, and seen as seeking to "dignify human culture" (Martínez Tórtola 1996: 46). As regards foreign policy issues related to Spanish behavior in Flanders during the reign of Philip II, the use of force was totally justified. The following text illustrates a demagogic and biased approach:

> The conspiracies of secret societies are not political bodies of our times. It can be proven that they operated in Europe in the sixteenth century with the aim of destroying Spain. *Don Felipe* was aware of it, but was not deterred in his determination to defend Flanders against the rebels that all the forces of evil hid behind. This is why our passage through the Netherlands is idealistic and noble and of universal goodness, and this is also why it has become a point of attack against our history. (quoted in Martínez Tortola 1996: 91)

The eighteenth century was usually the object of harsh criticism because it represented decadence for Spain. The appreciation and prominence of France in this century were seen as something negative. The nineteenth and twentieth centuries were usually limited to the history of Spain because it was when Spain acquired the role of fighting, as it had done in the past, against the political and social revolution. Major historic events were disguised, hidden, and distorted.

The Gradual, Slow, and Finally Strategic Recovery of Memory

Since the 1950s, the hegemonic fraction of the regime accepted that the autarchic way was not the best solution for the survival of the system, and a slow "liberalization" process began. It started with the economy. Consequently, the Falangist fraction, which was the political and ideological bastion of the dictatorship, was progressively removed from decision-making levels, to the benefit of the technocrats who were the majority. The objective, as described early on by the Opus Dei member Professor Florentino Pérez Embid (1949: 159), was "to use Europeanizing means to achieve purely Spanish goals." It involved modernizing the economic system but maintaining exactly the same political and ideological bases. In education, there was a progressive decrease of national Catholic exaltation. Yet, the denominational character of education was upheld and strengthened by the signature of the Concordat with the Holy See in 1953, which reaffirmed the church's right and control of education. This incipient economic change of course required adapting the skills of the work-force to the new requirements. Hence, in 1953, when a Christian-democratic oriented politician, Joaquín Ruiz Giménez, was the Minister of National Education, a new *Bachillerato* was approved by means of the secondary education act known as *Ley de Organización de la Enseñanza Secundaria* [Act of the Organization of Secondary Education]. It replaced that of 1938, which had come into existence during the war. Although the first four years of elementary *Bachillerato* became general studies for students until the age of fourteen, access to upper *Bachillerato* was reserved to a minority. It was, therefore, as classist as the previous one, and had very low female participation.

In the 1950s, textbooks started to feature photographs and realistic drawings with many captions. They were published by publishing houses.[6] Books published by the publishing house *Bruño* presented the history of Spain from a positivist approach and included a series of historic facts in chronological order across different periods and ages. However, they still exuded a clear national Catholic influence as evidenced by the following: "The knowledge of our patriotic history is of great importance, not only for Spaniards but also for all educated people, since Spain is one of the nations that has contributed the most to civilization and had a major influence for several centuries" (Carreras 1995: 213).

However, considerable progress can be glimpsed in school texts in the 1970s. These changes carry the hope of recovering historic memory. The textbook *Historia de España y Universal* [History of Spain and of the World] (Arenaza and Gastaminza 1965), for example, insisted upon the need to move away from the discourse of earlier years where a national conception of history prevailed. The errors of the past started to be admitted, and there was an implicit self-criticism that tended to draw a veil over the tragedy of the civil war. The "national reconciliation" process thus began (Carreras 1995: 214).

The great qualitative leap was the contribution made by the historian Jaume Vicens Vives. He introduced the ideas collected in the French journal *Annales* into Spain via the publishing house *Teide*, whose first edition dated from 1960. In other words, he included economic, social, and religious elements into history. Historic facts were no longer anchored in the positivist tradition but analyzed and studied from a broader perspective provided by the auxiliary sciences of history—demography, economy, and sociology. The end of the 1960s was the prelude to broad educational reform undertaken by means of the education act *Ley General de Educación* [General Act of Education].[7] At that time, local historians such as Alberto Compte, who followed the works and thought of the Catalan historian Jaume Vicens Vives, also wrote history textbooks. In these books from the end of the Franco dictatorship, an ideological and methodological opening replaced the old positivism. These were identity signs in a process of change. Democratic legitimacy turned physical violence into symbolic violence, and progress was reached through education and social inequality. According to Cuesta Fernández, a form of education called technocratic education for the masses, or a new form of curricular control, gradually appeared. In this new system, the Cuesta Fernández believes truth was constructed by means of the technical and instrumental opinion of experts and sanctity was reached through efficiency (Cuesta Fernández 1998: 63–65). The new technical changes were an attempt to redefine the subject as living history instead of traditional history. The classical model of history teaching, based on learning about dates, events, and historic cycles, started to be replaced by the analysis of the context as a new interdisciplinary way to organize contents in the broad framework of social sciences.

The unpublished research carried out by Hita Marín (1997) on the transmission of sociocultural and sociopolitical values in formal educational systems by means of the narration of history in textbooks printed by teaching publishing houses, shows unprecedented categories. They are essentially economic (see Table 8.1).

Table 8.1 *Economic and Non-economic References to Europe*

Publishing houses	% with reference	Average % with reference	% no reference	Average % no reference
Anaya	56.1%		43.9%	
Miñón	42.4%	47.2%	57.6%	52.8%
S.M.	42%		58%	
Santillana	48.4%		51.6%	

Source: Hita Marín (1997: 170).

The following are some of the most significant economic references to European countries: "At the end of the reign of Louis XIV a great economic crisis ravaged the country. It was due to different causes: wars, the lack of precious metals, low agricultural prices and Court expenses. Agriculture had to endure very low prices and heavy taxes. Several years of cold winters, droughts and poor harvests also contributed to the impoverishment of France" (Hita Marín 1997: 174).

Compulsory education school texts used before the new education act, *Ley General de la Educación* came into force gave considerable importance to economic factors in the development of history. During the last years of the Franco dictatorship, textbook authors even started to use the Marxist concept of "class struggle" within a social class analytical approach (see Table 8.2). The term was found on average 13.2 percent of the times in the coverage of the historic period known as *Edad Moderna*, the period from the last decade of the fifteenth century until the French Revolution, and on average 17.6 percent of the times in the coverage of the period known as *Edad Contemporánea*, the period from the French Revolution to the present day (Hita Marín 1997: 184).

Table 8.2 *Percentage of References to Social Classes, by Publishing Houses and Historic Periods*

Publishing house	Ancient World %	Average %	Middle Ages %	Average %	Edad Moderna[1] %	Average %	Edad Contemporánea[2] %	Average %
Anaya	12.2		19.5		21.9		24.8	
Miñón	14.6	9.7	24.9	20.2	9	13.2	16.7	17.6
S.M.	2.7		16.9		6.6		12.7	
Santillana	9.2		19.7		15.4		16.1	

Notes:
1. From 1490 to the French Revolution.
2. From the French Revolution to the present day.

Source: Hita Marín (1997: 184).

The explanation provided by Hita Marín (1997) about the paradoxical use of this terminology, especially considering that the textbooks were subject to censorship and prior authorization, is the need of the regime to "disguise itself." The author also mentions that the regulations about text authorization may have become more flexible.

The following are some examples of allusions to class struggle in Europe (in Hita Marin 1997: Appendix, 38–57).

● "Representativeness in eighteenth-century England was very reduced, only landowners could be elected to the Chamber…" (*Anaya*, vol. 2: p. 196).

● "Nobility against bourgeoisie in eighteenth-century continental Europe" (*Anaya*, vol. 2: p. 188).

- "The problem of Ireland, which depended on Great Britain, was not only about religious disparities. The agricultural situation was also pitiful. The exploitation of Irish farmers by British landowners was one of the greatest injustices witnessed by the modern world" (*Miñón*, vol. 3: p. 87).
- "Although the European war made a minority of tradesmen, manufacturers, landowners and speculators suddenly rich, it worsened the situation of farmers, blue collar workers and middle classes, thus increasing social discontent, which violently exploded in the year 1917" *(Santillana*, vol. 3: p. 408).

The ideological turn that was taking place in the Spanish society at the end of the Franco dictatorship was undoubtedly present in school texts, although the idea of Europe was still distant.

The Image of Europe in Social Science Textbooks: Historic Background

In the educational system controlled by the 1970 *Ley General de Educación*, which preceded the act introduced in 1990 by the Socialist Party government, the image of Europe was linked mainly to interdisciplinary social science textbooks. The subject was taught in the sixth, seventh, and eighth years in the *Segunda Etapa* [second level] of compulsory comprehensive education known as *Educación General Básica* or EGB (ages 12 to 14).

In a detailed study of the social science texts of the now extinct EGB, Rafael Valls (1994) rigorously analyzed their greater or lesser "European dimension" as well as their peculiarities and approach. The textbooks analyzed by Valls were the ones most widely used by Spanish primary education students in the early 1990s (published by Anaya, Vicens Vives and SM). Half of the content of the sixth- and seventh-year textbooks was devoted to geography. As for history, the Ancient World was studied in the sixth year, whereas *Edad Moderna* was studied in the seventh year. The eighth year textbook was devoted exclusively to the study of *Historia Contemporánea*. According to López Facal (2000: 50) the changes in the education content introduced by the *Ley General de Educación* are the most relevant since the educational system was established in Spain in the nineteenth century. This is especially due to the inclusion of historic contents in the area of social sciences of primary education, and also because social and economic contents were included in history, at the expense of descriptive ones in the *Bachillerato*.[8]

Distribution of Contents

As table 8.3 shows, the manuals published by Vicens Vives featured the greatest amount of historic information. According to Valls (1994), their typographical composition and content were inspired by French manuals. Their content was mainly based on the historiographic trend of the *Annales* school, which included social history topics such as samples of everyday life, culture, and the ideas of the times.

The three manuals studied had impeccable presentation. They included plenty of maps, pictures, sketches, drawings, and diagrams. Several chapters at the end of the books were devoted to ethical and civic education, but never exceeding 5 percent of the total content. As shown in Table 8.3, more content was devoted to Spain than to the rest of countries, especially in *Anaya* manuals which, unlike the other two, included the history of the region where the book was to be used. This gives us an idea of the kind of strategy following the guidelines and provisions of the new educational reform.

Table 8.3 *Global Distribution of Contents Studied in the Textbooks of the Second Level of Primary Education (EGB)*

Area studied	Anaya (%)	Vicens Vives (%)	S.M. (%)
Spain	43.5	26.8	26.6
European countries	9.3	22.7	9.5
Europe in general	32.7	33.9	40.8
Rest of the world	14.5	16.6	23.1

Source: Valls (1994:6)

Little attention (around 10 percent) was given to the different European countries, as the idea was to complete it in secondary education, which had a more encyclopedic character and a more Eurocentric approach. Still, the little space devoted to countries outside Europe is worth highlighting. The priorities in content learning are illustrated in figure 8.1.

Figure 8.1 *Degree of Importance Given to Contents*

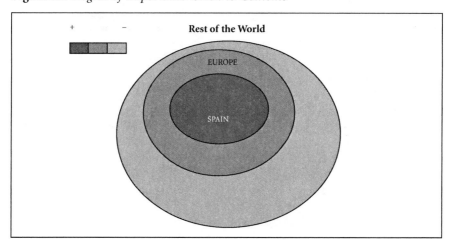

This is a sample of the successive replacement of contents with objectives and methods. Scientific knowledge became science that was taught, and textbooks were no longer considered as the only essential element in learning. The use of the book by the teacher became crucial (Torres Bravo 2000: 45).

Historiographic Evolution: From Content to Procedure

According to Rafael Valls (1994), the change in history textbooks was not only due to the political changes undergone by Spain over the last twenty years. The author believes there are other collateral questions that have also influenced this change of course. New teaching and pedagogical trends were being tested in some Western European countries. France, for example, was influenced by *l'éveil* or the predominance of local elements. In Spain, and particularly in Catalonia, groups of secondary education teachers were very soon familiar with the project *History 13/16,* developed in the United Kingdom (Schools Council 1972).[9]

These trends influenced the pedagogical understanding and the methods of teachers: a type of education that aimed at allowing students to learn by understanding started timidly to permeate educational systems. Regulated history progressively gave way to imagined history, where contents were replaced by methods so as to make teaching more rational. Instead of the product, the project became important, and textbooks started to be known by the name of their publishing house instead of that of their authors. This approach grew in importance in Spain with the enactment in 1990 of the new *Ley de Ordenación General del Sistema Educativo* [Act General Arrangement of Educational System], also known as LOGSE, whose main feature is to insist on working methods rather than on the transmission and learning of purely historiographic contents.

With the depreciation of a positivist historic conception related to conservative positions, and therefore with marked "neo-dictatorial" hues, a more social historiographic view has arisen in which events are interpreted. Data and historic facts, which were seen as related to noncritical and memory-based learning, have been left aside. One of the consequences is that students now have insufficient information about other cultures and countries to the benefit of local knowledge. This type of situation is reflected in a new approach about the meaning of history, the type of knowledge, its appropriateness and permeability and the way it should be taught. This has led scholars and teachers to advocate for compulsory secondary education the inclusion or integration of classic subjects such as "history" and "geography" in the current teaching area of "social sciences: geography and history" (see González Muñoz 2002: 32).

A Restricted View of Europe

The textbooks studied by Valls reflect how complex and difficult it is to have a clear criterion about the understanding of Europe. This was already noted by the French philosopher Edgar Morin (1994: 24), who said, "the notion of Europe must be understood according to a multiple and full complexity." In Spanish EGB primary school books, Europe had a physical-geographic meaning, although specific cultural matters—ways of life, thought, political behavior, and cultural manifestations—were sometimes dealt with in an isolated way. They were approached from a pro-Western interpretative perspective, in which Mediterranean countries and cultures and historically Romanized areas were allowed a greater importance. The image of Eastern European countries such as Russia or the Balkan countries was quite diluted, yet Latin America was included in the Western framework of analysis.

The univocal concept of Europe, as a noun or an adjective, was the one that appeared the most in textbooks, albeit vaguely. In spite of the widespread use of the terms "Europe" or "European," either the geographic area referred to was not delimitated, or the different geographic, cultural or political areas in the European mosaic were, in fact, mixed and intertwined. The Vicens Vives manual was the least imprecise, since it clearly marked the geographic and cultural areas in focus.

The following is a selection of quotations showing the impreciseness of the concept of Europe (sited in Valls [1994:12])

- "Many European cities were founded by the Romans" (Anaya, 6º curso: 116).
- "When the Roman Empire disappeared, the church was the only strong power that remained in Europe" (SM, 6º curso: 241).
- "Some of the reigns created by (Germanic migrations) disappeared quickly and violently. But others were luckier, and slowly gave rise to new countries that currently form Western Europe, such as France, England, Italy..." (Vicens Vives, 6º curso: 265).
- "At the beginning of the twentieth century, Europe owned the world. When we refer to Europe, we are talking about the five great powers: Great Britain, Germany, France, Russia and Austria-Hungary" (Vicens Vives, 8º curso: 137).

In general, school books did not clarify the section that corresponds with Western Europe enough, taking into account its economic, social, and cultural differences (González Muñoz 2002: 368–71).

An Obsolete Pro-European Historic Dimension

The historic approach of school books that was directly related to a European dimension was that of the Middle Ages, especially the importance given to the Carolingian Empire, which "built a European empire similar to the Roman empire." The joint context of the European countries thus reappeared. The "pro-European" approach was reiterated, albeit from a "cultural" point of view, at the beginning and during the development of *Edad Moderna*. The praise of patriotism and the triumphalism of earlier manuals disappeared and Spain was linked to the main artistic and cultural trends of European society in the sixteenth and seventeenth centuries, and even part of the eighteenth century, with a unitary perspective. A joint image of Europe was also provided in complementary maps and diagrams.

The same approach prevailed in the chapters devoted to *Edad Contemporánea*. All matters related to the nineteenth century and the first-half of the twentieth century—the development of the new European states, imperialism, and the onset of the world wars, for example—were analyzed with a marked Western approach. However, European history after the Second World War was given less space and attention. Most analyses were carried out from a pro-economic and political point of view, as two contrary positions or blocks but with a geo-economic treatment. This was not the case with Latin America, Africa, Southeast Asia or the Arab world.

There were frequent confusions between the whole of Europe, which was very vague, and to a lesser extent the more restricted area of Western Europe and Central Europe. A conceptual ambivalence also stems from the use of two imprecise and undefined frameworks such as Western Europe and Eastern Europe. Table 8.4 shows the main European countries referred to regarding political or cultural changes or movements, according to school textbooks.

Table 8.4 *Main Subjects Studied and Related Countries*

Subject	Countries
Gothic art	France, Italy, and Great Britain
Medieval trade	Flanders and northern Italy
Universities	Flanders and northern Italy
Religious reform	Germany, Great Britain, France, and Italy
Nineteenth-century nationalism	Germany and Italy
Political changes of the twentieth century	Soviet Union, Germany, and Italy

Source: Valls (1994:19)

In eighth year of EGB, the syllabus was devoted to the study of *Historia Contemporánea* (nineteenth and twentieth centuries). It included a chapter about what was then known as the European Economic Community (EEC). The chapter had a descriptive approach and referred almost exclusively to economic factors. The historic configuration process of the EEC, which began in 1957, was also dealt with, but to a lesser extent, as well as the most important phases, decision-making bodies, expansion, and crisis. The difficulty of reaching agreements because of the different criteria of the member countries was underlined. The new expectations and convergence possibilities of the member countries were not mentioned, and a somewhat pessimistic tone about the future of the European Economic Community prevailed.

Generally speaking, Europe was studied from a segmented perspective. Its totality and identity were not appreciated, and the relevant aspects for understanding the European dimension were not studied either. The stereotypes of our urban and pro-state culture were reproduced in an essentially political and economic approach. Little value was given to other social realities that might show the achievements of people as a driving force of humanity.

Current Knowledge of Europe through Textbooks

In current texts, there is a clear methodological and procedural approach to the detriment of proper contents. The change of discourse involved placing many expectations upon teachers, the driving forces of social change by means of innovative classroom working techniques. Methodological aspects are given the greatest importance. As Cuesta Fernández (1997 and 1998) suggests—following a theoretical framework devised by Swedish educational theorist Ulf P. Lundgren (1991)—the new hopes of pedagogical renewal and the longing for an imagined history are reflected in a new regulated history and a renovated disciplinary code, set apart from historiographic knowledge. There is an even greater belligerence against contents that have to be learned by heart, and a predominance of local and regional issues. The appropriateness of studying other regions of Spain or other countries is disregarded.

The implicit rhetoric in the new regulations boasts that history "has to provide the students with the necessary knowledge and methods to understand issues of social realities in their temporal dimension" in the same way as geography must do so in its "spatial dimension." In other words, the point is to build a new body of historic-geographic knowledge linked to education about democratic values and related to the problems of the world that surrounds the students. The aim is for the students to be able to understand these matters at least, which thus contributes to developing critical awareness. However, this is only a new illusion. The new minimum contents in geography and history are designed to build a non-conflictive and functional identity that fully respects authority and hierarchy, where continuity symbolically and strategically supersedes change, and where academic knowledge prevails over critical thought. The central structure is still ethnocentric, male-oriented and obsolete, and a linear, chronological, and outdated view of historic evolution still prevails. The new individual and collective identity is formed in the context of cultural homogeneity, which is a unitarian and formalist view that legitimizes the nation-state (González de Molina 1998; Valls 2002).

Curricular Appropriateness or a New Cosmetic Treatment

The official and regulated knowledge of European reality in primary education takes place in the subject *Conocimiento del Medio* [knowledge of surroundings], which means "social and cultural knowledge of the natural, social and cultural environment." It offers the possibility of a globalized approach, beginning with local knowledge and moving on to Europe and the world. The subject is not exclusively limited to local approaches and its content aspires to more general perspectives, although in a limited and descriptive way. Most of the textbooks consulted show general images of Europe through maps, through which the students, especially those in *tercer ciclo* [third level: fifth and sixth years], are invited to learn about the countries of the European Union. Still, it is surprising to see that primary education books do not include information about the Euro, the common currency that has been in use for more than a year, especially considering that the regions, or Autonomous Communities, of Spain had to publish complementary materials to increase public awareness about the Euro.

In secondary compulsory education, known as *Educación Secundaria Obligatoria* (ESO), knowledge about European reality is included in the subjects of *Ciencias Sociales, Geografía e Historia* [social sciences, geography, and history], which are compulsory for all students. The minimum content of this educational level grants a special importance to geography and history with respect to the remaining social subjects in the area—economics, sociology, anthropology, and art history. This is mainly due to the weight traditionally given to these disciplines as sciences in charge of the regulated knowledge of society (Mencía de la Fuente 1996: 47).

As regards contents and evaluation criteria, different territorial levels are considered: municipality, autonomous community or region, Spain, the European community, and the international community. The Spanish and European levels are clearly privileged, though the content blocks are open to the reality of other countries and cultures. A Eurocentric and, especially, ethnocentric view still prevails, as well as the concentric design of contents. If the contents really referred to the diversity they mention, the treatment should be polycentric at least and celebrate contrast rather than difference. In recent research about how Europe and the European Union are studied in secondary education, Europe appears as an endlessly changing concept, and its presence in school books, with no exceptions, goes way beyond the prescriptions of the respective educational bodies (Prats 2001).[10]

Joaquín Prats' research involved analyzing five leading or representative publishing houses (Anaya, Santillana, Vicens Vives, Ecir, and Barcanova, the latter being broadly present in Catalan schools). Their materials account for more than 80 percent of the textbooks used in the teaching of social sciences, geography, and history in Spanish schools. Prats especially underlines that "the concept of Europe, either as a noun or an adjective or in its more restrictive meaning as referring to Western Europe, is probably one of the most frequent concepts found in Spanish textbooks, especially in history books." The quantitative asymmetry between the different European regions and especially between Western and Eastern Europe is significant (see Table 8.5 and Table 8.6). There are also twice as many references to Spain than to Europe. All the books include a chapter about the European Union, which underlines the advantages of Spain's membership in the EU, but does not mention the future enlargement of the EU to include other countries.

Table 8.5 *Presence of European Geography in ESO Textbooks*

Contents	Percentage of European geography
General analysis of Europe	43
Western Europe—European Union	45
Eastern and Southeast Europe	12

Source: Prats (2001: 57)

Table 8.6 *Presence of European History in ESO Textbooks*

Contents	Percentage of European history
General analysis of Europe	43
Western Europe—European Union	46.5
Eastern and Southeast Europe	10.5

Source: Prats (2001: 81)

The contents that exclusively refer to the European dimension are still imprecise, marginal, and vague. The trend of times prior to the educational reform continues. Even though the chapters that refer directly to the European Union have been updated, they still have the same Eurocentric approach as earlier ones.

In the analysis of history textbooks, the conceptual vagueness of Europe is even greater, since the concept itself is in a constantly evolving process. What Europe are we referring to? What period are we talking about? In his research, Prats (2001) mentions that textbooks normally use the concept of Europe with a territorial meaning. They simply aim at listing historic phenomena in a linear way, with no greater precision. Another less frequent procedure is to present new images of Europe where other auxiliary subjects also participate in the explanation of the concept. Thus, there is Christian Europe, medieval Europe and Renaissance Europe, for example. These points are analyzed with the help of other auxiliary subjects that broaden the meaning and tackle the subject with a more open and interdisciplinary approach (Prats 2001: 62).

Most textbooks consider the Middle Ages as the time when a new Europe was created, and make certain references to present-day Europe such as: "It was in the Middle Ages that the Europe of today was born: different languages, different countries ... " (Prats 2001: 63). Still, attention is almost exclusively given to Western Europe, and Eastern Europe is disregarded. Roman-Western culture prevails over Eastern-Orthodox culture in the texts, following the Schism of Christianity. The research carried out by Prats confirms that, in current history textbooks, medieval Europe is dealt with in the most pro-European way with respect to all other historic periods, even though it is still dominated by the history of western Europe.

The period known as *Edad Moderna* is different from other periods in that the most representative nations—especially England, France, and Spain, followed by Germany, the Netherlands, and Italy—are dealt with in a differentiated and individual way. Demographic and economic matters are those presented with the most integrated and pro-European approach. The most common issues in textbooks are geographic discoveries, the shaping of the modern state and the consolidation of national monarchies, the schism of Christianity between Catholics and Protestants, and the concept of Old Regime.

In the period known as *Edad Contemporánea*, the view of Europe is ambivalent. It is sometimes seen as a unit where the historic phenomena of certain nations prevail. On other occasions, it is seen as a totality. About nineteenth-century colonialism, we read that: "During the nineteenth century, a few countries in Europe controlled the greater part of the planet with their power, their influence or their business ... In the nineteenth century, Europe shared the African continent and set out to use its resources systematically" (Prats 2001: 77). Sometimes a more unitary view of Europe is given in *Edad Contemporánea*, as can be seen in the following quotation: "Contemporary History begins with the 1789 French Revolution and the British Industrial revolution...in only half a century, the European world changed its appearance radically" (Prats 2001: 75). The rest of *Edad Contemporánea* revolves around the two world wars, considered disastrous for the whole of Europe, and the European decline that contributed to the rise of the new power blocks after the Second World War. The books conclude with the fall of communism and the creation of a new world order.

History textbooks in *Bachillerato* [noncompulsory secondary education] devote much more space to facts and concepts than to the great variety of procedural contents and attitudes introduced by LOGSE. More enriching and functional mechanisms have gradually been introduced to replace the classical transmission procedures. Recent research carried out in the region of Catalonia about the appropriateness of *Bachillerato* history books points out that the contents refer both to the Catalan autonomous community and to the Spanish state, in accordance with the distribution made by official regulations. Looking at the contents in more detail, such books devote a greater space to political history, whereas economic and social contents are present to a lesser extent.[11]

Conclusions

The progressive institutionalization of European Citizenship has entailed a major effort to close ties between European Union institutions and European citizens, and had built solid foundations for a joint project. However, despite the various attempts outlined in this chapter, this is not explicitly reflected in current textbooks.

In Spanish textbooks, geography and history are presented in a linear way. Geography highlights the physical and political features of Europe, whereas history is structured as a chronological and homogeneous set of periods from ancient times to the present day, with a traditional view that does not take modern historiographic trends into account. Textbooks are set in a "pro-European" context, albeit from a Eurocentric point of view. This is patent in the abundance of maps of Europe that attempt to point out joint features, but do not show a common European history and, therefore, a shared heritage. The Spanish view of history has always been linked to that of the rest of Western European countries and focused on artistic and cultural features instead of economic, social, and political traits, thus masking an ambiguous collective memory at the service of political goals. Before Spain's full membership in the European Union, textbooks were imbued with the inferiority complex of Spain with respect to Europe. They highlighted the features that made Spanish history different, especially the Christian Reconquest and the colonizing influence in America. There was a vague and faded view of European history and culture. Certain facts were handled with a complacent attitude and lack of self-criticism, whereas other socially and culturally irrelevant matters were treated with excessive belligerence.

In the new textbooks brought about by the new education act of 1990, known as LOGSE, considerable progress has been made toward offering an image of totality. Still, local and regional matters prevail over European ones, which are now considered complementary in the syllabi.[12]

At present, in compulsory secondary education, one chapter is devoted to the European dimension, but it lacks contextual information. It focuses on descriptive features from an economic point of view, and disregards other important matters such as the cultural, political, and social dimensions. The new teaching materials do not show an image of Europe as a whole. The view of a joint Europe vanishes. In geographic topics, priority has been given to matters that highlight economic differences and leadership issues, to the detriment of historic roots and development possibilities in a multidimensional, non-exclusive and intercultural framework where we can live together in freedom.

At the end of this chapter we have to go back to what initially we said about reality and the possibilities of turning Europe into a significant learning process for our youth. We are not talking about idealisms or utopias. We are talking about developing a European identity which can transcend the limitations of the "official history" configured in school knowledge, and create a plural space of bonds and guiding and socializing knowledge that may help us read and interpret the complex current world. The idea is to "reoccupy the territory of our history as a civil ideology" (Boyd 1997: 266), especially in the case of Spain, an old European country that has created its nation-state between three civil wars, the most recent of which led to a cruel dictatorship the country still has not completely recovered from. In order to achieve the above, we believe knowledge and experience of the past are essential: this is precisely the catapult that will allow us, as Nietzsche thought, to "make a great spring."

We consider all this should be done rigorously, without vain idealisms looking for a solid conception of a unique Spain, and not a cultural plural vision of the territories and regions that reached out to form one of the first states in early modernity. To begin with, the concept of identity itself is questionable—self-images and images of the "other" are not static entities, but elements in a continuous process. The concept of "European identity" is debatable as well, unless we overcome the essentially and even mythicized views of the past and its memory, and highlight instead the opening of the concept of identity. The idea is to think about it and imagine it as a "floppy" concept that describes realities in a flux with no clear borders and with internal oppositions and contradictions, discursively shaped in contentious social bargaining processes (see Delanty 1995 and 1999, and Stråth 2002). In this context, the metaphors provided by some authors are really productive, such as that of conceiving identity as a "nested identity" (Marks 1997: 35), as a question of multiple coexisting identities where local elements have a certain weight as do the other entities or communities that configure supraterritorial identities, vital spaces in the development of a genuine cosmopolitan self in an emergent global society.

However, we should not overestimate the role of school knowledge and its effects on the education of our youth. In this sense, the "academic" views of school knowledge—either taught or included in school textbooks—which have prevailed so much in Spain in the near and distant past are limited.[13] The legitimacy of school knowledge is not guaranteed just because it is conceived through scientific processes mostly linked to the world of university science. As Popkewitz (2000, 2002) has been arguing, we can think of the curriculum as performing an alchemy on disciplinary knowledge (as the sorcerer of the Middle Ages sought to turn lead into gold, modern curriculum theory produces a magical change as it turns the specific intellectual traditions of historians or physicists, for example, into teaching practices). To understand the alchemies of the curriculum, we can approach humanities and social science—and also science and mathematics—as systems of knowledge produced within complex and pragmatic sets of social relations (for example, knowledge accepted as history, sociology, or anthropology involves particular institutional relations and systems of reasoning about research, teaching, and professional status) (Popkewitz 2000 and 2002; Luis Gómez 2001, for a translation of that into the curricular field of history and social sciences).

Finally, there is always the fact that, in order to teach, it is not only necessary to have scientific training but also pedagogical training. As one of the best known and most veteran specialists in educational and school reforms and innovations believes, this is because, "if teachers do not fulfill the conditions for productive learning, they will not be able to create and maintain these conditions for pupils" (Sarason 2002: 103). Spain, which has the second largest academic community of educational theorists after Germany—according to the number of posts held in its teacher education institutions—still has a long way to go.

Notes

1. In this chapter we focus only on "official history": history that is spread through the teaching the school subject contents of history and geography, and in others related to the social sciences context. We focus on textbooks as the most efficient tools for analysis, and not on "unofficial histories," those produced through informal education (e.g., oral tradition, religious institutions, meetings and discussions, etc.) (Carretero et al. 1994). "Official history" has at least three main functions: providing a cognitive instrument for envisioning the nation; enhancing group identity; and fostering loyalty among citizens.
2. María Luz Morán (1998: 158) highlights the progressive institutionalization of three myths: reconciliation with respect to the mirage of the civil war; Europeanization as an antidote against anti-European "Hispanism"; and finally, modernization and democratization. She considers these elements to be a synthesis of earlier processes, and also the legitimizing principles of the new collective "ethos" of Spanish citizens.
3. As mentioned in the Conclusions of the 5th meeting of school councils involving the Spanish Autonomous Communities and the central government, on "European educational policy and the European dimension of education," there is a clear need to produce educational material and resources aimed at developing the European dimension at different educational levels. This is considered a priority issue in the different actions undertaken by the European Commission.
4. SPICAE was established in Valladolid (Spain) in 1997. Its first meeting was held in Cassino (Italy) at the end of 1999, with the theme "The image and idea of Europe in textbooks between 1900 and 1945." See Genovesi (2000) for the papers from this meeting.
5. Synthesis of the most representative definitions of the manuals mentioned by Albacete (2000), which are: *Atlas-Geografía* [Atlas-Geography], Barcelona: Librería Católica, 1905; *Geografía para niños. Ciclo geográfico primer grado* [Geography for children. Geographic cycle: first level], by Osés Larumbe, published by Hijos de Santiago Rodríguez, Burgos, 1923; Geografía *General. El cielo, la Tierra y el Hombre* [General Geography. The Sky, the Earth and the Man], by Giner de los Ríos, published by Juan Ortiz, Madrid, 1935; *Iniciaciones. Libro activo de primeras nociones* [Iniatiations. Active book of first notions], by A. Fernández, published by Salvatella, Barcelona, 1936.

6. The printing press *Teide* published a black-and-white edition of the book *España-ampliación* [Spain–an expanded version] by ,Santiago Sobrequés in 1953. The catholic publishing house *Bruño* also appeared, but we must not forget that the texts had to be approved by the government authorities and the Church (Carreras 1995: 208).

7. Modern mass education is a relatively recent phenomenon in Spain. It was really a creation of Franco's dictatorship, toward the end of the regime in the 1970s, with the introduction of the *Ley General de Educación*. At that time it was intended to produce a degree of social and political change that would help to maintain the precarious legitimacy of the regime. Franco's educational reforms in that period are a good example of how to use a reform as a matter of what Hans Weiler (1983) has called "compensatory legitimation" (or as it was privately called in the political spheres of Franco's regime, "an oxygen cylinder" for the regime). Considered by the elite of technocrats leading the reform—with the support of the leading Opus Dei ministries of Franco—as a kind of "silent revolution," the previous traditional elitist system was abolished. A comprehensive school system following the Swedish pattern was introduced—*Educación General Básica* (EGB) [General and Basic Education], then recommended by international organization such as UNESCO, the World Bank and the OECD—along with a sweeping curricular reform. The 1970 was mainly implemented after Franco's death, during the so-called period of transition to democracy. In 1990, the newly democratic Spain embarked on a new modernization of the system led by the Socialist party, and the new education act —the *Ley Orgánica de Ordenación General del Sistema Education* (LOGSE) [Act of General Arrangement Educational System]—was passed. Comprehensive school became more important, and compulsory schooling was extended from age 14 to 16. Curriculum reforms created new interdisciplinary areas with an emphasis on social learning and issues of gender and multiculturalism.

8. Also see Gómez Rodríguez (2000: 172–4). The author states that, in the face of the social, cultural, and ideological changes undergone by society, the minimum contents recently established as an alternative for secondary compulsory education (*Enseñanza Secundaria Obligatoria—ESO*) will soon be obsolete or inappropriate. Considering the new political structure that is taking shape in Europe and in the world, the author suggests placing the analysis of social problems at the core of the history syllabus. This approach is similar to that of John Dewey, who advocated "education for citizenship". The idea is that most explanatory and interpretive approaches can be included in the area of social sciences by looking at social problems.

9. We do not have space here for looking at the role of teachers in the renewal of history teaching. In Spain, there are still what are known as pedagogical renewal groups, some of which were formed at the end of the Franco dictatorship. In the specific case of history and geography, understood as intertwined with other social sciences and not as a single discipline, the relation of these groups with the academic or scientific community of historians and geographers is very competent and courageous. Such is the case of FEDICARIA, a federation of ten groups from all over Spain, formed by teachers from all levels of the Spanish education system. It produces a rigorous and rich yearbook entitled *Con-Ciencia Social.* See Morgenstern (1992) for a critical approach to the situation in Spain in the field of teacher education and the role of pedagogical renewal groups; and Boyd-Barrett and O'Malley (1995) for an overview in English of the Spanish education reform until the conservative party, *Partido Popular*, came to power in 1996. For an analysis of the different views held by the Spanish academic history and historians in relation to the teaching of this field, see Luis Gómez (1999), who is one of the leaders of

FEDICARIA. Another important journal on the teaching of history and social sciences in Spain is *Íber (Didáctica de las Ciencias Sociales, Geografía e Historia)*, printed by *Graó* in Barcelona. It is edited by leading members of the academic community of curriculum and didactics educationists in these fields at the different schools of education at Spanish universities. See in particular Alonso (1998), for a critical view of the *Partido Popular* reform of Humanities, and the special issue on *Europa en las aulas* [Europe in the classroom] (2000).

10. The legal context of the different non-university educational levels, their general objectives, and the provisions governing them, are still those of the act known as LOGSE until the legal and regulatory framework of the recently passed *Ley de Calidad de la Educación* [Quality of Education Act] is fully developed (see Article 4 of LOGSE, Royal Decrees establishing the minimum contents of Primary Education (Royal Decree 1006/1991, 14th June) and compulsory secondary education (Royal Decree 1007/1991, 14th June), and those of the new *Bachillerato* or noncompulsory secondary education (Royal Decree 1178/1992, 2nd October)]. The process to reform the minimum contents began in 1996 and concluded at the beginning of 2001 with the publication of the new Royal Decrees (3473/2000 and 3474/2000), which establish the minimum contents in compulsory secondary education (ESO) and noncompulsory secondary education, known as *Bachillerato*, (BOE, 16–1–01)]. Bluntly speaking, the model of curricular adaptation proposed by LOGSE has not been accepted in practice by most teachers. Instead, publishing houses are the ones that have adapted the minimum contents, with all the meaning and symbolism this entails.

11. However, López Facal (2000: 50) considers that, in spite of the fact that LOGSE represents a great progress in the organization of education, there is a lesser presence of history in its contents than in the earlier act LGE. Still, the author underlines that the contents have been adjusted to the new structure of Autonomous Communities and the administrative decentralization of the state, which has increased the weight of specific contents in geography and history and literature of the different Autonomous Communities. This plurality has not easily been accepted, and it has not always matched the proposals of the regions in the struggle to obtain a national identity. The consequence was an intended reform of humanities, which later produced the *Decreto de enseñanzas mínimas* [Decree of minimum contents], where the contents have been greatly increased and evoke the old and obsolete syllabi of the past.

12. For more information, see Burguera (2002).

13. Space constraints do not allow us to explain the heated controversy in Spain about the teaching of history and humanities that was started in 1998 by the statements of Esperanza Aguirre, the Conservative Minister of Education and Culture, who expressed concern about the inadequacies of history teaching in secondary education (ESO), and deemed it to be "calamitous." The echoes of the past reemerged when the proposal was put forward to return to an education based on the prevalence of syntactic or disciplinary elements over semantic or social ones, that is, to the teaching of history and humanities with a more disciplinary character. The idea was to recover the memory of tradition by breaking off with the previous socialist stage, and revive once again the obsolete "positivist historicism," where the events, great historic characters, chronology and encyclopedic knowledge of the old history become the central elements of the new education. Among the different writings, books, scientific publications and, above all, newspapers articles (more than 400), see the interesting editorial of *Con-Ciencia Social* (vol. 5, 2001) for an assessment of the debate raised about these issues in Spain over the last years.

References

Arenaza, Ignacio, and Fermin Gastaminza. 1965. *Historia de España y Universal* [History of Spain and the World]. SM.

Albacete, Catalina. 2000. "La ausencia de un concepto integrado de Europa en los anuales escolares de geografía escolar." In *L'immagine e l'idea di Europa nei manuali scolastici (1900–1945)*, ed. Giovanni Genovesi. Milano: Franco Angeli.

Alonso, M. 1998. "Humanidades: Crónica de un estrepitoso proyecto". *Íber. Didáctica de las Ciencias Sociales, Geografía e Historia*, vol. 17, 85–108.

Beneyto, José María. 1999. *Tragedia y razón. Europa en el pensamiento español del siglo XX*. Madrid: Taurus.

Boyd, Carolyn. 1997. *Historia patria. Politics, history and national identity in Spain: 1875–1975*. Princeton: Princeton University Press.

Boyd-Barrett, Oliver, and Pamela O'Malley, eds. 1995. *Education Reform in Democratic Spain*. London and New York: Routledge.

Burguera, Jordi. 2002. "Los libros de historia del bachillerato en Cataluña: análisis de contenidos." *Íber: Didáctica de las Ciencias Sociales, Geografía e Historia*, vol. 33, 95–108.

Cámara Villar, Gregorio. 1984. *Nacional-Catolicismo y escuela. La socialización política del franquismo*. Jaén: Hesperia.

Carreras, Agustín. 1995. "L'histoire dans les manuels scolaires franquistes." *Revue Européenne d'Histoire*, vol. 2, 201–216

Carretero, Mario. 2002. "Learning history through textbooks: are Mexican and Spanish students taught the same story?" *Learning and Instruction*, vol. 12, 651–65.

——— 1994. "Historical knowledge: cognitive and instructional implications." In *Cognitive and Instructional Processes in History and the Social Sciences*, ed. Mario Carretero and James Voss. Hillsdale, NJ: Erlbaum Associates.

Cereceda, Feliciano. 1943. *Historia y Geografía de España: Quinto curso de Bachillerato*. Madrid : Razón y Fe.

Con-ciencia Social. 2001. "Entre el revival y el festival contrareformista: el retorno de la historia escolar a ninguna parte." Vol. 5, 9–23.

Consejos Escolares.1994. *La política educativa europea y la dimensión europea de la educación. La participación como factor de calidad*. Vitoria: Departamento de Educación del Gobierno Vasco.

Costa, Joaquin. 1903. *Reconstitución y europeización de España: Programa para un partido nacional*. Huesca: V. Campo.

Cuesta Fernández, Raimundo. 1997. *Sociogénesis de una disciplina escolar: la Historia*. Barcelona: Ediciones Pomares-Corredor.

——— 1998. *Clío en las aulas*. Madrid: Akal.

Delanty, Gerald. 1995. *Inventing Europe: Idea, Identity, Reality*. London: Macmillan.

——— 1999. "Social Integration and Europeanization." *Yearbook of European Studies*, vol. 12, 221–38.

Delgado, Consuelo. 2000. "La imagen de Europa en la formación histórica de los maestros en España." In *L'immagine e l'idea di Europa nei manuali scolastici (1900–1945)*, ed. Giovanni Genovesi. Milano: Franco Angeli.

Escolano, Agustín. 2000. "Europa en el caleidoscopio. La representación de Europa en los manuales escolares (1900–1939)." In *L'immagine e l'idea di Europa nei manuali scolastici (1900–1945)*, ed. Giovanni Genovesi. Milano: Franco Angeli.

Genovesi, Giovanni, ed. 2000. *L'immagine e l'idea di Europa nei manuali scolastici (1900–1945)*. Milano: Franco Angeli.

Gómez Rodríguez, Ernesto. 2000. "Modernidad, postmodernidad y enseñanza de la Historia en la escuela obligatoria." *Historiar*, vol. 4, 162–75.

González Muñoz, Carmen. 2002. *La enseñanza de la historia en el nivel medio. Situación, tendencias e innovaciones.* Madrid: Anaya.

González de Molina, Manuel. 1998. "Sobre los contenidos de una nueva Historia de España." *Ayer*, vol. 30, 241–70.

Hita Marín, José Antonio. 1997. *La transmisión de valores socioculturales y sociopolíticos en los sistemas educativos formales de tres sistemas políticos contemporáneos y arquetípicos: la España franquista, la Rusia soviética y la República italiana. Estudio comparativo de la narración de la Historia en los libros de texto de la enseñanza obligatoria.* Granada: Universidad de Granada.

Iber. 2000. *Europa en las aulas.* 23 (special issue).

Lamo de Espinosa, Emilio. 2001. "La normalización de España. España, Europa y la modernidad." *Claves de Razón Práctica*, vol. 111, 8–13.

López Facal, Ramón. 2000. "Pensar históricamente. Una reflexión crítica sobre la enseñanza de la historia." *Íber: Didáctica de las Ciencias Sociales, Geografía e Historia*, vol. 24, 46–55.

Luis Gómez, Alberto. 2001. "Tradiciones curriculares, innovaciones educativas y función social conservadora del conocimiento escolar: la primacía de los temas sobre los problemas." *Biblio 3W. Revista bibliográfica de Geografía y Ciencias Sociales*, vol. 337, 1–11, at www.ub.es/geocrit/b3w-337.htm.

———1999. "Conocimiento académico y enseñanza: Las preocupaciones de los historiadores españoles por los niveles no universitarios." *Biblio 3W. Revista Bibliográfica de Geografía y Ciencias Sociales*, vol. 162, 1–5, at www.ub.es/geocrit/b3w-162.htm.

Lundgren, Ulf P. 1991. *Between Education and Schooling: Outlines of a Diachronic Curriculum Theory.* Victoria, Australia: Deakin University Press.

Marks, Gary. 1997. "A Third Lense: Comparing European Integration and State Building." In *Europe, the Search for European Identity*, eds. Jytte Klausen and Louise A. Tilly. Lanham: Rowman and Littefield.

Martínez Tórtola, Esther. 1996. *La enseñanza de la historia en el primer bachillerato franquista (1938–1953).* Madrid: Tecnos.

Mencía de la Fuente, Emiliano. 1996. *La educación cívica del ciudadano europeo. Conocimiento de Europa y actitudes europeístas en el currículum.* Madrid: Narcea.

Morán, M. Luz. 1998. "La cultura política de los españoles." In *España, sociedad industrial avanzada, vista por los nuevos sociólogos*, ed. Salustiano Del Campo. Madrid: Real Academia de Ciencias Morales y Políticas.

Morgenstern, Sara. 1992. "Teacher Education in Spain: A Postponed Reform." In *Changing Patterns of Powers. Social Regulation and Teacher Education Reform*, ed. Thomas S. Popkewitz. New York: Suny Press.

Morin, Edgar. 1994. *Pensar Europa. Las metamorfosis de Europa.* Barcelona: Gedisa.

Nóvoa, António. 2002. "Ways of Thinking about Education in Europe." In *Fabricating Europe. The Formation of an Education Space*, eds. António Nóvoa and Martin Lawn. Dordrecht, The Netherlands: Kluwer Academic Publishers.

Pérez Embid, Florentino. 1949. "Ante la nueva realidad del problema de España." *Arbor*, vol. 45–46, 149–60.

Pérez Garzón, Juan Sisinio. 2000. *La gestión de la memoria.* Barcelona: Crítica.

Popkewitz, Thomas S. 2000. "The Denial of Change in Educational Change: Systems of Ideas in the Construction of National Policy and Evaluation." *Educational Researcher*, vol. 29, 17–29.

——— 2002. "How the Alchemy Makes Inquiry, Evidence, and Exclusion." *Journal of Teacher Education*, vol. 53, 262–67.

Prats, Joaquin. 2001. *Los jóvenes ante el reto europeo.* Barcelona: Fundación La Caixa.

Revuelta, Clara. 2000. "La idea de Europa en los textos de formación política del bachillerato. Primera etapa franquista." In. *L'immagine e l'idea di Europa nei manuali scolastici (1900–1945)*, ed. Giovanni Genovesi. Milano: Franco Angeli.

Sarason, Seymour B. 2002. *La enseñanza como arte de representación*. Buenos Aires: Amorrortu (original in English).

Schools Council. 1972. *What is History: Schools Council History 13–16 Project*. Edinburgh: Holmes McDougall.

Soysal, Yasemin. 2002. "Locating European Identity in Education." In *Fabricating Europe. The Formation of an Education Space*, eds. António Nóvoa and Martin Lawn. Dordrecht, The Netherlands: Kluwer Academic Publishers.

Stråth, B. 2002. "A European Identity. To the Historical Limits of a Concept." *European Journal of Social Theory*, vol. 5, 387–401.

Therborn, Goran. 2002. "Space and Learning." In *Fabricating Europe. The Formation of an Education Space*, eds. António Nóvoa and Martin Lawn. Dordrecht, The Netherlands: Kluwer Academic Publishers.

Torres Bravo, Pablo Antonio. 2000. "Qué Historia y qué profesorado de Historia secundaria en el siglo XXI." *Didáctica de las Ciencias Experimentales y Sociales*, vol. 14, 33–52.

Valls, Rafael. 1994. "La imagen de Europa en los actuales manuales escolares españoles de Ciencias Sociales." *Didáctica de las Ciencias Experimentales y Sociales*, vol. 8, 3–26.

———— 2002. "No basta con oir y repetir: la ampliación de las enseñanzas mínimas y sus efectos." *Íber: Didáctica de las Ciencias Sociales, Geografía e Historia*, vol. 33, 52–57.

Vicens Vives, Jaume. 1960. *Historia Universal y de España*. Barcelona: Teide.

Weiler, Hans. 1983. "West Germany: Educational Policy as Compensatory Legitimation." In *Politics and Education*, ed. Mattew Thomas. Oxford: Pergamon Press.

Wertsch, James V. 1997. "Narrative tools of history and identity." *Culture & Psychology*, vol. 3, 5–20.

Part III

Global Frameworks and
Approaches to World History

Chapter 9

❖ ━━━━━━

World History and General Education: How to Bring the World into the Classroom

Michael Geyer

After more than a century of disinterest and, indeed, disdain, world history has regained attention and recognition. It has reemerged as the central impulse for revitalizing general education—and it seems that general education itself is staging something of a comeback (Bentley 1996; Comparativ 2002). Over the past two decades, an exponentially growing number of colleges and universities have begun to introduce survey classes in world history/global studies or have moved toward building a general education curriculum along these lines.[1] A variety of new history programs have emerged in order to prepare graduate students how to teach world history more effectively.[2] Most importantly, secondary education in the United States has shifted toward a world history curriculum, which complements an American history curriculum that itself is opening up to the world. World history has made a remarkable comeback.

However, the question of how to bring the world into the classroom remains unsolved. To be sure, there is a growing number of textbooks for college-level teaching to choose from, whose quality has improved dramatically over the past ten years or so.[3] The change is palpable compared to the beginning of the 1990s, when one could think of world history as a vast, uncharted terrain. But there are limits to this endeavor. World history, for all its practitioners have achieved, is not quite a "field" of scholarship yet, notwithstanding impressive efforts.[4] Despite a proliferation of textbooks, the jury is still out whether or not there is a sufficient body of thought—as opposed to accumulated knowledge—that supports teaching courses in world history. The discrepancy between the quick success of world history as a teaching field and the much slower growth of thought about world history as a sub-discipline of history, and the discrepancy between the power of the former and the poverty of the latter, is palpable. If the return of world history is an accomplished fact, the question remains what to do with it now that it has arrived.

The short answer to this question is threefold: (1) that world history succeeded because it responded pragmatically to a growing disorientation within academia in the face of the accelerated globalization during the last quarter of the twentieth century; (2) that the difficulties of bringing the world into the classroom necessitates a choice of subject for world history; and (3) that the goal of teaching and thinking world history consists in understanding the human condition in a global age. A long answer would require a book, given the state of the art in world history. What I can try to do, though, is to elaborate each of these claims so as to suggest both the reasons for and the difficulties with bringing the world into the classroom.

Why the Sudden Academic Interest in World History?

The recurrence of world history emphatically was not a renaissance of older world historical thought. Rather, its most striking feature was the historiographic innocence, if not its outright agnosticism concerning previous thought about the world. It is for the most part unaware of and surely disinclined toward the Western traditions of world history, even though they may enter subterraneously.[5] The same can be said about non-Western traditions of thinking about the world. It is not that a historiography on thinking the world is missing; it just does not matter all that much for world history.[6] Hence, we may conclude that, for better or worse, current interest in world history is less the product of any one of these traditions than a result of the tangible and immediate, and matter-of-fact recognition that the "world" has invaded almost everybody's life. The renewed interest in world history reflects first and foremost a pervasive and, indeed, global experience of the world being compressed into a global space. More theoretically inclined scholars speak of a radical acceleration of "time-space compression" in order to characterize this situation (Harvey 1989).

The public recognition of this global condition is inseparably linked to the political events during the past ten years. As a result of the collapse of the Soviet Union, the dissolution of communist regimes in Eastern Europe, the prosecution of major, high-tech wars in the Middle East and elsewhere in the former Third World, the simultaneous rise of global processes of democratization, and the emergence of ethnic nationalisms and fundamentalisms – in the face of not just the multitude but the magnitude and the unexpected nature of these current events, a growing number of scholars thought of the current period not simply as a phase of turmoil and adjustment but as a period of major historical transformation(s). Increasingly, it was interpreted as a period of "world historical crises" (see Jakob Burckhardt 1978; Maier 2000).

The thrust of these transformations is twofold. First, the hold of Europe on the world and its imagination is being replaced by a new and, as yet, undetermined configuration of competing hemispheric powers, whether the latter are based on territorial power (China), religion (Islam), military might (United States) or, alternatively, on a multilateral regime of trade. Second, the world is being interlinked more closely through communication and transportation irrespective of competition and rivalry. Hence, lateral influence is competing everywhere with heritage in the regeneration of societies and civilizations, it seems that we are more keenly attuned to the disasters that this imbrication produced and have yet to develop a better sense of what a successful combination of engagement of the world and renewal of traditions entails. But even if the outcome is open, it is plain enough that these two developments have quite dramatically reshaped the world—so much so that an older world historical imagination no longer captures the actual changes in the world. The consequence is a high degree of disorientation, a kind of global vertigo in which world image and global reality are "out of sync".

The events of 9/11 (the attack on the World Trade Center and the Pentagon) and its aftermath have reinforced this global vertigo and have put world history to the test. For academically, world history gathered steam as a progressive project (even when and where it was taught in conservative places). It developed in part out of Cold War area studies, which had run into a dead end. It reflected more generally a rise, across the board, of non-Western histories in contention with Western civilization or European histories. And it derived from a vivid sense among Europeanists that Europe was but one region among others (Chakrabarty 2000). This kind of world history was interested, to a fault, in proving the existence of a global ecumene and, notwithstanding initiatives in international (or formerly, diplomatic) history, was rather blue-eyed when it came to power and global imperial reach (compare Appadurai 1996, and Kennedy 1993). Typically, world-systems theories did not have much traction among world historians, who rather preferred the language of global flows of people, goods, and ideas (Bentley 1993; Bentley and Ziegler 2003). Perhaps this picture is somewhat too wholesome. But clearly world historians were caught quite unawares by the gathering post-9/11 wave of neo-imperial studies (Ferguson 2001 and 2003). These latter enterprises, in turn, compete with a revivified American history, which has now also taken a distinctly international turn (Bender 2002). The world has become a much tougher place and world history seems to be toughening up as well.

Still, the initial incentive for a revival of world history is worth recalling because it is one of those incidents where a new and puzzling kind of experience—the experience of globality—generated a novel field of inquiry and, above all, of teaching. This emergent field was always tied to a variety of often cross-cutting interests, academic, political, and otherwise. But its most compelling and, one might add, confusing feature was the *pilotage à vue* in the effort of making sense of a world that fits none of the preponderant models of academic thought, and to disseminate this new knowledge to a changed and changing audience of college students. The most exciting aspect of the endeavor was that everyone was changing in the process. William McNeill, the most senior of the world historians, was perhaps the most reckless in this regard—and his critique of a (civilizational) world history he had himself endorsed for so long is one of the most impressive documents to characterize the scene (McNeill 1990). It is emblematic for the field that he began as a historian of Western Civilization in a global context and has moved on to a human history as "evolution from simple sameness to diversity and then toward complex sameness" (McNeill 1963; the quote is from the cover of McNeill and McNeill 2003). Right or wrong, the 2003 history of *The Human Web* tells a radically different story from his 1993 *Rise of the West*. In this difference we can capture the spirit of world history.

Three further aspects of this transformation may help to explain what was happening. First, world history satisfied the demand for diversification beyond the Eurocentrism of twentieth-century American academia. The latter has become a loaded term that has generated an acrimonious debate about the politically correct teaching machine. (D'Souza 1991 on one hand and Spivak 1993 on the other). It is inextricably linked to Edward Said's notion of "orientalism" (Said 1978). However, while the public debate—commonly dubbed the "culture wars"—suggests a confrontation between pro-Westerners and anti-Westerners, the fault-lines were in fact more complex. Without wanting to underestimate a persistent European bias, the main tensions in working out a world history agenda developed between localists and globalists. The insistence on an irreducible difference of culture and civilization and on its autonomy ran up against the world-historical inclination to emphasize the import of connectivity (see the debate in Young 2001). In the 1990s, this debate spilled over into the streets in the rising tide of antiglobalization riots (Smith and Johnston 2002). The net effect was, though, that in this competition of locales on one hand and of localists versus globalists on the other, "the West" shrank to another global locality. All the while some of the locales, whose transcendent and identity-forming authentic values were celebrated in the 1980s, developed their own, distinct global reach (Turner, 1991 was one of the first reflections on this subject).

World historians were successful because they approached the heated debates of the 1980s and 1990s pragmatically. They argued that the story of the world in which we live can no longer be told as a Eurocentric story and, hence, the story of where "we" come from can no longer be told as a European story nor as a story of Westernization (von Laue 1987; on the American debate: Hollinger 1993; generally, Balibar and Wallerstein 1991). There was, however, a great deal of uncertainty about how to replace this history of a region writ large. For some, it seemed enough to have 'a thousand flowers bloom'—to represent the sheer diversity of human endeavor (Greaves et al. 1997). Others emphasized the ties of migration, travel and exchange, the transfer of knowledge, and the commodity trade to shape a world history of a new kind (Stearns 2001; many of the trend-setting arguments come from Sassen 1998). Rather than seeing the world as a succession of civilizations, either developing concurrently or replacing each other in an endless succession, these new world histories came to see the world as a web of relationships (Castells, 2000; the most successful textbook following this approach is Bentley and Ziegler 2003). This latter view has, by and large, prevailed.

The second aspect of the transformation is that world history responded to the global reach of local communities in developing its own comparative history of expansions (Pomeranz and Topik 1999 and Pomeranz 2000). This was one of the more intriguing cases of an emergent world history backing into a useful concept by way of experience rather than any particular thought. In fact, thought on world history initially moved in the predictable direction of a revamped universalism. One of the initial claims that led to a considerable debate was the notion of a "global consciousness" (Robertson 1992). Initially, world historians were very attracted by this idea which they traced back into a genealogy of long-distance travel (for example, Helms 1988 or Pratt 1992; on transfer of knowledge see Headrick 1988). It seemed to provide a shortcut to what they wanted. But it turned out that something was claimed here that was difficult to prove in reality: "Global consciousness" was a hollow concept.

It proved far more effective to explore the multiple overlays that shaped or influenced local societies. The fashionable term for this was "hybridity," but there was more to it than fashion. For the incipient history of multiple overlays opened up the tightly closed "container" nation with its controlled parallel genealogies back in time that had dominated historical thought. Where standard history emphasized the genealogy of nations in a deep history, world historians came to highlight the—often enough catastrophic—mixtures of peoples, ideas and artifacts that made up societies at any one moment. Overall, world history textbooks retained a chronological structure, but within this, the synchronous development of fusing and generating cultures came to be far more central. In this, they linked up with the localists who had come to mix up the nation from within—perhaps most famously in Duara's (1995) *Rescuing History from the Nation*. The challenge and the possibility of this approach—which in many ways has become "the" world history approach—consists of exploring society and culture as persistently creating and generating bonds of belonging and togetherness. Forget a certain naivete of this approach that tends to gloss over domination. What matters is the recovery of a sense of society—not as some categorical entity sliced up into race, gender, class etc.—as a generative and vastly creative, interactive subject. What we (re)discover here is the notion of culture as "cultivation" (Arendt 1977).

Third, world historians struggled hardest in coming to terms with the world as an integrated whole. The most difficult question to answer was to figure out what was global about the world? How, if at all, did the world fit together?

The challenge here consisted first and foremost in overcoming professional codes without dropping out or being dropped from academia. For answering the question about globality meant challenging the prevailing strategies of knowledge in academia. Specialization has been the way of producing new knowledge in the twentieth-century academy. (This, incidentally, affected all of general education, which gained its reputation of being unscholarly because of asking general questions.) And, lest there be any doubt, specialization has yielded results. Yet, there has always also been a fear that the continuing specialization of knowledge would lead into a dead-end, in which we know more and more about less and less, as the adage goes. But these frights have regularly come and gone. Why then should there be an interest in "very big structures" (Charles Tilly), if specialization has proven to be so effective a tool in producing new knowledge?

Above all, the renewed initiative to think "big" is a result of a crisis of paradigms. That is to say, that all the while scholars specialized in their research, there had been a remarkably effective big picture in place that was more or less explicit, albeit often unreflected (Adas 1989). "Modernization" was perhaps the most successful of them. It was an elaborate regime of theory as well as a political and cultural *imaginary*. But it succumbed—not so much to internal, academic criticism, although that was vicious at times—to the growing recognition that this regime of thought, while good at certain things, did not grasp the condition of globality and the process of globalization. It had few of the heuristic and none of the predictive qualities to make sense of the world in which we lived and it had tremendous difficulties in fathoming how the different parts of the world found their way into the present. It fell apart in the latest wave of accelerated globalization. With its paradigmatic grip on reality slipping, specialized knowledge production was at a loss and began to flounder.

Hence, it was back to the drawing boards everywhere—and this search for explanatory strategies helped world history over its own doldrums. For it was quite uncertain, if the reconstituted world history was indeed any more successful in exploring anew the changing condition of globality over time. It cannot be said that world historians had a good grip on the subject of world history, let alone globalization (Mazlish 1998). World historians have come to accept only hesitantly that "globalization" and "globality" cannot be seamlessly developed out of world history after all (Arrighi 1994; Geyer and Bright 1995; Hopkins 2002). They have yet to discover that the notion of the "world" in world history itself needs historicizing. But, again, their general orientation has been a productive one. They have increasingly wagered their project of world history, not on the world in all its variety, but on global spaces or corridors in which many centers are stitched together and in which individuals and social groups can be in many places at the same time, being stretched across vast distances and intersecting, interacting, colliding with cultural heritages from all parts of the world, although they tend to perceive of themselves as living in one space and one space alone. The critical mapping of these global spaces and their precedents constitutes perhaps the most important aspect of research and learning in world history over the last decade.[7] It challenged quite radically the situatedness and autonomy of any culture and the settled nature of knowledge. Instead, it highlighted a history of persistent unsettlement.

Of course, this idea or argument –it is yet to be formulated into a stringent theory—appears to be so quintessentially American (which it is). But the nice thing about world history is that the idea is there to be challenged and, if need be, to be replaced by a better one. What counts is that the lead-argument makes sense of where the world is at and how it got there. In the end, it is better to have one halfway good idea that works than a perfect one that does not.

How to Bring the World into the Classroom?

Where ever world historians may stand with regard to the difficulties of escaping or rethinking world historical traditions within or without various civilizational paradigms, the sheer scope of the world and its past remains the basic obstacle for teaching world history. The very basic problem is that there is just too much history out there for it to be crammed into the limited "real time" of world history in the classroom. There will always be too much history. Hence the key problem of world history is how to make the world's pasts fit into the very limited space and time that is available for any intellectual endeavor, let alone the history of the world in a semester or two.

As long as world history is the history of everybody and everything, all the time, it amounts to less than nothing. This kind of world history condemns world historians to know little about nothing. It reduces them to concepts and ideas that are derivative and makes them the purveyors of platitudes. The result is a history that stacks up civilization snippets from prehistory to the present global age.[8] The world as such and all its pasts cannot be the subject of world history—and more recent world histories have by and large shunned this course of action. Again, world historians fared best when they avoided recourse to older civilizational models, even if the curricular logic of academic politics pushed them in that direction.[9]

Still, a good case has been made for world history as "total history." It would be preferable, though, to speak, more properly, of world history as history of humanity. This kind of history comes in two broad streams, that flow in different directions. One emerges from the interest in global crosscultural interaction (one of the pioneers of this approach is Philip D. Curtin 1984; see also Lockard 1994). While much of this history is currently engrossed in showing in empirical detail the nature of these interaction, William McNeill on one hand and Jerry Bentley on the other have shown that a more systematic (or, for that matter, theoretical) take on this evidence may well develop into a general history that focuses on the perennial tension between settlement and unsettlement. This world history would have the benefit of a long and worldwide history of conflict as well as a tradition of articulating this tension in myth, images, and texts.[10] If this history were to transcend the dichotomous self-fashioning either into great imperial civilizations or nomadic control of communications, it would have to approach anew one of the key questions of political thought: What does it take to bring people together and to hold them together? The issues at stake are solidarity/community, civility, taste, and manners on one hand, and state building and power in a world of permeable boundaries on the other.

The second stream cuts into the problem of a history of humanity by looking at the grand ecological changes that shaped the world and its people and, in turn, were shaped by them (see, for example, J.R. McNeill, 2000). This is a world history that explores the ecological bonds of human existence. It approaches humanity within the context of nature and explores human history as nature, as is the case in the history of communicable human diseases (Crosby 1986). This history struggles with older questions such as nature and nurture, but also newer ones of a comparative ecology of human history, and may well proceed to revive the venerable topic of a history of nature and of ecological change (Diamond 1999). Somewhat surprisingly, this return to world history as natural history has been remarkably unfazed, so far, by otherwise flourishing sociobiological or, for that matter, neo-Darwinian approaches. Likewise, a genetics-inspired history of populations has not taken root in history, although it has surely captured the public imagination.[11]

Both a *history of un/settlement* (where would we put "modern" and, for that matter, American history in this context?) and a *natural history of the human condition* may well turn out to be the stuff a future "grand" world history is made off. These histories have immediate relevance while at the same time articulating a human condition and reflecting upon a venerable legacy of human thought. I tend to think of this pair of histories as the legitimate successor of civilizations programs—building necessarily on the local knowledge of area studies—and thus the privileged subject for general education. They aspire to what the latter had done in the nineteenth and twentieth centuries. It is a philosophical or, "scientific" history, deeply committed to the traditions of human thought, and yet reflecting on the present world in a meaningful fashion. In a sense, these histories of humanity truly deserve the name of "world history." Yet, despite the work of William McNeill, world historians have just barely begun to chart this terrain (W. McNeill, 1976).

Most world histories, though, fit a rather different mold and might better be labeled "global histories." The latter are histories that make visible—in concrete detail as much as in theoretical reflection—those practices that hold together the world and thus shape the lives of individuals and communities. It is a history of space rather than place and of practices of making connections rather than establishing roots. It spans the real world, but does not need to encapsulate it in its entirety.[12] While there are many ways to go about this history, it entails three essentials of global mapping.

There is first and foremost the challenge of identifying agents and their practices that link together discrete places into an interconnected space. Such global spaces are held together in a grid of communications, capital flows, exchanges of goods, and military confrontations. Societies are similar to islands within these spaces and, like them, have distinct properties. Much can be said to qualify this observation. But the main point here is that globalism—and the study of global history—is not a matter of universalizing abstraction. It is rather the domain of traders, financiers, entrepreneurs, entertainers, soldiers, sailors, professionals like lawyers or medical doctors, bureaucrats, and of the occasional historian (like Polybios) who marvel over the effective interconnection between discrete places and wonders about degrees of integration and separation. This is not least a space that is populated by religious activists who expand their local and regional appeal—and turn out historically to be among the most effective globalizers. The colonizers, of course, may rival them. They act in a world that does not emerge from local knowledge systems in universalizing images, backed up by the select knowledge of the few who venture out beyond the frontiers. Instead, the global world comes into being as a multitude of tangible networks that shape local experience and remake local inequality.

There is, second, the experience of profound—and indeed, catastrophic—unsettlement as a result of global interconnection. While grids of global transactions (however far they may reach in actual practice and however dense they may be) synthesize space-time, there is very little that would suggest a homogenization of societies over the long run. If anything, interconnectivity furthers migration in a global landslide that mixes together races, colors, and regional and civilizational identities. Even if people stay put (and that option often means either an extraordinary privilege or a calamity), they are confronted with and apprehend no longer just their own heritage, their own values, norms, and artistry but a multiplicity of concurrent influences. Their outcome is more often dramatic redifferentiation than homogeneity. Even the most powerful linguae francae, such as Chinese or English, had a way of splintering up. But people are caught up in powerful forces that cut across places and align themselves in unpredictable fashions to reproduce local communities and solidarities. By the same token, artifacts, music, and dance, from very different cultural environments, mix much as ideas and beliefs do. The emerging "global" culture reassembles goods from all parts of the world. Syncretism, the fusion of dissimilar artifacts, and processes of creolization, nonauthentic fusion of disparate elements into one among many microexperiences, this is the key expression of this development (Hannerz 1987; Rowe and Schelling 1991).

Third, there are skills to be explored—this is, unfortunately, the weakest link in world history so far—that are indispensable in creating and surviving in such global spaces. In an academic context they oscillate between disciplines. For simplicity's sake, let us call them skills of transcoding (Jameson 1991: 394–99).

These are based on modes of inquiry that encompass, on one level, strategies of coping with the fear of otherness while honoring difference. They could be made prominent features of the curriculum and form a scholarly and educational site for bringing together a great variety of disciplines in common projects such as intercultural reading or explorations in symbolic exchange. But often there is too much of a mystique attached to practices that allow for interpersonal and intercultural exchange. These approaches underestimate the very instrumentality of so much of the traffic that connects people and places. The fact of the matter is that expertise and the trade in knowledge and skills have always been a key aspect of the global past—and may well be the main assets of global culture. Exploring and teaching such skills of transcoding in world history ultimately requires a rethinking of epistemology—one that is able to acknowledge different referential universes and yet does not abandon a sense of linkage and commonality.

In contrast, prevailing scholarship pits settlement against unsettlement, the city against nomads, the nation against migrants, and a world of places against a world of global spaces. Academic scholarship has come to cherish the idea of culture as an autonomous and indigenous process of unfolding norms and values, grounded in the unity of language, society, and territory. Scholarship is at a loss in explaining an interconnected world. It is unable to make sense of a configuration that is anchored in many local worlds with their own and discrete processes of socialization that are nonetheless tightly connected. It is unable even to depict the multiplication of radically different local worlds, forged from a melange of elements from all parts of the world. It has tremendous difficulties in coming to grips with a world in which societal boundaries are redrawn in diasporas across the world, in which identities are pieced together and social codes and meanings are created from scraps. This moment of extraordinary creativity of humankind consists in piecing together a human existence beyond the imagination of civilizational studies.

Beyond civilizational histories there is a great deal of room for maneuver in bringing the world into the classroom in the form of global history that ranges from straightforward history of global spaces to learning the skills of operating in them. However, the bottom line is that global history shatters the silence surrounding global transactions by tracking them, describing them, and making them visible and accountable. By the same token, it facilitates a knowledge that actively uses and develops the means of global communication in encountering and envisioning an interconnected world. This is, in my view, the proper subject of world history as global history.

What Does it Take to Imagine "Globality"?

Terms such as globalism, globalization, global politics, global history, and even global consciousness have gained currency in recent years. There is surely no lack of definitions and explanations for the phenomenon hiding behind these words, although there are quite a few scholars who rather doubt the concept and, occasionally, the reality.[13] Most of the time, reference to globalization or the condition of globality is simply used to express amazement over the ability to connect at an instance over huge spaces and time zones, to effect actions on the other end of the world, to transport people, things, and images (as well as bacteria and viruses) to virtually any part of the physical world. This wonderment in the face of a human-made infrastructure of communication and transportation and of the people and things that occupy it is surely not the worst way to start an exploration. However, being confronted with the experience of globality, world historians rarely inquire what the condition of globality entails.

Simply put, globality is a condition in which every part of the world is linked and responsive to every other part, although in very different measure and in very different states of density. As suggested above, it is useful to distinguish between the formation of global spaces, which captures the loose webbing of the world, and the actual process of globalization. The former is a process that occurs across time. There is a great deal still to be learnt about the ups and downs of this development as well as about the highways and byways that make up global connectivity. Globalization is usefully limited to the moment in time when the "world" has truly become a "globe" in that it lost its outer boundaries of physical space and was becoming an interior space of interactions—a space, to be sure, with new internal peripheries and centers, but bounded together by interactions that increasingly take place in "real time." While we may debate, when exactly this happened, and while we need to know much more about the way in which it did, the special quality of globalization deserves attention.

For with globalization being attained, human existence has come fully into the purview of all human beings. This is what I would call the "condition of globality." In contrast to the "human condition" it is not something that is always already there. Rather, it is the product of human action at a specific moment. While globalization occurred gradually and remains incomplete, it constitutes an uncanny leap.[14] In a state of globality, "humanity" is no longer a natural or an imagined totality. It comes into being no longer through thought or sheer imagination (like the universalist imagination of the West asserts).[15] Neither does humanity come into being as a (natural) species. Rather, humanity comes into existence in a multiplicity of discrete economic, military, and informational practices, whether or not it is thought. Globality exists as daily practice, which is why the old universalism has so little to say about the conditions of globality.

Take, for example, the future market in downtown Chicago as one of these hands-on realities of a new globality. There is no reason to think that the people working in "global futures" have a global vision of what they do. But their transactions exert a global reach, whatever their consciousness may be. One may even doubt that they would be better traders for having a different and more global consciousness. Yet, in order to understand what they set in motion it takes global thought, a mapping of the world, which traces their actions within a global network of exchanges. By the same token, the future market's next-door neighbors, mostly Mexican and Puerto Rican immigrants, form another such network of global exchanges, although of a very different kind. At first sight there is nothing new about these (im)migrants. As always, the newest immigrants are at the bottom of the pile. And yet there is a difference. Many of these immigrants have the chance of staying in close, even daily contact with their former community. The density and reciprocity of these connections makes a difference, because there is no longer a presumption that, with the dust of immigration settling and the disinterested or unwilling parties remigrating, an automatic adjustment and acculturation would set in, especially if supported by appropriate education. To be sure, the difference between people who are tied to "the world" by trusts or pension funds (future exchange) and those tied to "the world" by personal memory and family interactions is immense. Yet both reflect a pervasive and practical globality, which they imagine in their own way, making do with a cultural repertory that is fitted to the situation.

The challenge of a history of globalization—and by extension, the challenge of a global history—consists in and elucidates the daily practices that consti-tute globality. For it is only in the act of mapping the divisive reality of global interconnection that it is articulated as a commonality of human existence. In mapping the human condition at the end of the twentieth century, the study of global affairs makes explicit and visible—it traces—both practices of global regimes and the imbrications of local communities in global space. It makes transparent and accessible, through knowledge, the lineaments of wealth and violence, underpinned by information, that compress humanity into a single humankind. It critically accompanies the imagination that enjoins the efforts of orienting oneself in an interconnected world (whether it is the expertise of traders or the imaginary world of migrants). And it lends presence to the diverse human labors, splintered up into so many particularities, that go into creating and maintaining an interconnected world. This is all the more impor-tant because, as a human-made condition, globality can no longer be approached as a merely physical and natural or metaphysical and divine condi-tion. It is, indeed, in the purview of human beings, and thus becomes accessible to history.

Why then is it so difficult for historians to visualize, as a whole, this state of globality? The simplistic answer is to say that the world is much too big and global transactions much too complex. But ethnologists tell us that this is true for the smallest communities—and so do natural scientists when they try to understand cells or subatomic particles. The real question is what the particu-lar difficulty is of reducing complexity under conditions of globality (when one should think that everybody has some sort of "global consciousness," but in fact has none of it). The reason is, as already Hegel alerted us, a deceit built into the division of labor that is made possible by linking two otherwise separate parts (of the world). The division of labor draws the world together through a myriad of human actions, but it sets every locale apart—so much so that every locale may very well imagine itself separate and autonomous, contemplating its own wants and needs.[16] And yet fulfillment of these wants and needs is dependent on the participation in a globalizing division of labor. The classic term for this condition is "alienation," but this term is by now so abused and misused that it is not very useful, except to remind us that there are ways of thinking and imagining the process of a divisive integration of the world.

Globalization as a process of divisive interconnection may help us to make more sense of what I called global vertigo. In the first instance, it is merely a metaphor to describe a certain unease and disorientation, more or less strongly expressed, in the face of rapid globalization, which, in turn, was the main source for a vivification of world history. It seemed nothing but a certain dizziness in the face of very rapid processes that have spun out of control. Obviously, this situation also produces its own excitements—and both feelings mark the "sense" of the current interest in world history very well. But now it appears possible to explore this experience of world history sensibly and analytically (without denying the indubitable powers of emotions in this process). We are living in a world that is drawn together in global practices, but we have few suitable representations of the process or, for that matter, narratives, images or scholarly analyses to achieve that end. Neither do we have a politics to guide or inform the processes of globalization. The interaction and exchange between the various elements of an integrated world is raw. While this exchange is mediated by each individual actor, it remains unpolitical and, hence, unimagined. Since Hegel has already made an appearance, we might at this point also appeal to Habermas. What is missing, is a public imagination that connects a world that is interlinked in all manner of real and imagined transactions. For only this public imagination constitutes commonality. Historians would be ill served if they did not recognize that this is what history has always provided, a public imagination—only now the scope is global rather than national.

To put this point in line with political theory: the problem at stake in the disoriented experience of the world as global construct and, hence, the challenge of world history is one of representation. For what is missing to date is representation in its triple meaning of *Vorstellung* (objectification>imagination), *Darstellung* (imagination>figuration) and *Vertretung* (figuration> political participation). The world exists in so many discrete and interacting parts, but we have no map of their interconnectedness (*Vorstellung*), or ways of translating this map into vivid narratives of transactions (*Darstellung*), or ultimately the power to shape and influence them (*Vertretung*)—and hence no responsibility or accountability for our actions. This is the reason why so many people think of globalization as either something of a natural force (for example, earthquake or avalanche) or a supernatural reality (a subject of cyber fiction). But it is neither.

Globality is not earth/nature nor is it cosmos/imaginary. Instead, it has become an integrated global space of human activities—a "nature" and an "imagination" that works off and articulates a man-made world of linkages. This argument is really rather simple if we keep in mind that in order to grasp the world as an object (*vorstellen*, meaning: to put before you in your mind), universalist thought had to project the world as an image. This totalizing and universalizing imagination was an amazing leap, which some associate exclusively with the West. Wrong or right, today we have the world before us not simply in photographic images from outer space, but in the form of e-mail messages, or sweatshirts, or, for that matter, aboriginal art—whether we imagine it or not. Hence, mapping this global space and shaping it into a global imagination is the main challenge of world history in an age of globality. It entails making visible and transparent (tracing) the imbrication of localities in global networks of exchange. It necessitates paying particular attention to those institutions that hold together and coordinate aspects of these processes, whether they are transnational or national, public or private. For the task is to make transparent and accessible the lineaments of wealth and violence that compress humanity into a single humankind. The purpose of world or global history is to make this reality visible to all who partake in the diverse human labors, which are splintered up into so many particularities, and thereby create an awareness and consciousness of the actual integration of the world.

Notes

1. The World History Bulletin 1, 1983, is the best source of information on world history teaching, (available from the World History Association, Sakamaki Hall A 203, 2350 Dole Street, Honolulu, HI 96822–2283).
2. Among the graduate programs, note University of California, Riverside; University of California, Santa Cruz; University of Hawaii; Idaho State University; The Johns Hopkins University; University of Minnesota; Northeastern University; Ohio State University; Washington State University; the University of Victoria; and, most recently, the University of North Carolina. See also Manning (2003).
3. The list of new textbooks has become bewilderingly large and diverse. I have consulted the following texts in particular: Stearns et al. (1992); Bulliet et al. (1997); Craig et al. (2000); Tignor et al. (2002); Bentley and Ziegler (2003).
4. The most consistent overview of research and research interests in world history is provided by the *Journal of World History* 1 (1990) – which is the official journal of the World History Association.
5. See the somewhat sensationalist account of Blaut (2000).
6. Here, I am thinking especially of the contribution of Marshall G.S. Hodgson (1993).
7. While more concerned with parallel histories than global space the textbook by Robert Tignor et al. 2002 serves as a good example for this trend.

8. The comprehensive-highlights approach that strings up grand events of grand civilizations like beads is the problem particularly of an older generation of world histories that have been reissued in new editions. I am thinking here particularly of J.M. Roberts (1993) or Philip Lee Ralph et al. (1991).
9. The introduction of world history courses has rather ambivalent consequences for academic politics, particularly in times of fiscal crisis. Whereas in good times it was used to diversify staff and to expand coverage (with the result that most universities and colleges now have a significant group of "non-Western" historians), the same tool may as well be used to shrink area expertise—on the presumption that one world historian can do what five area experts have done. Of course, the alternative is to reduce European history to the level of area studies. In any case, the problem with an all-encompassing world history is both intellectual and political.
10. An intriguing reminder of the historiographic and intellectual tensions is Thom (1995).
11. See, for example the highly readable Cavalli-Sforza (2000).
12. I would distinguish this global history from a "history of globalization," which is the relatively recent history of interaction in an effectively integrated world. See Geyer and Bright (1995).
13. Held et al. (1999) provides the most useful introduction.
14. On the notion of such "leaps" and 'axial times" as well as on the new condition of globality see Jaspers (1953).
15. Here, I differ "categorically" with Headley (2002), because as important as a universalist imagination was for globalization—and surely for Western expansion—it is not imagination that constitutes globality, but transactions. The problem is that this multitude of transactions remains largely unimagined and that the older universalist imagination of Europe does not capture them.
16. An application of this principle is Calhoun (1993). See also his *Nationalism* (1997).

References

Adas, Michael. 1989. *Machines as the Measure of Men; Science, Technology, and Ideologies of Western Dominance*. Ithaca and London: Cornell University Press.

Appadurai, Arjun. 1996. *Modernity at Large: Cultural Dimensions of Globalization*. Minneapolis and London: University of Minnesota Press.

Arendt, Hannah. 1977. "The Crisis in Culture: Its Social and Its Political Significance." In *Between Past and Future*, ed. Hannah Arendt. Harmondsworth and New York: Penguin, 197–226.

Arrighi, Giovanni. 1994. *The Long Twentieth Century: Money, Power and the Origins of Our Times*. London and New York: Verso.

Balibar, Etienne, and Immanuel Maurice Wallerstein. 1991. *Race, Nation, Class: Ambiguous Identities*. London and New York: Verso.

Bender, Thomas, ed. 2002. *Rethinking American History in a Global Age*. Berkeley: University of California Press.

Bentley, Jerry H. 1993. *Old World Encounters: Cross-Cultural Contacts and Exchanges in Pre-Modern Times*. New York and Oxford: Oxford University Press.

——— 1996. *Shapes of World History in Twentieth-Century Scholarship, Essays on Global and Comparative History*. Washington, D.C.: American Historical Association.

Bentley, Jerry H. and F. Ziegler. 2003. *Traditions and Encounters: A Global Perspective on the Past,* 2nd edn. Boston: McGraw-Hill.

Blaut, J.M. 2000. *Eight Eurocentric Historians.* New York and London: Guildford.
Bulliet, R.W. 1997. *The Earth and its People: A Global Experience.* Boston: Hughton Mifflin.
Burckhardt, Jacob. 1978. *Weltgeschichtliche Betrachtungen.* Stuttgart: Kröner.
Calhoun, Craig. 1993. "Nationalism and Ethnicity," *Annual Review of Sociology,* vol. 19, 211–39.
——— 1997. *Nationalism.* Minneapolis: University of Minnesota Press.
Castells, Manuel. 2000. *The Rise of the Network Society,* 2nd ed. Oxford; Blackwell.
Cavalli-Sforza, Luigi Luca. 2000. *Genes, Peoples, and Languages,* trans. Mark Seielstad. Berkeley: University of California Press.
Chakrabarty, Dipesh. 2000. *Provincializing Europe: Postcolonial Thought and Historical Difference.* Princeton and Oxford: Princeton University Press.
Comparativ: Leipziger Beiträge zur Universalgeschichte und vergleichenden Gesellschafts-forschung 2002. Special edition, "Weltgeschichtsschreibung im 20. Jahrhundert" vol. 12, no. 3.
Craig, Albert, et al. 2000. *Heritage of World Civilizations,* 8th edn., 2 vols. New York: W.W. Norton.
Crosby, Alfred W. 1986. *Ecological Imperialism: The Biological Expansion of Europe, 900–1900.* Cambridge, U.K. and New York: Cambridge University Press.
Curtin, Philip D. 1984. *Cross-Cultural Trade in World History.* Cambridge and New York: Cambridge University Press.
Diamond, Jared. 1999. *Guns, Germs, and Steel: The Fates of Human Society.* New York: W.W. Norton.
D'Souza, Dinesh. 1991. *Illiberal Education: The Politics of Race and Sex on Campus.* New York: Free Press.
Duara, Prasenjit. 1995. *Rescuing History from the Nation: Questioning Narratives of Modern China.* Chicago and London: University of Chicago Press.
Ferguson, Niall. 2001. *The Cash Nexus: Money and Power in the Modern World, 1700–2000.* New York: Basic Books.
——— 2003. *Empire: The Rise and Demise of the British World Order and the Lessons for Global Power.* New York: Basic Books.
Geyer, Michael and Charles Bright. 1995. "World History in a Global Age." *American Historical Review,* vol. 100, no. 4, 1034–60.
Greaves, Richard L. et al. 1997. *Civilizations of the World: The Human Adventure.* New York: Addison-Wesley.
Hannerz, Ulf. 1987. "The World in Creolization." *Africa,* vol. 57, 546–59.
Harvey, David. 1989. *The Condition of Postmodernity: An Enquiry into the Origins of Cultural Change.* Oxford: Basil Blackwell.
Headley, John M. 2002. "The Universalizing Principle and Process: On the West's Intrinsic Commitment to a Global Context." *Journal of World History,* vol. 13, no. 2, 291–321.
Headrick, Daniel. 1988. *The Tentacles of Progress: Technology Transfer in the Age of Imperialism, 1850–1940.* New York and Oxford: Oxford University Press.
Held, David et al. 1999. *Global Transformations: Politics, Economics and Culture.* Stanford: Stanford University Press.
Helms, Mary W. 1988. *Ulysses' Sail: An Ethnographic Odyssey of Knowledge, Power, and Geographic Distance.* Princeton: Princeton University Press.
Hodgson, Marshall G.S. 1993. *Rethinking World History: Essays on Europe, Islam and World History,* ed. Edmund Burke III. Cambridge, U.K. and New York: Cambridge University Press.

Hollinger, David A. 1993. "How Wide the Circle of the 'We'? American Intellectuals and the Problem of the Ethnos since World War II." *American Historical Review*, vol. 98, no. 2, 317–37.

Hopkins, A.G. 2002. "The History of Globalization - and the Globalization of History." In *Globalization in World History*, ed. A.G. Hopkins. New York: Norton, 12–44.

Jameson, Frederic. 1991. *Postmodernism or, the Cultural Logic of Late Capitalism*. Durham, NC: Duke University Press.

Jaspers, Karl. 1953. *The Origin and Goal of History*, trans. M. Bullock. New Haven: Yale University Press.

Kennedy, Paul M. 1993. *Preparing for the Twenty-First Century*. New York: Random House.

von Laue, Theodore H. 1987. *The World Revolution of Westernization. The Twentieth Century in Global Perspective*. New York: Oxford University Press.

Lockard, Craig A. 1994. "The Contributions of Philip Curtin and the 'Wisconsin School' to the Study and the Promotion of Comparative World History," *Journal of Third World Studies*, vol. 11, 180–223.

Mazlish, Bruce. 1998. "Crossing Boundaries: Ecumenical, World, and Global History." In *World History: Ideologies, Structures, and Identities*, eds. Philip Pomper, Richard H. Elphik, and Richard T. Vann. Oxford, U.K. and Malden, MA: Blackwell Publishers, 41–52.

McNeill, J.R. 2000. *Something New Under the Sun: An Environmental History of the Twentieth-Century World*. New York: W.W. Norton.

McNeill, J.R. and William H. McNeill, 2003. *The Human Web: A Bird's-Eye View of World History*. New York and London: W.W. Norton.

McNeill, William H. 1963. *The Rise of the West: A History of the Human Community*. Chicago: University of Chicago Press.

———— 1976. *Plagues and Peoples*, 1st ed. Garden City, N.Y.: Anchor Press.

———— 1990. "The Rise of the West after Twenty-Five Years." *Journal of World History*, vol. 1, 2–21.

Maier, Charles S. 2000. "Consigning the Twentieth Century to History: Alternative Narratives for the Modern Era," *American Historical Review*, vol. 103, no. 3, 807–31.

Manning, Patrick. 2003. *Navigating World History: Historians Create a Global Past*. New York: Palgrave.

Pomeranz, Kenneth. 2000. *The Great Divergence: Europe, China, and the Making of the Modern World Economy*. Princeton, N.J.: Princeton University Press.

Pomeranz, Kenneth and Steven Topik. 1999. *The World That Trade Created: Society, Culture, and the World Economy, 1400–the Present*. Armonk, N.Y.: M.E. Sharpe.

Pratt, Mary Louise. 1992. *Imperial Eyes: Travel Writing and Transculturation*. London and New York: Routledge.

Ralph, Philip Lee et al. 1991. *World Civilizations: Their History and Their Culture*, 8th ed., 2 vols. New York: W.W. Norton.

Roberts, J.M. 1993. *A History of the World*. New York and Oxford: Oxford University Press.

Robertson, Roland, 1992. *Globalization; Social Theory and Global Culture*. London: Sage Publications.

Rowe, William and Vivian Schelling. 1991. *Memory and Modernity. Popular Culture in Latin America*. London: Verso.

Said, Edward. 1978. *Orientalism*. New York: Pantheon Books.

Sassen, Saskia. 1998. *Globalization and Its Discontents: Essays on the New Mobility of People and Money*. New York: The New Press.

Smith, Jackie and Hank Johnston, eds. 2002. *Globalization and Resistance: Transnational Dimensions of Social Movements*. Lanham: Rowman & Littlefield.

Spivak, Gayatri Chakravorty. 1993. *Outside in the Teaching Machine*. New York: Routledge.

Stearns, Peter N. 2001. *Cultures in Motion: Mapping Key Contacts and Their Imprints in World History*. New Haven and London: Yale University Press.

Stearns, Peter N., Michael Adas and Stuart B. Schwarz. 1992. *World Civilizations: The Global Experience*. New York: Harper Collins.

Tignor, Robert et al., 2002. *World Together, Worlds Apart: A History of the Modern World from the Mongol Empire to the Present*. New York: W.W. Norton.

Thom, Martin. 1995. *Republics, Nations, and Tribes*. London and New York: Verso.

Turner, Terry. 1991. "Representing, Resisting, Rethinking: Historical Transformations of Kayapo Culture and Anthropological Consciousness." In *Colonial Situations: Essays on the Contextualization of Ethnographic Knowledge*, ed. George Stocking. Madison, WI: University of Wisconsin Press.

Young, Robert C. 2001. *Postcolonialism: An Historical Introduction*. Oxford: Blackwell Publishers.

Chapter 10

Cartographies of Connection: Ocean Maps as Metaphors for Inter-Area History

Kären Wigen

Recent years have witnessed a veritable sea change in the practice of history in the English-speaking world. Where most historians traditionally studied stable national cores, more and more today find themselves drawn to the mobile and the marginal. Impatient with the space-time grid of their professional training, a growing group of scholars identifies with a thematically defined agenda: one concerned with the global circulation of people and ideas, money and microbes, social movements and institutional responses. What all these phenomena have in common is their transnational geography. None can be satisfactorily investigated within the bounds of a single state, and most spill across even the macro-regions of area studies.

Collectively, the ascendancy of such topics has begun to configure a new field of inquiry, one that might be termed *inter-area history*. In fundamental ways, inter-area history troubles the foundational categories of the discipline, for areas and states constitute not only the intellectual apparatus through which we think about the world, but also the units in which we organize our curriculum and train our students. Investigating farflung connections is thus a daunting project, both professionally and conceptually, and has prompted a searching conversation about the origins, uses, and limits of received geographies (Lewis and Wigen 1997).

If that conversation has taught us anything, it is that ours is not the first generation to confront a bewildering new world with an outmoded map. As historians today set about bending, bridging, and otherwise improvising on inherited categories to accommodate new findings and new questions, we might be well advised to look to an earlier moment of cartographic improvisation, when another group of thinkers was forced to bend and stretch their inherited metageographical framework to accommodate new findings and new questions.

The precedent that I have found most instructive is the mapping of the world's oceans in the early modern era. Starting in the late fifteenth century, as every schoolchild learns, European navigators discovered continents that previously had been uncharted. They also made simultaneous discoveries of vast sea spaces. The process of mapping water-bodies may not have drawn as much attention as the assimilation of new landmasses into the medieval continental scheme. But conceptually, the challenge of maritime cartography was more complex—for reasons that go to the heart of our current predicament.

Like the global connections that draw our attention today, the ocean is a crossroads, a site of interaction; a space of passage, rather than a place to settle and control. By its nature, sea space has to be shared. This in turn makes its geographical identity hard to fix; the usual rules of geopolitical nomenclature— naming by claiming—do not readily apply. Moreover, ocean space has few clear boundaries. Winds and currents might organize the earth's waters into various subsystems, but all of them are connected, and fixing their limits in any durable, objective way has proved impossible. As a result, oceans have posed a conceptual challenge very similar to that of transnational history: neither one can be carved up definitively into discrete, bounded domains. Atlas makers since the early modern period have thus faced a conundrum similar to our own: how does one go about mapping a global commons? By what principles might areas be delimited in an interconnected, interstitial, inter-area domain?

The answers to those questions have been a long time coming. As Martin Lewis (1999) has documented, European maritime geography effectively remained in flux for almost half a millennium. Between 1450 and 1950, Western cartographers experimented with four fundamentally different models for mapping ocean space: national seas, maritime arcs, bounded basins, and a single global ocean. It is my contention that each of these four ocean schemes constitutes a useful metaphor for a specific paradigm in the emerging field of inter-area history.

To the extent that scholars of transnational phenomena can be thought of as explorers in a similarly borderless, interstitial domain, revisiting these early oceanic geographies might help us to see broader patterns in the way that new scholarship is "mapping" inter-area history. Accordingly, the remainder of this chapter fleshes out these four paradigms, drawing on an earlier cartography of interactive sea space to shed light on the emerging geographies of connective history. Most of the literature discussed here consists of scholarly articles and monographs, where the new transnational approaches first appeared. But in recent years, connective perspectives have begun to reshape textbooks and reference works as well. The final section of this chapter focuses on one particularly promising, pioneering new work, the DK *Atlas of World History* (Black 2000).

National Seas

The first way that European cartographers attempted to apprehend ocean space was by carving it up into national seas. In this early model, maritime territory was essentially appropriated as an extension of national territory; coastal waters were simply named after the states that abutted them. Thus maps of the North Atlantic might show a "British Ocean" and a "Scottish Ocean"; the Western Pacific was typically labeled a "Chinese Sea"; and the waters off the coast of South America were routinely segmented into a "Sea of Peru," a "Sea of Chile," a "Sea of Brazil," and so on. Not surprisingly, enterprising map makers in Western Europe tended to extend European national claims conspicuously farther than the rest. A map from 1553 by Pierre Desceliers, for instance, represents the North Atlantic as a striking succession of horizontal bands, projecting a "Sea of France," a "Sea of Spain," and a "Sea of the Antilles" thousands of miles into open waters (see figure 10.1).

This kind of cartography serves as a useful metaphor for our most venerable inter-area fields: diplomatic and imperial history. Operating in the same way as the toponyms on Desceliers's map, labels such as "Spanish Empire" or "American diplomacy" effectively extend a national claim over a big swath of transnational space. The resilience of this kind of categorization can be seen not only in higher education but also in the publishing industry that supports it. Consider the organization of a recent catalogue from Penguin Books. According to Penguin, the spice wars in the Indian Ocean—featured in a recent paperback called *Nathaniel's Nutmeg* (Milton 1999)—constitute an episode in "British history." Likewise, a reprint of *The Voyages of Captain Cook* is also identified as a book about Britian, rather than, say, as a work of Pacific studies (a category that Penguin does not yet recognize) or "world history" (a category that appears to include only developments in Asia and Africa). These cases reveal a common paradigm: one where transnational entanglements are framed in national terms.

This model obviously has its limits, and many historians in the past few years have made a powerful case for the need to go beyond the perspectives of traditional imperial and diplomatic historiographies. But it is worth noting that the habit of identifying great swaths of world history as de facto "national seas" has its uses. If nothing else, this habit can serve to alert national historians to transnational concerns. Such is the case in British history, where the past decade has given rise to a whole new body of scholarship, focusing less on the British Empire than on "imperial Britain." Bringing imperial history back home, as it were, this scholarship documents in case after case how developments in the metropole were profoundly shaped by the needs, the resources, and the lessons of the colonization project.[1]

Similar stirrings are afoot in my own field of East Asian history. In new work on China, Korea, and Japan, diplomatic and imperial relations are being recast, not as peripheral concerns suitable for separate specialties, but as central concerns and crucial preconditions for the assertion of state legitimacy.[2] The same is true for the premodern era. Where comparative sociologists argued in the 1980s for "bringing the state back in" (Evans, et al. 1985), Tokugawa and

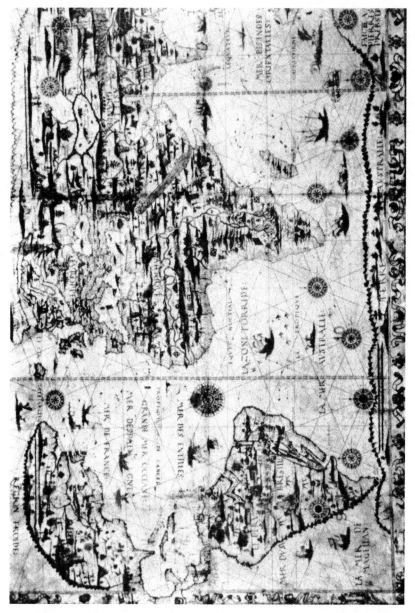

Figure 10.1 *World Map Showing National Seas, by Pierre Desceliers.* Note the horizontal toponyms extending westward from the Eurasian continent into the Atlantic ocean (to read these labels, orient the map with south at the top). From *Die Weltkarte des Pierre Desceliers von 1553*, reproduction published in 1924 by the Vienna Geographical Society. Reprinted with permission of the American Geographical Society, Milwaukee, Wisconsin.

Qing historians in the same years began bringing the *world* back in to the history of the nation-state.[3] To be sure, many textbooks still reflect an older perspective (describing the Tokugawa period as "an era of seclusion," for instance, and segregating discussions of empire from chapters on domestic development). But a new emphasis on the interconnectedness of East Asia has already begun to reshape the materials through with historians teach about this region.[4]

Ocean Arcs

Just as diplomatic and imperial paradigms are not the only way to approach inter-area studies, however, so national seas are not the only way to conceptualize sea space. During the European Enlightenment, French cartographers developed a new model, embedding national seas in long ribbons of water that might wrap around or between whole continents. The result was a two-tier configuration, incorporating local seas into longer *ocean arcs*.

A 1719 map by Nicolas Sanson shows this new principle at work (figure 10.2). Like his predecessors, Sanson identified a dozen national seas, bordering the coastlines of every continent. But farther from shore he demarcated a single "Occidental Ocean," curving from northern Europe around the Horn of Africa; its counterpart, the "Indian or Oriental Ocean," was shown as flowing from the Bay of Bengal to the Banda Sea. Between these two, he identified a "Meridional or Ethiopian Ocean" that wrapped around the entire southern half of Africa. Similar ribbon-like arcs (some with the same names) can be seen on a 1696 map by Jacques-Dominique Cassini (figure 10.3). But Cassini also added a dramatic, sinuous "Sea of the North," extending all the way from the Caribbean Sea to the North Pole and beyond, linking up with the Pacific in the vicinity of Kamchatka.

While it is not entirely clear how these ocean arcs were derived, it appears that they were meant to mark pathways of interaction. Both Cassini's and Sanson's "oceans" roughly denote trading circuits in the age of sail. Their Indian or Oriental ocean, for instance, corresponds to the old segmentary trading system that extended from the Swahili coast to the South China Sea. Likewise, their Occidental arc approximates the first leg of the triangular trade in the North Atlantic, which was already well established when their maps were published at the turn of the eighteenth century. Finally, their Meridional or Ethiopian Ocean denotes the hazardous passage around the Cape of Storms, where European ships braved the hazardous Agulles Current to forge a direct link between the Indian Ocean and the Atlantic world.[5] Cassini's "Sea of the North" is a more fanciful projection, but the intended implication even here may be that this stretch of sea, too, marks a *potential* pathway of interaction (the elusive "northwest passage" that the French, in particular, were so eager to find).

Figure 10.2 *World Map Showing Ocean Arcs, by Nicolas Sanson.* From Sanson's "Mappe-monde géo-hydrographique, ou description générale du globe terrestre et aquatique, en deux plans-hémisphères" (Paris: Hubert Iaillot, 1719). Reprinted with permission of the American Geographical Society, Milwaukee, Wisconsin.

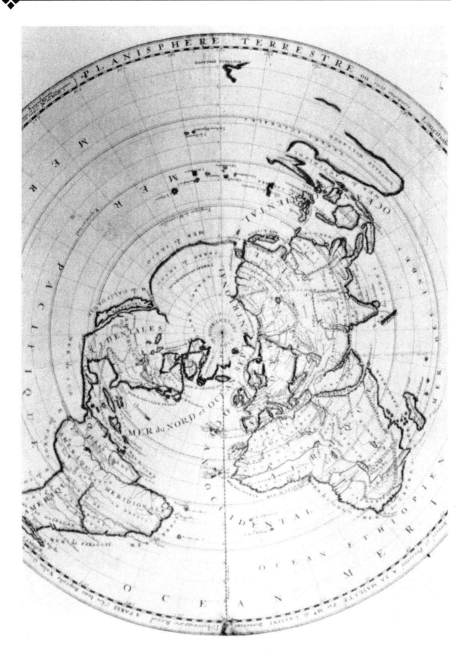

Figure 10.3 *Polar Projection Showing Ocean Arcs, by Jacques-Dominique Cassini.* Detail from the Cassini world map of 1696. Reprinted with permission of the American Geographical Society, Milwaukee, Wisconsin.

For whatever reason, ocean arcs had a relatively brief life on European maps, and their very existence is mostly forgotten. Yet their contours remain provocative, inviting us to think about pathways of connection as demarcating meaningful 'areas' within the wider expanse of the sea. That sensibility, I would argue, has a clear counterpart in inter-area history today: the study of transnational networks. Like Cassini, the network historian starts from the geography of interaction, framing an area on the basis of historical human linkages. Such an approach can illuminate an enormous variety of associations: from feminist sisterhoods to Sufi brotherhoods, from governmental bodies such as the East India Company to non-governmental bodies such as the Red Cross.[6] But of all the transnational networks on the planet, the one with the greatest grip on our profession's imagination at the moment is undoubtedly the diaspora.

Considered from a geographical standpoint, diaspora scholarship has a compelling feature: it effectively creates new domains for historical research. In methodological terms, what is novel about this approach is the way it has allowed scholars to frame fields on an ad hoc basis, crossing conventional borders in pursuit of particular patterns of interaction. The prototype here is Paul Gilroy's famous *Black Atlantic* (Gilroy 1993). Notably, Gilroy did not propose to study one empire; nor did he tackle all of Atlantic history; nor did he posit an "African Atlantic" (a colonial inversion of the "national seas" paradigm). Instead, Gilroy identified a cultural archipelago as his area, stretching his frame to include all black people and their cultural forms, on whatever side of the Atlantic he might find them.

This is a fascinating way to think about areas, and one that has clearly struck a deep chord. In the last few years, diaspora scholarship has rocked the academic world. Its burgeoning scholarship, headlined in the new journal *Diaspora* (but spilling over into area- and discipline-specific journals as well), propeled a five-year Ford Foundation initiative called "Crossing Borders," and has issued a profound challenge to the institutional and pedagogical segregation of ethnic and area studies.[7] Indeed, it is worth pondering why this approach has gained such a following at this historical moment. What social forces might be converging to make the diaspora paradigm so compelling to Anglo-American academics in the late twentieth and early twenty-first century? Certainly, the reactivation of global diasporas as important economic and political forces in our time, following the liberalization of U.S. immigration laws in the 1960s, and the tremendous surge of migration world wide in subsequent years, has played a crucial role (Luibheid 1997 and more broadly Appadurai 1996). The growing power of diasporic identities in our own classrooms has unsettled our mental maps of the past.

For all their power, however, networks and diasporas are not the only new principles for mapping world history, just as ocean arcs were not the final answer for mapping the world's seas. Over the course of the twentieth century, both national seas and ocean arcs largely gave way to a third paradigm: that of the discrete ocean basin.

Ocean Basins

By the 1950s, most atlases and geography textbooks recognized only three "true" oceans: the Atlantic, Pacific, and Indian. These labels were not new in themselves; all three toponyms had appeared on European maps since at least the 1400s. What was novel was the way they were deployed. Rather than sharing space with national seas and maritime arcs, the Atlantic, Indian, and Pacific oceans now extended right up to the shoreline. A true ocean had come to be defined as a bounded body of water, vast in scale, abutting the surrounding landmasses on most sides. This remains our normative ocean prototype today (figure 10.4).

For those who seek to reconfigure areas in history, the basin paradigm might at first seem hopelessly retrograde. After all, discrete, bounded oceans are the conceptual counterpart of discrete, bounded land areas—the very grid that inter-area history is trying to transcend. But I would submit that, when extended to sea space, this paradigm undergoes a subtle but important shift. At sea, it functions to frame interstitial spaces of passage as autonomous places with their own names. Giving such spaces an independent identity marks them as worthy of study in their own right.

In this sense, the basin model is a useful metaphor for yet a third approach to inter-area studies: the study of contact zones, frontiers, and borderlands. The essence of this approach is to focus on interstitial places: zones of particularly intensive cross-cultural exchange, including not only conquest and assimilation

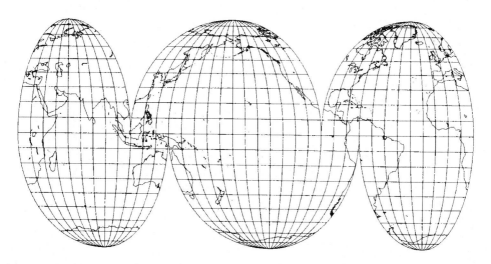

Figure 10.4 *World Map Showing One Global Ocean, by Athelstan Spilhaus.* From *Atlas of the World with Geophysical Boundaries, Showing Oceans, Continents and Tectonic Plates in their Entirety* (1991). Reprinted with permission of the American Philosophical Society, Philadelphia.

but also translation and creolization, cosmopolitanism and hybridity. What makes this approach distinctive is that, while shifting attention away from national cores, it retains a primary emphasis on place. Empires and diasporas, fortune-seekers and pilgrims, germs and ideas might pass through, but in this approach, the geographical frame is fixed, and the perspective is resolutely regional.[8]

A recent interdisciplinary conference on "Interactions in History," sponsored in part by the Ford Foundation's Crossing Borders initiative, featured three different manifestations of this approach which together help convey both its breadth and its subtlety. John Mears, reflecting on borderlands as a comparative analytical category, made the important point that "borderlands" have been historically made into "bordered lands" by the actions of nearby states. Stephen Rapp, focusing on the Caucasus, turned the same point around, insisting that, if we want to understand places like Caucasia in their own terms, we must view them through local eyes as a "crossroads" rather than as someone else's frontier or periphery. Finally, geographers Palmira Brummett and Lydia Pulsipher zoomed in even further. Focusing on individual islands and port cities, they showed that maritime cities often serve simultaneously as nodes in a wider system of exchange and as the locus of complex, cosmopolitan communities in their own right, with distinctive and durable identities that mark them off (sometimes starkly) from the nations that surround them (see Bentley and Bridenthal forthcoming).[9] Together, these papers not only show the promise of crossroads/border studies, but make a very important methodological point: namely, that scale of analysis is not a given that can be read off from historical processes, but a critical scholarly choice. Since inter-area interactions manifest themselves at every scale, from the micro to the macro, teaching about such interactions calls for both flexibility and care in choosing the lenses for our lectures.

The Global Ocean

The final metaphor for inter-area studies might be seen as either a refutation or a transcendence of the earlier models. This is the approach where national seas, ocean arcs, and maritime basins are subsumed into a single global ocean. Both Elisée Réclus and Carl Ritter, two of the nineteenth century's most systematic geographical thinkers, insisted that the earth's oceans were really one great, globe-girdling water-mass, dominating the southern hemisphere (just as the bulk of Eurasia and North America dominated the northern hemisphere). From this perspective, the Atlantic, Pacific, and Indian oceans are merely giant embayments of a single, interconnected sea (figure 10.5).

This vision of a single ocean readily serves as a metaphor for a fourth paradigm in transnational history: the global approach. This can take a number of forms. Global historians can trace the path of a particular mobile thing,

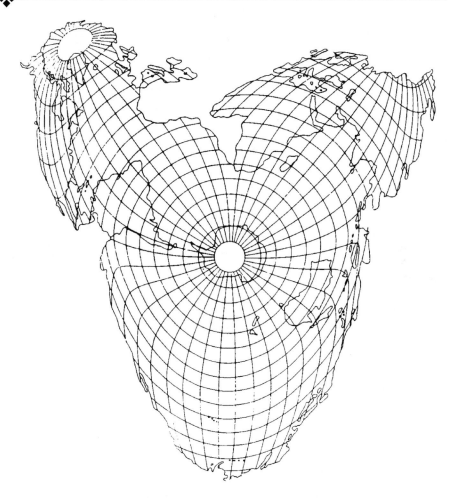

Figure 10.5 *World Map Highlighting Individual Ocean Basins, by Athelstan Spilhaus.* Spilhaus notes that this "interrupted Mollweide projection cuts all continents to show oceans to best advantage." From *Atlas of the World with Geophysical Boundaries, Showing Oceans, Continents and Tectonic Plates in their Entirety* (1991). Reprinted with permission of the American Philosophical Society, Philadelphia.

whether a germ, an idea, or a commodity. This biography-of-things approach has given world history some of its most powerful, vivid material for classroom use, bringing home to students in a concrete way the extent to which globalization pervades their daily life (Appadurai 1981; Clunas 1999; Crosby 1983). But globalists can also take other tacks. For instance, they might focus on *responses* to mobility: attempts by situated actors (whether workers or consumers, states or local communities) to regulate, channel, or disrupt global flows. French historian Matt Matsuda, for instance, has drawn attention to the tremendous levels of energy that modern European states had to invest in a system of identification designed to keep track of the movements of their increasingly mobile citizens, workers, and outlaws (Matsuda 1994; revised and with illustrations 1996: chap.6). Adam McKeown's new book adopts a similar focus, documenting the enormous and unwieldy institutions designed either to control or to facilitate Chinese immigration across the Pacific (McKeown 2001). Both of these recent works effectively answer Lauren Benton's call for a new "institutional world history" (Benton 1996). So too does the work of Charles Bright and Michael Geyer, represented in the *American Historical Review* in a provocative paper on "Regimes of World Order" in the twentieth century (Geyer and Bright 1995).

Nor does this exhaust the possibilities of the global paradigm. A third way to do global history is to identify a moment in time and take a truly catholic interest in everything that happened in the world during that moment. The temporal slice might be as wide as a century or era, or as narrow as a single year.[10] While a narrow slice may be the only manageable one to tackle in scholarly writing, more expansive units of time can clearly be productive frameworks within which to organize courses, conferences, and scholarly journals.[11] And then, for those who desire a truly panoptical view across eras as well as areas, there is yet another way to do global history: namely, to analyze the shifting kinds, degrees, and registers of globalization over time.[12]

This brief inventory suggests at least four ways to do global history: tracking specific flows, analyzing responses to flows, taking a slice of time, and narrating successive modalities of globalization. Admittedly, these are disparate studies to group under one paradigm. But what unites them is their truly global reach. To the extent that historians working in this vein are analyzing processes rather than places, and dealing with truly globe-spanning regimes, they take us effectively beyond inter-area to "pan-area" history.

In short, just as cartographers after 1492 conceptualized sea space from four very different perspectives, so historians have approached inter-area connections in four corresponding ways: as extensions of national history, through transnational networks, by focusing on contact zones, and by analyzing global flows or processes. Each of these approaches generates a different metageography for inter-area history, so that in a sense we have four competing models for organizing this emerging subfield. But I would insist that there is no need to privilege one of these approaches over another. All four models can and should be retained and deployed simultaneously for different sorts of projects. To go back to the ocean metaphor, national seas are useful frameworks of analysis for some purposes; grouping them into ocean arcs or basins will reveal other sorts of processes and dynamics; and these in turn need to be conceptually combined for still other analytical purposes into a single global framework.

Bringing the World to Students

The foregoing discussion brings us finally to the pedagogical issue that is at the core of this collection: how is the new inter-area perspective being incorporated in curricular materials? How are teachers who are excited by this new research bringing transnational perspectives into the classroom?

One answer, of course, is to incorporate inter-area perspectives into the national history surveys that constitute our bread-and-butter courses. This is being done in a wide variety of ways across the discipline, often through subtle but powerful shifts in the nature of assigned readings.[13] A bolder option, being explored on many campuses, is to develop new courses that tackle a wider canvas: diasporic spheres, ocean basins, or indeed world history as a whole. Indeed, the last decade has seen a burgeoning of such courses across the United States—and a parallel profusion of textbooks and teaching aids for their instructors and students.[14]

A hallmark of this new literature, and one of the most promising publications of the decade, is a pioneering new historical atlas edited by Jeremy Black (2000), the DK *Atlas of World History*. The first notable thing about the DK *Atlas* is its novel organization. The book is divided into two roughly equal parts, with elaborate cross referencing between the two. Part I, "Eras of World History," maps the world as a whole from prehistory to the present, taking successive temporal snapshots that illustrate a variety of themes (agricultural origins, urban growth, organized religion, oceanic exploration, trade and biological diffusion, empire, migration, and the like). This is followed by an equally substantive Part II, "Regional History," which slices the subject along a different axis altogether. This section devotes conscientiously parallel treatment to developments in eight areas: North America, South America, Africa, Europe, West Asia, South and Southeast Asia, North and East Asia, and Australasia and Oceania. The atlas's general editor, Jeremy Black, has previously published sharp critiques of the ethnocentric world views represented in national atlases (Black 1997). That background has served him well here, judging from the remarkably even-handed way in which the DK *Atlas* represents the globe. Every regional section, for instance, follows the same sequence, beginning with a two-page spread on "Exploration and Mapping." This reveals exploration to have been a truly global project, placing the familiar charts of European discovery alongside equally detailed treatment of non-European voyages, and showing a tantalizing sample of premodern maps from every world region.

Complementing the novel organization of this atlas is its creative cartography. The maps are visually stunning, with sharp graphics, subtle colors, unusual projections and scales, and innovative framing tailored to the themes at hand. Not surprisingly, those themes correspond closely to the various paradigms of inter-area history discussed above. Prominently featured are transnational flows (whether of peoples, languages, religions, or biota), commercial and social networks (including criminal syndicates), and transoceanic diaspora (including a variety of slave migration streams). Overall the coverage is less weighted toward wars and geopolitics than that of most previous atlases, with greater amplification of economic, social, and cultural developments. But even in the geopolitical domain, clever use of overlays and shading allows unusually subtle mapping of boundaries and frontiers. Given the level of detail and the relatively affordable price, it is likely that this atlas will be used, not just in world history courses, but to contextualize regional histories as well.

Taken together, the DK maps reveal that, while locations on the globe may endure, the human configurations that we call "places" effectively come and go. If thriving centers can be turned into backwaters under a new regime, peripheries too are subject to inversion; and a cultural "middle ground" of the kind identified by Richard White is highly vulnerable to chance and change (White 1991). These examples drive home geographer Doreen Massey's point that the localities we inhabit are temporally as well as spatially delimited; all places, at whatever scale, are temporary "envelopes of spacetime" (Massey 1995). By my reading, this message increasingly underlies college-level history pedagogy across the United States, in virtually every subfield of the discipline.

Conclusion

Inevitably, the recent turn to inter-area history raises challenges for historical practice. To paraphrase Jeff Wasserstrom's (2001) recent manifesto in *Perspectives Online*, historians may increasingly want to "read globally," but we still need to "write locally." One question this poses is, how do we operationalize this in training the next generation? What configuration of fields best prepares an apprentice historian for pursuing grounded yet globally minded research? A second question has to do with incorporating indigenous voices into our work. Inasmuch as "one person's periphery is another person's homeland," part of the project of inter-area studies must be a critical analysis of location from many different perspectives. As a recent University of Chicago report puts it, "world regions" are also "regional worlds": places from which local people articulate their own world views.[15] In other words, "areas" are not just objects but also active participants in knowledge production. This too has implications for historical practice. I suspect that taking this insight seriously may entail changing the way we work; in particular, it points toward collaborative research with scholars in the areas we study. But this in turn raises logistical questions: how can such collaborative work be supported? what are its difficulties? and if it is indeed worthwhile, how can we get it recognized by tenure and promotion committees?

A final challenge is that of making world history truly inclusive. By dint of their training and professional pressures, practitioners of U.S. and European history (at least in the United States) tend to focus their lenses more narrowly than do those of Asia, Africa, and Latin America. Perhaps as a result, they tend to be underrepresented in conversations about global history. Yet historians who operate at a micro-scale are everywhere revealing local evidence of hybridity and multiculturalism—the outcomes and engines of the very global interactions charted in works like the DK *Atlas*. Surely, "local" historians working near home and "global" historians studying distant lands are both viewing similar processes, just at a different scale of resolution: we may be using different ends of the telescope, but we are all looking at the same interactive world. Both of these perspectives are needed, and specialists from *all* areas must be in on the conversation if this field is to move forward. Otherwise, the "world" of world history may end up rather like the world of world music: a truncated category produced by the marketing department, rather than an inclusive intellectual domain.

Notes

1. For examples, see Cooper and Stoler (1997).
2. For a review of this literature, see Katzenstein and Shiraishi (1997), Schmidt (2000), and Wigen (1999).
3. See Wigen 1995, ["Bringing the World Back In: Meditations on the space-time of Japanese early modernity," Research Papers in Asian/Pacific Studies, Asian/Pacific Studies Institute, Duke University. An expanded version of this paper, under the title "Japanese Perspectives on the Time/Space of 'Early Modernity'"] was presented at the XIX International Congress of Historical Sciences, Oslo, Norway August 7, 2000. The paper can be accessed on the web at www.oslo2000.uio.no/english/index.htm (under Major Themes 1a, "Is Universal History Possible?").
4. Two excellent works that synthesize the new perspectives in a manner suitable for college-level introductory courses include Hudson (1999) and Morris-Suzuki (1998).
5. For information on the difficulties of navigating in this region (and much else on oceans and seafarers in the early modern period), see the fascinating "Latitude" website created by Patricia Seed of Rice University, at www.ruf.rice.edu/~feegi.
6. Papers on these and other network topics were presented at the "Interactions" conference, 1–3 February 2001, at the Library of Congress. A complete program, with abstracts, is available on the web at www.historycooperative.org/proceedings/interactions/index.html.
7. For how these trends have affected Asian-American studies, see *positions* 7, no. 3 (1999), a special issue on "Asian Transnationalities." On related developments in African-American studies, see Shea 2001. For more on the Ford Foundation's "Crossing Borders" initiative, see www.fordfoundation.org/publications/recent_articles/crossingborders.cfm.
8. An important subfield where this perspective has been worked out is the new Western history of the United States. Leaders in this field include Patricia Limerick, William Cronon, and Richard White.

9. See the abstracts of papers by John Mears, Stephen Rapp, and Palmira Brummett and Lydia Pulsipher on the "Interactions" website at www.historycooperative.org/ proceedings/interactions/index.html. The conference proceedings will be published in Bentley and Bridenthal (forthcoming).
10. For a lively example of the latter, see Wills Jr. (2001).
11. On the latter point, see the journals *Eighteenth Century Studies* and *Early Modern History*, both of which strive for global representation within a temporal frame.
12. This is the approach taken by C.I. Bayly in his keynote address for the "Interactions" conference mentioned in note 6.
13. On resources for this kind of pedagogical innovation in the Japan field, see note 5.
14. An excellent gateway to these resources for world history is the webpage of Northeastern University's World History Center, at www.whc.neu.edu.
15. "Area Studies, Regional Worlds: A White Paper for the Ford Foundation." (The Globalization Project, University of Chicago Center for International Studies, June 1995.) Available on the web at regionalworlds.uchicago.edu/pub.html.

References

Appadurai, Arjun, ed. 1981. *The Social History of Things: Commodities in Cultural Perspective*. Cambridge: Cambridge University Press.

——— 1996. *Modernity at Large: Cultural Dimensions of Globalization*. Minneapolis: University of Minnesota Press.

Bentley, Jerry H., Renate Bridenthal, and Anand A. Yang, eds. 2005. *Interactions: Transregional Perspectives on World History*. Honolulu: University of Hawai'i Press .

Benton, Lauren. 1996. "From the World-systems Perspective to Institutional World History: Culture and Economy in Global Theory." *Journal of World History*, vol. 7, 261–96.

Black, Jeremy. 1997. *Maps and History*. New Haven: Yale University Press.

——— ed. 2000. *Atlas of World History: Mapping the Human Journey*. London: DK Publishers.

Clunas, Craig. 1999. "Modernity Global and Local: Consumption and the Rise of the West." *American Historical Review*, vol. 104, no. 5, 1497–511.

Cooper, Frederick and Ann Laura Stoler. 1997. *Tensions of Empire: Colonial Cultures in a Bourgeois World*. Berkeley: University of California Press.

Crosby, Alfred. 1993. *Ecological Imperialism: The Biological Expansion of Europe, 900–1900*. Cambridge: Cambridge University Press.

Evans, Peter, Dietrich Rueschemeyer and Theda Skocpol, eds. 1985. *Bringing the State Back In*. Cambridge: Cambridge University Press.

Geyer, Michael and Charles Bright, 1995. "World History in a Global Age." *American Historical Review*, vol. 100, 1034–60.

Gilroy, Paul. 1993. *The Black Atlantic: Modernity and Double Consciousness*. Cambridge, Mass: Harvard University Press.

Hudson, Mark J. 1999. *Ruins of Identity: Ethnogenesis in the Japanese Islands* Honolulu: University of Hawaii Press.

Katzenstein, Peter J. and Takashi Shiraishi, eds. 1997. *Network Power: Japan and Asia*. Ithaca: Cornell University Press.

Lewis, Martin. 1999. "Dividing the Ocean Sea." *Geographical Review*, vol. 89, no. 2, 188–214.

Lewis, Martin and Kären Wigen. 1997. *The Myth of Continents: A Critique of Metageography*. Berkeley: University of California Press.

Luibheid, Ethne. 1997. "The 1965 Immigration and Nationality Act: An 'End' to Exclusion?" *positions: east asia cultures critique*, vol. 5, no. 2, Fall, 501–522.

Massey, Doreen. 1995. "Places and their Pasts." *History Workshop Journal* vol. 39: 182–92.

Matsuda, Matt K. 1994. "Doctor, Judge, Vagabond: Identity, Identification, and Other Memories of the State," *History and Memory*, vol. 6, 73–94.

——— 1996. *The Memory of the Modern.* Oxford: Oxford University Press.

McKeown, Adam. 2001. *Chinese Migrant Networks and Cultural Change: Peru, Chicago, Hawaii, 1900–1936.* Chicago: The University of Chicago Press.

Milton, Giles. 1999. *Nathaniel's Nutmeg, or, The True and Incredible Adventures of the Spice Trader who Changed the Course of History.* New York: Farrar, Straus and Giroux.

Morris-Suzuki, Tessa. 1998. *Reinventing Japan: Time Space Nation.* Armonk: Sharpe.

Schmidt, Andre. 2000. "Colonialism and the 'Korea Problem' in the Historiography of Modern Japan." *Journal of Asian Studies*, vol. 59, no. 4, 951–75.

Shea, Christopher. 2001. "A Blacker Shade of Yale: African-American Studies Takes a New Direction." *Lingua Franca* 11, no. 2: 42–49.

Wasserstrom, Jeff. 2001. "Eurocentrism and its discontents." *Perspectives Online*, January 2001, www.theaha.org/perspectives.

White, Richard. 1991. *The Middle Ground: Indians, Empires, and Republics in The Great Lakes Region, 1650–1815.* Cambridge: Cambridge University Press.

Wigen, Kären. 1995. "Bringing the World Back In: Meditations on the Space-time of Japanese Early Modernity." Research Papers in Asian/Pacific Studies, Asian/Pacific Studies Institute, Duke University.

——— 1999. "Culture, Power, and Place: The New Landscapes of East Asian Regionalism." *American Historical Review*, vol. 104, no. 4, 1183–201.

Wills, John E. Jr. 2001. *1688: A Global History.* London: Granta.

Chapter 11

World History: Making Sense of the Present

Hanna Schissler

How people imagine the world, construct historical time, and position themselves and society in time and space has changed over time, sometimes dramatically so. Ways in which the past has been constructed have always provided plenty of reasons for disagreement and conflict. Curricula and textbooks have been major battlegrounds for these conflicts, because it is there that societies write their own histories and project themselves into the future. Whether, and how, textbooks are used to promote an understanding of the world at large is crucial. The message to students varies depending on whether they hear about their communities and regions; whether the focus on national history is so strong that the rest of the world hardly comes into focus at all; whether national history is juxtaposed to world history, as in the United States (and most countries for that matter); or whether it is implicitly integrated into and subsumed to the national and European narratives as in Germany.

The romantic German poet Novalis wrote at the end of the eighteenth century: "History always is world history; and only in relation to all of history is it possible to comprehend any singularity."[1] While Novalis argued for a broad universal mindset from which one's own history derives its meaning, I would like to turn his argument around and make an argument on the ways in which every history conveys implicit information about "the world": History shapes people's imagination of the world in which they live, of its geographical scope and of its overall importance. A message about the world at large and about the meaning of things is always conveyed in teaching, be it in the implicit assumption that the world "out there" does not matter (because what "really" matters is "our country" or "our community") or in claims that what takes place beyond the boundaries of our "container" is similar or less important, fundamentally different or threatening, than what takes place inside it.[2] What is hidden constitutes as much meaning as that which is said. This chapter argues that in order to make sense of the world, especially of today's world, textbooks and curricula must embrace world history. That is easier said than done, and it requires some deliberation about the positioning as well as the methodology of historical thinking and writing.

The Deconstruction of "History" and the Emergence of "Histories"

The historiographical revolution that has changed the writing of history over the last decades (Novick 1988) and which, to a certain degree, has left its mark on school textbooks, reveals diverse and changing needs for orientation in a rapidly changing world. It was the national narrative, which had been unquestioned for the longest time, and which to this day continues to be history by default, that has been seriously challenged by the historiographical revolution of the last decades. The changing needs for historical orientation refer in particular to three realms of historical inquiry: its geographical scope; notions of time; and to historical agency. These categories can, in fact, be applied to the writing of history at all times. What people deem important in the past is closely linked to the present in which they live, shaping assumptions and making people ask certain questions, focus on certain agents, ignore others, and address history in smaller or larger scope. Frequently enough, the assumptions that influence historical inquiry remain unconscious (or are pushed into some kind of "natural" and objectified mode, thus rendering its own historicity invisible) and can only be deciphered in retrospect. National history, the history by default par excellence, is no exception. Neither is world or global history,[3] which has become increasingly popular in recent years in the United States (Allardyce 1982; Schissler 2002; see in particular Michael Geyer, chapter 9 in this volume; on developments in Europe see Middell) and is about to make its way also into European curricula and textbooks. If the scope of inquiry, notions of time (chronology), and agency respond to demands of the present, then historical narratives tell us a lot about issues of the present, which these narratives address.

During times of nation building, the focus on national politics has been at the center of historical inquiry. Agency has been attributed mainly to politicians and political leaders—the "great men make history"—approach. Or states themselves have been promoted to the status of actor: Germany did this or that; England responded by doing such and such. Nations seem to function like people, they even have emotions: Germany felt threatened by England building up its navy. National narratives follow a model of society that, as Charles Bright and Michael Geyer have argued, "tends to take the nation as a presumptive and preexisting unit of containment at the center of the story." Nations for the most part are imagined as "freestanding entities," as "containers" (Bright and Geyer 2002: 64). The "container model" of national history powerfully marks boundaries and gives meaning to issues. For most historians even in the present, it is hard to image that it could be otherwise. However, historians have always gone beyond national history. During times of international conflict and competing national interest, the main motor of change frequently has been ascribed to international relations. This international relations approach, however, has little in common with the transnationality of the current global age, because it continues to be wedded to national histories. Nations as quasi-subjects continue to function as agents in international relations. The national as well as international relations approaches to historical writing responded more to worldviews of the nineteenth century, while in the twentieth century—at least during the second half—these approaches were more and more challenged from standpoints below and beyond national levels. It was in Western Europe and North America that in the last third of the twentieth century, the needs of the present left their imprint on historiography and moved history writing beyond a focus on national history. Historians attempted to gain greater perspective on people's concrete lives and to turn away from national history, focusing on the local, the *Heimat*, and on regional developments. While these changes refer to the geographical scope of historical inquiry, they also reflected newly empowered "agents" in history who might have had an even more lasting effect on our understanding of historical processes. Histories that focus on social classes, women, minorities and ethnic groups have most radically questioned older versions of agency in history and have spoken to previously neglected groups striving to have a political impact on the present.

These more recent approaches to regional history, to social, gender, ethnic, and more broadly speaking cultural history, which coexist with older or more established narratives, mainly took issue with the geographical scope of inquiry and constructed new subject positions in history. Meanwhile, other approaches promoted ideas about the direction of history, thus conveying teleological assumptions about the purpose and the goal of history. Not only the Enlightenment of the eighteenth century, but also modernization theories of the 1960s had more or less fixed ideas of where history was going or should be going. In addition to assumptions on the direction of political, social, and economic development, modernization theories had a clear notion of cause and effect, driven by what seemed an inexhaustible optimism about economic growth and modern abilities to shape society. In its most clearly articulated version, modernization theories of the 1960s assumed that development takes place in more or less clearly defined stages (Rostow 1971). The assumption prevailed that if only "Third World" countries followed certain steps and took certain political or economic measures, they would soon reach the level of Western countries and reach the haven of modernity. Modernization theories thus promoted ideas about the sequence and predictability of social, economic, and political development. Modernization theories also tended to think in terms of nation-states sometimes supplemented by transnational regional approaches. Today, as the "model societies" of the West face more and more difficulties (of economic growth, ecological disaster, political delegitimization, social integration, and cultural rupture), scholars have clearly become much less enthusiastic as well as less optimistic about goals and stages of historical development in general and about the possibility of prescribed steps to achieve sustained development over the globe. Since the publications of the Club of Rome's report on the limits of growth in 1973, an increased awareness of modernity's costs has shattered naive beliefs in the blessings of Western style development. So has the emergence of a quite powerful postcolonial discourse. Modernization theories were popular for some time mainly among sociologists and economists. Historians scorned them, for a mixture of good and not so good reasons. They were for the most part skeptical of the teleological as well as of the theoretical constructs that inspired modernization theory. What made historians in the 1960s even more apprehensive, was that they were for the most part fixated on quite narrow national paradigms, thus rejecting any broader or comparative outlook on historical processes.

While modernization theories in their endless optimism were quite short lived, the deconstruction of the national narrative that focused on social classes, groups, genders, ethnicities, and locales is here to stay. While the challenge that the multiplicity of new histories posed to "History" mainly focused on historical processes and agents "below" the national narrative as the dominant form of historiography since the nineteenth century, this now is about to change. Educators understand that they must address issues of a globalizing world and its complexities, economic exchange on a worldwide level, politics and communication, and transnational migration and its transforming impact on host societies. Except for the United States, where world history in the classroom has gained prominence in recent years (Bentley 1996; Dunn 2000; Geyer, chapter 9 in this volume), usually promoting an approach where one civilization follows another,[4] the frameworks to conceptualize world-wide developments are for the most part random and poorly developed. This is not the place to assess critically the world history course that is being taught at colleges and in high schools in the United States and that has emerged from the Western Civilization course (Allardyce 1982; Segal 2000). However, as Michael Geyer has shown in his chapter, world history has had a lasting impact on historical thinking in the United States at all levels. World history has not only made its way into the classroom, but has also begun seriously to transform American history departments. While an overall trend on transnationalizing history can hardly be overlooked, and is clearly to be seen in textbooks, in Germany unification has triggered debates among scholars on questions of national history, yet again (Conrad 2002). While in Germany a national focus is still counterbalanced by other influences, especially Germany's European outlook, many East European countries after 1989 have developed outright narrowly nationalistic views on their own history. What looks like a leap back into the nineteenth century, however, seems to be a protest against long-endured communist internationalism, and thus, among other things, is a reaction—although not one that anybody would welcome—toward a confusing present. In spite of such re-nationalizing tendencies, overall Europeans are beginning to warm to the idea of history beyond national and European levels. Slowly they understand that they have to broaden their views and encompass a perspective on the world, which transcends national history on the one hand, and a preoccupation with the process of integration and enlargement of the European Union on the other. However, it is only when people understand that their lives are closely connected with an increasingly transnational world that debates on world history will fall on fertile ground.

The Enlightenment Approach toward Universal History

There was a precursor to world history: namely, a notion of universal history that is deeply embedded in the European Enlightenment and that has little to do with world history as it is understood today (Allardyce 1990; Geyer, chapter 9 in this volume). This is so because the European Enlightenment of the eighteenth century promoted the secularization of historical time. Philosophers claimed that it was humans who made history—a history that was no longer determined by "divine providence" (Koselleck 1975: 687). This reasoning fits with an enlightened view of the world, in which the individual was constituted in dramatically different ways. It also reflects the optimism of the time, which conveyed a sense of reason as much as feasibility. Universal history was, like any history, deeply anchored in assumptions about the present. Friedrich von Schiller was well aware of that connection when he gave his inaugural lecture on "Was heißt und zu welchem Ende studiert man Universalgeschichte" at the University of Jena in the year of the French Revolution in 1789: "From the totality of events, the historian, who engages in universal history, focuses on those, which have a clear, easily determined and important influence on today's generation. It is the relationship of a historical fact to today's constitution of the world that needs to be examined in order to collect material for world history."[5]

Schiller was part of the European movement of intellectuals who strove to liberate themselves from what Immanuel Kant had called the self-imposed minority status of humanity. For Schiller, the European focus of his universal history project was as much taken for granted as the notion of progress and agency that resided in the historical process itself. In the wake of the French Revolution, the Eurocentric view of the world—of direction and agency in history, with which modern world history takes issue, did not constitute a problem as it does in today's world. For the European intellectuals of the time it was clear that it was men who were the historical agents—white, educated men, that is. Women, slaves, and ethnic minorities (Jews) did not have citizen status, and thus could not act in (and on) the world, in the full sense of the word, as responsible individuals. The imaginary world of the Enlightenment was not, as is the case today, hopelessly decentered. Center and periphery were clearly defined. So were actors and non-actors. In today's world, the idea that only men make history and shape the world has been challenged as much as the idea that every region of the world has yet to rise to European levels. We are no longer quite as certain that it is Europe (or the United States for that matter) that sets the standards which every country and every region of the world has to attain in all respects. The many drawbacks of a unilinear developmental scenario, briefly revived in modernization theories, have since become abundantly clear.

The Enlightenment concept of universal history was a transnational concept with a broad universalistic program, programmatically shaped by a Eurocentric view of the world. Universal history was never quite forgotten; in fact, it became part of general education around the turn of the nineteenth century in the United States as much as in Germany and other countries (Allardyce 1982). But universal history became less and less attractive as historiography became more professional on the one hand and more national on the other during the nineteenth century, especially during its second half. In fact, the professionalization of historical research and its nationalization went hand in hand (Novick 1988; Allardyce 1990; Koselleck 1975: 690, Middell 2002).

Challenges of Canonized Knowledge

Historiography in general, especially for instruction in schools, and the nation-state have traditionally had an intimate relationship. As we have hinted in the introduction to this book, schooling for the general population and state control of curricula and textbooks in the eighteenth and nineteenth centuries were part of the process of nation building (Assmann 1995), as was the enforcement of the state's monopoly of power. Academic historiography in Germany, as elsewhere, enthusiastically succumbed to the national craving for recognition and put itself willingly into the service of the nation-state—the less secure the nation was or felt, the more this was the case. Because history and geography textbooks and curricula show a special affinity for the state-controlled production of knowledge, it is there that the process of canonization and instrumentalization for state purposes can most clearly be studied up into the present. (Since the Second World War, social studies textbooks have joined history and geography in producing the kind of knowledge that is close to a society's self-understanding.) In fact, from the outset of obligatory schooling in Europe, the production of knowledge in history in particular was closely wedded to the process of nation-building. However, the nation-state's influence on education had consequences that have to be dealt with to this day. It has favored (through its formal control of or informal influence on curricula and textbooks) a view of history that mirrored its (idealized) perception of itself. This pertains particularly to nation-states' formative years, but is by no means restricted to them. As the historian Gianna Pomata wrote:

> The textbook is not a neutral form. It is a form created with a specific pedagogic intent, when history was introduced into the schools. The fundamental message entrusted to the textbook seems that of transmitting a "universal" and synthetic image of history. How is this universal dimension constructed? By means of generalizations that do not explicitly deny, but implicitly omit as irrelevant, certain differences in historical experience, such as the difference between men and women. This is the reason why the chronological format is fundamental in this kind of text. The textbook needs a universal and abstract standpoint from which to organize the historical material. The idea of historical time as neutral time (the time of chronology) allows events to be represented through an "objective" medium, independent from the points of view of the people who experienced them. Thus, the illusion of a "general" and unified vision of history is created. (Pomata 1993: 42)

In other words, the national narrative has promoted a certain level of abstraction, ignoring points of view that were not compatible with it. It has been tied to a particular notion of chronology, and has promoted an objectivist stance of historical inquiry following that "noble dream" (Novick 1988). Ever since history has been taught in schools, creating and transporting synthetic, objectivist images of history, textbooks have conveyed a kind of knowledge that has helped to generate loyalty toward the state and the community. However, the unifying and objectivist character of historical knowledge in schools has not been without drawbacks. Historical approaches that go against the grain and are not easily subsumed under the synthesis of national history have been excluded or marginalized, because they stress the particular, or because they promote subversive knowledge, which sometimes might come down to one and the same thing. The consequence has been that such perspectives and standpoints that do not fit either are ignored in the process of producing canonized historical knowledge or have been pushed aside as irrelevant. Inclusion and exclusion of knowledge, however, are political decisions made by those who construct curricula and control textbook production, and who have an interest in promoting or suppressing certain kinds of knowledge.

Gianna Pomata (1993) has criticized the unifying view of textbooks from a feminist point of view and argued for an inclusion into textbooks and curricula of partial histories below the level of national narrative. Objections to synthesizing or unifying forms of historical knowledge have since the heyday of feminism broadened considerably: issues of gender, class, ethnicity, generation, region, and religion that have inspired historical scholarship have also, if only in rudimentary ways, made it into school textbooks. The national narrative, however, is not easily pushed aside. It continues to be history by default. It is the straightforward iteration of one's own history in national terms that most people continue to view as the most "natural" mode of telling the story. This is true in spite of the thorough deconstruction of the national narrative "from below," from feminist, ethnic, and other viewpoints that have made a decisive mark on the ways in which we think about history, and which no longer can be ignored. Fragmentation of "the" historical narrative has been a concern in recent years—more on the academic level, to be sure. Textbooks and curricula have been lagging in the deconstruction process of master narratives for reasons that have been discussed earlier. In the end, however, decentered views of history, welcomed by some and deplored by others and even the fear of a loss of "History," may also have reached the classroom, and all the more so where the teaching of history in schools and on the lower levels of college came to resemble academic history. However, for the time being it is safe to assume that the much-feared fragmentation has not yet done its "evil deeds" and that canonized knowledge prevails in classrooms.

The fact is that states as the entities that provide education for the masses have an interest in the messages that textbooks convey, and that has not changed in principle from the eighteenth and nineteenth centuries to the present. However, the contents as well as the processes of knowledge production have changed greatly, not only in Western Europe and the United States but also on a worldwide level (Frank et al. 2000, and Julian Dierkes, chapter 4 in this volume). While history "from below" was very successful in deconstructing national narratives, for quite a while now it is transnational narratives that have been and are being discussed. Transnational narratives, however, have as much difficulty asserting themselves against the dominance of national histories as have "partial histories," or history "from below." The trend for the most part is to soften the focus on national history, and, indeed, what might be called "worldization"[6] of national history might be our best bet in the classroom. (By "worldization" I mean the deliberate effort to set national histories in relation to world developments and to focus on such developments that transcend national boundaries). In some Western European countries today national dominance is considerably less rigid than it used to be, for example, during the time of heated national competition leading to the First World War. Transnational organizations such as the European Union surely play a role here (see the case studies in part I of this volume, "Europe Contested"). However, in many countries all over the world the national focus remains pervasive. Especially in Eastern European countries, the nation has been "reinvented" after 1989. National history is being reclaimed and history is being reconstructed to serve national purposes. It would be a mistake, however, to attribute such developments only to Eastern European countries, and especially the Balkans. The role of national history in the United States also does not seem to loosen its grip on the profession and on teaching, and trends to internationalize American history are quite recent (Bender 2000 and Bender 2002; Guarneri 2002; Osborne 2003). National history in the United States always has been contested. Especially during the 1990s, the United States went through major controversies in the

field of curriculum development and teaching, particularly over the National
Standards for American history and for world history (Appleby 1995; Jones
1995; McDougall 1995; Nash 1994/95; Nash et al. 1997; Nolte 1997; Stearns
1994/95).[7] These culture wars, however, did not prevent, and in fact might
have aided, world history in making serious inroads into classrooms everywhere. However, the nationalists do not surrender easily. In 2002, President
Bush signed the Education Bill, which again ordains a strengthening of
national history in schools.[8]

According to the UNESCO guidelines of 1949, to which textbook
researchers have since agreed, it was (and continues to be) the insistence on
the uniqueness of one's own nation at the exclusion of all others that continues to heat up conflict. This is particularly so with countries, which perceive
themselves as ethnically "pure" nations (for example, Germany during the
Second World War; the falling apart of former Yugoslavia mostly along ethnic
lines; and any number of other cases all around the world). Because national
narration has all too easily descended into national stereotypes, feeding
hostilities that have led to war and genocide, a focus on a narrowly conceived
national history is highly problematic. While relativizing national and ethnic
particularities in textbooks and curricula might not prevent conflict, it might
contribute in modest ways to a more peaceful coexistence between people
(Jeismann 1979; Pingel 1999; Schissler 1991).

Ways of Understanding History in the Age of Globalization

History has provided striking arguments to broaden contexts and to develop
models for a better understanding of the world at large, beyond the all too
lightly referred to "globalization." While world historical events frequently
reveal their significance only in retrospect, sometimes our awareness that the
world and our place in it has changed is instantaneous. Examples are the
coming down of the Berlin wall and the rapid disintegration of the Soviet
Union after 1989 with the subsequent end of the bipolar world as well as the
terrorist attacks of 11 September 2001. Such events had immediate effects on
the ways in which we perceive the world. These events and following developments have made the world in which we live much more complex and less
predictable. Increasingly, people are becoming painfully aware that they can
no longer do without a thorough understanding of the world beyond their
own locales or nations, and of global connections and other cultures. A world
history that makes sense to students and responds to new needs for orientation in the present would be an appropriate response to the demands of an
interconnected and globalizing world.

Globalization, however, is an ambiguous as much as a seductive term. It
covers everything and nothing. When I speak of globalization, I certainly do

not mean what Peter Stearns has called "the loud approval of the forces of contemporary capitalism and American foreign policy" (Stearns 2003: 153). That is an aspect of globalization against which more and more people try to mobilize annually when the world's political and economic leaders meet in posh Swiss resorts. Globalization in this sense is also the target of scathing analysis by postcolonial writers (Chakrabarty 2000; Guha 2002). "There is understandable resistance to the notion of globalization, especially in its more exuberant iterations, on the suspicion that it is but the latest formulation of a continuing 'Westernization' or 'Americanization' of the world" write Charles Bright and Michael Geyer (2002: 65). Globalization might yet be the latest concept to justify domination. Instead of such colonizing usage, the term should be used analytically and historically, much as Geyer and Bright (1995) have proposed in their important article "World History in a Global Age." Globalization has its forerunners in historical processes of the past. It is not a recent phenomenon that pertains exclusively to the present. The world has been globalizing for centuries, particularly in the shaping of the "world system" during the fifteenth and sixteenth centuries (Wallerstein 1974–1989), the discovery of new continents, the setting up of international trade relations, and most particularly during the imperialist and colonial periods of the nineteenth century. However, there are unquestionable developments that pertain only to the present and have accelerated globalization in unforeseen ways. Resulting from that dramatically increased speed is a change in the notion of historical time on the one hand and a process of "decentering" of individual life trajectories on the other. To understand the current situation requires a lot more than relativizing nations and international relations. Transnational connections encompass more than international relations, because international relations continue to rely on nations as quasi-subjects. To broaden one's historical horizon, to shift interest away from the "container model" of the nation, and to focus instead on transnationality requires any number of empirical as well as theoretical operations. World history conveys an idea of connectedness and exchange between people on local and global levels. Karen Wigen, in her contribution to this volume (see chapter 10) distinguishes four ways of doing global history: tracking specific flows, analyzing responses to flows, taking a slice of time, and narrating successive modalities of globalization. Michael Geyer (see chapter 9) has developed elaborate ways to narrate "globality" and to bring world history into the classroom. While world history responds to real changes in historical time and transcends national narratives, it clearly does not render the nation-state irrelevant, as Benedict Anderson has pointed out (Anderson 1991). In fact, nation-states historically were a response to ongoing processes of globalization in an attempt to gain some control over these processes (Bright and Geyer 2002: 66; Middell et al. 2003). Empirically, the nation-state is, to use a Hegelian term, *aufgehoben* [included and transcended] in the process of globalization, and conceptually it must have its place in world history. In this sense world history is yet another deconstructionist endeavor, because it relativizes and contextualizes national narratives and strips them of their exaggerated claims to make sense of history.

Even if new attempts at teaching world history and of writing world history textbooks are not entirely successful because, as Daniel A. Segal has pointed out, world history textbooks follow Western civilization textbooks with an evolutionist model of cultures (Segal 2000), in principle world history takes issue with Eurocentric views of the past. In Dipesh Chakrabarty's term it tries to "provincialize Europe" (Chakrabarty 2000; Wasserstrom 2001). In its programmatic statements, world history radically questions claims of the universality and validity of Western thought. As it has developed in the United States, world history implicitly (and sometimes explicitly) responds to a new understanding of what the United States is all about. While Western Civilization spoke to the European roots of the United States, world history acknowledges the multi-ethnic composition of the American population. As the legitimacy of "white (male) America" and the hegemony of its history has been under fierce attack since the days of the civil rights and the women's movements scholars have been uncovering non-European roots of the United States. It is cultural diversity and the acknowledgement of difference that sets world history apart from the unifying tale of enlightened universal history (Allardyce 1982). Before it becomes an organizing narrative, world history has to go through the deconstructionist endeavors of historical writings of the last decades. At least on a programmatic level, this has occasionally been achieved, and reads as follows in a much-used textbook in the United States:

> The reasons [to teach world history] are immediately evident. First, the composition of the American population perpetually changes, adding to our need for international understanding. The European heritage, though still vital, now logically shares attention with our sources in Africa, various parts of Asia, and Latin America. Second, American involvement in world affairs continues to grow. Long a Pacific, Caribbean, and Atlantic power, the United States nevertheless has tended to define its primary interests in terms of Europe. In the second half of the 20th century, after participation in three wars in Asia, plus massive economic and cultural interaction around the globe, the United States and its citizens have embraced a global perspective. This perspective involves emphasis on international currents and on a full range of civilizations. [...] We also share a firm commitment to include social history that involves women, the nonelite, and experiences and events outside the spheres of politics and high culture. (Stearns et al. 1992: XIII)

The argument, then, is for a world history that has immersed itself in the deconstructionist endeavors of the last decades and resists the "parade of civilizations" approach (Linveldt 2001), which clearly can not satisfy any need for orientation and does nothing but overwhelm students and teachers alike.

Although globalization itself is not a historically new phenomenon, much is indeed historically new. This newness discredits the nation as the (main) producer of meaning as much as it defies a sense of security that previous containment might have produced. It provides arguments for globalizing history in the classroom. But what is new? According to Castells (1998:336) among others, the following are historically new: computers, the internet, the resulting revolution in communication technology and subsequent changes in communication patterns; social movements that have challenged the place of men and women and their relations with each other; changes in the profile of the labor force that have to do with new communication technology on the one hand and on the other with a dramatic change in the work force away from the model of the male breadwinner toward a considerable increase in women and minorities in the work force; as a consequence, changed relations between generations; a cultural revolution, which has not only relativized hierarchies that had for a long time been taken for granted, but also has promoted new ways of acquiring knowledge; dramatically altered educational requirements; transnational migration on a world wide level; the concentration of the majority of the world's population in metropolitan areas; international trade relations and global economic entanglements that leave no region of the world unaffected; global financial markets and an unrestrained capitalism world wide; and new forms of global and other forms of regional inequality, for which we have yet to develop concepts. The impact of these globalizing forces of the present on people's lives is enormous and has hardly yet been fully understood.

In the dramatically changing scenario of the present, people have been put into a position in which they must constantly learn new things. What was solid knowledge thirty years before, seems to be devalued today. Children and young people live in a world that is dramatically different from their parents'. Work lives have changed, and paid work has become a rare commodity (Sennett 1998). Family lives have changed not only through disruptive historical events like wars, but also through a worldwide attack on patriarchal structures. This has altered the ways in which women and men (and children as well) live, and has caused many individuals to fall out of family networks altogether. What in the second half of the twentieth century was thought to be secure, like economic status or prospects for the future and for old age, in many countries is either about to evaporate before peoples' eyes or at least to become highly insecure. This is true for the welfare states of the Western Hemisphere that have been going or are currently going through major cutbacks. It is even more true, although for quite different reasons, for people who emerged after 1989 from the influence of the Soviet Union. These people used to know what to expect from the future in state socialist societies, but now have been thrown into a state of uncertainty and, frequently enough, dire poverty.

People nowadays move at a much faster pace through time and space than they used to. Peoples' sense of orientation (and their need for it) all too often cannot keep up with new demands. Ruptures are ubiquitous, most pronounced in the lives of people who went through regime changes, or who are the victims of ethnic cleansing (or even genocide) and the disintegration of political, economic, and social structures all over the world (Castells 1998: chapter 2). In the countries that have emerged from the former Soviet Union, ways of doing things, of coping with life, of learning and processing information, of making sense of the world, have been dramatically devalued within only a few months. However, also in Western countries during the last thirty years or so, life trajectories have abruptly taken new turns everywhere. While these changes have opened new possibilities for many, they also have left any number of people behind. These are people who are not in a position to take advantage of the new possibilities, who are either too poor, or too old, or not educated enough, or who live in regions of the world that for some reason or other are at the periphery of the nodes of modernity. The process of a globalizing world, according to Bright and Geyer, on the one hand deepens integration and on the other proliferates difference. New forms of inequality are promoted: "Far from fostering a homogenization of the world, globalization has made the production of difference and inequality a much more proximate and intimate affair" (Bright and Geyer 2002: 68–9). Manuel Castells has aptly described the processes that privilege some and throw others into utter poverty, dependency, and ignorance as "fourth worldization" (1998: chapter 2). In this process, centers and peripheries at the community and global levels relentlessly attribute or withhold life chances for people. (Castells 1998, chapter 2). In the end there is "one world" indeed, but not a world where everybody has adjusted to the same (Western) standards of modernity. "The peoples of the world are pulled into processes of global interaction and emerge resegmented and transformed in their diversity." The result then is a world of "multiple modernities" (Bright and Geyer 2002: 68).

Ambiguity is the marker of globalization. While interconnectedness, an accelerated pace of life, broadened horizons, and the possibility of cosmopolitanism for the select few is one side of the story of the multiple modernities in which we live (or of postmodernity for that matter),[9] the other side is more ambiguous, if not outright sinister. The "postmodern condition," a condition in which "the center no longer holds," as Zygmunt Bauman has put it, forces people continuously to construct new identities, to adjust to a kind of "liquid modernity" (Bauman 1997; Bauman 2000; Giddens 1991; Giddens 1994). As much as the fluidity of meaning and the search for new identities is liberating for many that were suppressed by tradition, by religion, or by rigid gender constructions, the postmodern condition is not easy to endure. If the center no longer holds, freedom for some means disorientation and even disintegration for others. The same person might even experience freedom and disorientation simultaneously. Those who cannot easily embrace new freedoms might then look for crutches that give them some resemblance of stability. This situation can be a breeding ground for fundamentalisms of all kind, where people dig in their heels to protect them against the overcomplexity of the world.

The current situation requires the rethinking of education on many levels. With increased speed in the field of personal, economic, social, political, and global developments, the need for orientation and for new kinds of knowledge is on the increase and can no longer be ignored. Constantly changing demands on education dramatically altered ways of knowledge acquisition, and the ambiguity of modern life itself seriously overburdens educators. Education is all too often blamed for the insufficiency of young peoples' abilities and is held accountable for a kind of disorientation. However, the "crisis in education" is only the sign, not the culprit. Admittedly, the old ways will no longer do. If the old ways of making sense of the world, and especially if national history as a "container model" will no longer suffice because the world itself has changed dramatically, we must think about more appropriate, or simply more helpful, ways of learning about this changing world and our place in it. Education is at the forefront of a battle in which people attempt to prepare for the new challenges of multiple modernities and for an integrated world of unequal access. World history is an attempt at universities and schools to prepare students to cope with the demands of the present. World history might help teachers and students to understand that "the world" is not "out there" somewhere, but that it saturates our lives and that we are part of it; it might help to endure the ambiguities of this modern world, and it might aid in resisting the temptation to turn to fundamentalism. In addressing the present world in its historicity, world history might help teachers and students to gain a better orientation in this modern world, and perhaps to ease somewhat the inequalities that permeate a world in which knowledge has become a crucial means of participation. However, any attempt to cover world history in its entirety (usually conceived as from "prehistory" to the present), is a monstrous endeavor. This becomes abundantly clear when one looks at American world history textbooks, which frequently have more than one thousand pages, tables of contents that stretch over more than ten pages, and weigh 2.5 kilograms. A national mindset no longer serves us well. As we expect historians to be gender sensitive these days,[10] and to pay attention to difference, we now also expect that historians will broaden their views and find ways to teach their students in a manner that will enable them to move around this world and not get lost.

Notes

1. [Jede Geschichte muss Weltgeschichte sein, und nur in Beziehung auf die ganze Geschichte ist die historische Behandlung eines einzelnen Stoffes möglich.] Novalis, quoted in Koselleck (1975: 690).
2. On the notion of a "container" model of national history, see below in this chapter.
3. In this chapter, I do not distinguish between world history and global history, since that distinction would be irrelevant for this text. However, when I speak of universal history, I mean the Enlightenment concept. For further differentiation, see Koselleck (1975), who develops the meaning of the change in terminology in detail.
4. For a critique of the evolutionary model that informs the civilization approach, see Segal (2000).
5. The German reads: "Aus der ganzen Summe der Begebenheiten hebt der Universalhistoriker diejenigen heraus, welche auf die *heutige* Gestalt der Welt und den Zustand der *jetzt lebenden* Generation einen wesentlichen, unwidersprechlichen und leicht zu verfolgenden Einfluss gehabt haben. Das Verhältnis eines historischen Datums zur heutigen Weltverfassung ist es also, worauf gesehen werden muss, um Material für die *Weltgeschichte* zu sammeln" (Schiller 1970: 359).
6. This expression is owed to Carol Gluck, who teaches Japanese history at Columbia University.
7. See also the internet discussion in the *Chronicle of Higher Education* from the year 1998: "Are the Culture Wars Over? If so, Who Won?" with contributions from Todd Gitlin. "A Truce Prevails: For the Left, Many Victories are Pyrrhic"; Annette Kolodny. "If Harsh Realities Prevail, We All Will Continue to Loose"; Lawrence W. Levine. "Struggles are a Small Price to Pay for Diverse Universities"; Gertrud Himmelfarb. "The Vision of the University is Still at Stake"; Nell Irvin Painter. "Battles are Far From Over in Culture's Private Clubs"; Evelyn Hu-DeHart. "The Spotlight is Shifting to Students of Color"; Ray Suarez. "Too Many in Academe Stayed Grandly Above the Fray."
8. Notice in *Perspectives,* vol. 40, 2002, no. 2: 16.
9. This is not the place to discuss at length theories of postmodern society. I rely on the frameworks that have been developed by Zygmunt Bauman, Manuel Castells, Ulrich Beck, Anthony Giddens, and David Harvey.
10. For examples of how to combine gender and world history see Connell (1993), and Strasser/Tinsman (forthcoming).

References

Allardyce, Gilbert. 1982. "The Rise and Fall of the Western Civilization Course." *American Historical Review,* vol. 87, 695–725.

——— 1990. "Toward World History: American Historians and the Coming of the World History Course." *Journal of World History*, vol. 1, no. 1, 23–76.

Anderson, Benedict. 1991. *Imagined Communities.* London: Verso.

Appleby, Joyce. 1995. "Controversy of the National History Standards." *Organization of American Historians Magazine of History,* vol. 9, no. 3.

Assmann, Alaida. 1995. *Arbeit am nationalen Gedächtnis. Eine kurze Geschichte der deutschen Bildungsidee.* Frankfurt: Campus.

Bauman, Zygmunt. 1995. *Life in Fragments. Essays in Postmodern Morality.* Oxford: Blackwell.

———— 1997. *Postmodernity and its Discontents.* New York: New York University Press.

———— 2000. *Liquid Modernity.* Cambridge: Polity Press.

Bender, Thomas. 2000. *The La Pietra Report: A Report to the Profession.* Bloomington: Organization of American Historians.

———— ed. 2002. *Rethinking American History in a Global Age.* Berkeley: University of California Press.

Bentley, Jerry H. 1996. *Shapes of World History in Twentieth-Century Scholarship.* Washington: The American Historical Association.

Bright, Charles and Michael Geyer. 2002. "Where in the World is America? The History of the United States in the Global Age." In *Rethinking American History in a Global Age*, ed. Thomas Bender. Berkeley: University of California Press, 63–99.

Castells, Manuel. 1997. *The Information Age: Economy, Society and Culture, vol. II. The Power of Identity.* New York: Blackwell.

———— 1998. *The Information Age: Economy, Society and Culture, vol. III. End of Millenium.* New York: Blackwell.

Chakrabarty, Dipesh. 2000. *Provincializing Europe. Postcolonial Thought and Historical Difference.* Princeton: Princeton University Press.

Club of Rome (Dennis Meadows, Donella Meadows, Erich Zahn, and Peter Milling). 1973. *Die Grenzen des Wachstums. Bericht des Club of Rome zur Lage der Menschheit.* Hamburg: Rowohlt.

Connell, R.W. 1993. "The Big Picture: Masculinities in Recent World History." *Theory and Society,* vol. 22, 597–623.

Conrad, Sebastian. 2002. "Doppelte Marginalisierung. Plädoyer für eine transnationale Perspektive auf die deutsche Geschichte." *Geschichte und Gesellschaft,* vol. 28, 145–69.

Dunn, Ross E. 2000. "Constructing World History in the Classroom." In *Knowing, Teaching and Learning History. National and International Perspectives,* ed. Peter Stearns, Peter Seixas, and Sam Wineburg. New York: New York University Press, 121–42.

Eckart, Andreas. 2002. "Gefangen in der Alten Welt. Die deutsche Geschichtswissenschaft ist hoffnungslos provinziell: Themen jenseits der europäischen Grenzen interessieren die Historiker kaum. Eine Polemik." *Die Zeit,* no. 40, (26 September), 40.

Erdmann, Elisabeth. 1998. "Was verstehen wir unter 'Weltgeschichte'?" *International Society for History Didactics: Information, Mitteilungen, Communications,* vol. 19, no. 1, 14–26.

Frank, David John, Suk-Ying Wong, John W. Meyer and Francisco O. Ramirez. 2000. "What Counts as History: A Cross-National and Longitudinal Study of University Curricula." *Comparative Education Review,* vol. 44. no. 1, 29–53.

Geyer, Michael and Charles Bright. 1995. "World History in a Global Age." *American Historical Review,* vol. 100, 1034–60.

Giddens, Anthony. 1990. *The Consequences of Modernity.* Stanford: Stanford University Press.

———— 1991. *Modernity and Self-Identity. Self and Society in the Late Modern Age.* Stanford: Stanford University Press.

———— 1994. "Living in a Post-Traditional Society." In *Reflexive Modernization. Politics, Tradition and Aesthetics in the Modern Social Order,* eds. Ulrich Beck, Anthony Giddens, and Scott Lash. Stanford: Stanford University Press, 56–109.

Guarneri, Carl J. 2002. "Internationalizing the United States Survey Course: American History for a Global Age." *The History Teacher,* vol. 35, no. 1, 37–64.

Guha, Ranajit. 2002. *History at the Limit of World-History.* New York: University of Columbia Press.

Harvey, David. 1990. *The Condition of Postmodernity. An Enquiry into the Origins of Cultural Change.* Oxford: Blackwell.

Jeismann, Karl Ernst. 1979. "Internationale Schulbuchforschung. Aufgaben und Probleme." *Internationale Schulbuchforschung,* vol. 1, no. 1, 7–22.

Jones, Arnita A. 1995. "Our Stakes in the History Standards." *Organization of American Historians Magazine of History,* vol. 9, no. 3.

Koselleck, Reinhart. 1975. "Geschichte." section: "Von der 'historia universalis' zur 'Weltgeschichte'" 686–91 in *Begriffsgeschichtliches Lexikon,* eds. Otto Brunner et al., Stuttgart: Klett.

Lindtvedt, Ane. 2001. "Pluses and Minuses of a Secondary School World History Text." *The History Teacher,* vol. 34, no. 3, 383–7.

McDougall, Walter A. 1995. "Whose History? Whose Standards?" *Commentary,* vol. 99 (May), 36–43.

Middell, Matthias. 2002. "Europäische Geschichte oder *global history—master narratives* oder Fragmentierung?" in *Die historische Meistererzählung. Deutungslinien der deutschen Nationalgeschichte nach 1945,* eds. Konrad H. Jarausch and Martin Sabrow. Göttingen: Vandenhoeck & Ruprecht, 214–52.

Middell, Matthias, Susanne Popp and Hanna Schissler. 2003. "Weltgeschichte im deutschen Geschichtsunterricht. Argumente und Thesen." *International Textbook Research,* vol. 25, 149–54.

Nash, Gary B. 1994/95. "The History Standards Controversy and Social History." *Journal of Social History,* vol. 29, 39–49.

Nash, Gary B., Charlotte Crabtree, and Roß E. Dunn. 1997. *History on Trial. Culture Wars and the Teaching of the Past.* New York: Knopf.

Nolte, Paul. 1997. "Ein Kulturkampf um den Geschichtsunterricht. Die Debatte um die National Standards in den USA." *Geschichte und Gesellschaft,* vol. 48, 512–32.

Novick, Peter. 1988. *That Noble Dream. The "Objectivity Question" and the American Historical Profession.* Cambridge: Cambridge University Press.

Osborne, Thomas J. 2003. "Implementing the *La Pietra Report*: Internationalizing Three Topics in the United States History Survey Course." *The History Teacher,* vol. 36, no. 2, 163–75.

Pingel, Falk. 1999. *UNESCO Guidebook on Textbook Research and Textbook Revision.* Hannover: Hahn.

Pomata, Gianna. 1993. "History, Particular and Universal: On Reading Some Recent Women's History Textbooks." *Feminist Studies,* vol. 19, 7–50.

Rostow, Walt W. 1971. *Politics and the Stages of Growth.* Cambridge: Cambridge University Press.

Schiller, Friedrich von. 1970. Nationalausgabe, vol. 17. Weimar: Böhlau.

Schissler, Hanna. 1991. "Der Beitrag der internationalen Schulbuchforschung zur Friedensforschung." In *Friedensforschung—Eine Handlungsorientierung zwischen Politik und Wissenschaft,* ed. Ulrike C. Wasmuht. Darmstadt: Wissenschaftliche Buchgesellschaft, 179–91.

———— 2003. "Weltgeschichte als Zeitgeschichte. Orientierungsbedürfnisse der Gegenwart am Beispiel der USA und Deutschlands." In: *Curriculum Weltgeschichte. Globale Zugänge für den Geschichtsunterricht,* eds. Susanne Popp and Johanna Förster. Schwalbach: Wochenschau, 173–95.

Schmidt, Marianne. 1991. "Was kommt nach Europa? Überlegungen zur Didaktik einer neuen Weltgeschichte." In: *Geschichtsunterricht im vereinten Deutschland. Auf der Suche nach Neuorientierung,* part 2, ed. Hans Süssmuth. Baden-Baden: Nomos, 121–31.

Segal, Daniel A. 2000. "'Western Civ' and the Staging of History in American Higher Education," *American Historical Review*, vol. 105, 770–803.

Sennett, Richard. 1998. *The Corrosion of Character. The Personal Consequences of Work in the New Capitalism*. New York: Norton.

Stearns, Peter, Michael Adas, and Stuart B. Schwartz. 1992. *World Civilizations. The Global Experience*. New York: Harper Collins.

Stearns, Peter, Michael Adas, and Stuart B. Schwartz. 1994/95. "The World History Standards." *The History Teacher*, vol. 28: 441–46.

Stearns, Peter, Michael Adas, and Stuart B. Schwartz. 2003. "Treating Globalization in History Survey." *The History Teacher*, vol. 36, no. 2, 153–60.

Strasser, Ulrike, and Heidi Tinsman. 2003. "Engendering World History." *Radical History Review*, forthcoming no. 91, Winter 2005.

Wallerstein, Immanuel. 1974–1989. *The Modern World System*. 2 vols. New York: Academic Press.

Wasserstrom, Jeffrey. 2001. "Eurocentrism and its Discontent." *Perspectives* (January).

Notes on Contributors

❖

Vasilia L. Antoniou completed her Ph.D. in Sociology, "Does history matter? Temporal and spatial projections of the nation and identity in post-1974 Greek elementary school history textbooks" at the European University Institute, Florence, Italy. She was a research officer in the project "Rethinking Nation-State Identities in the New Europe" at the University of Essex (1999–2002), funded by the British Economic and Social Research Council. She has taught undergraduate and postgraduate classes in the Department of Sociology at the University of Essex. She has written and presented a number of papers on history education and national identity and has contributed to several edited publications. Her research interests are in the fields of history education, identity, citizenship, and social integration in post-war Europe.

Teresa Bertilotti is a researcher at the European University Institute in Florence, where she is working on her thesis "female education in Italy from national unification until 1923." She is also a research assistant at the Chair of History of Education at LUMSSA University in Rome. She was a research officer in the project "Rethinking Nation-State Identities in the New Europe" at the University of Essex (2000–2002), funded by the British Economic and Social Research Council. She has been awarded a number of scholarships from the École Française de Rome and École des Hautes Etudes en Sciences Sociales (Paris). She has published several articles on the institution of the Italian school system and on female education in nineteenth- and twentieth-century Italy.

Julian Dierkes is Assistant Professor and the Keidanren Chair in Japanese Research at the Institute of Asian Research, and a faculty associate at the Institute for European Studies at the University of British Columbia. He received his degree from Princeton University and is currently revising his dissertation, "Teaching Portrayals of the Nation—Postwar History Education in Japan and the Germanys," for publication. Apart from his interests in the comparative political sociology of educational policy, he is continuing work examining changes in the organizational structure of large U.S. corporations, and beginning a new project on the shadow education system in Japan. Before coming to UBC he held a fellowship at the East Asia Institute of the University of Cambridge. He has been awarded several grants for his dissertation research.

Michael Geyer is Samuel N. Harper Professor of History at the University of Chicago. He specializes in German and European History, but has been teaching world history/history of globalization since 1979, together with Charles Bright (Residential College, University of Michigan). Among the most recent essays on world history is their "Where in the World is America? The History of the United States in the Global Age," in Thomas Bender, ed. 2002. *Rethinking American History in a Global Age.* Berkeley, University of California Press. 63–99. He is currently working with Charles Bright on a history of globalization in the twentieth century.

Jacques E.C. Hymans is Assistant Professor in the Department of Government at Smith College. His research explores the nature of national identity conceptions and their consequences for foreign policy. His work has appeared in such journals as the *European Journal of International Relations*; *Security Studies*; *The Nonproliferation Review*; and *French Politics and Society.* Hymans received his Ph.D. from the Harvard University Department of Government in 2001. He has held residential fellowships at Ohio State, Stanford, and the École Normale Supérieure in Paris.

Antonio Luzón is Lecturer of Comparative Education at the University of Granada, Spain. As a member of the Research Group "Educational Policies and Reforms" of the Junta de Andalucía, he has gained extensive experience as a social sciences teacher. His publications deal with adult education and comparative education.

Sabine Mannitz is Senior Research Fellow at the Peace Research Institute in Frankfurt on Main and currently works on socialization processes in the armed forces of democratic states. She studied ethnology and political science at the Universities of Hamburg and of Frankfurt on Main and specialized in urban anthropology, migration, and social learning and the construction of collective identities. As a researcher at the European University Viadrina of Frankfurt on the Oder, from 1996 to 1999, she engaged in the international research project "State, School, and Ethnicity," a comparative study on the civil enculturation of children from immigrant families in four European countries published by Berghahn Books in 2004, *Civil Enculturation: Nation-State, Schools, and Ethnic Difference in Four European Countries*, eds. Werner Schiffauer, Gerd Baumann, Riva Kastoryano and Steven Vertovec. She was research officer in the project "Rethinking Nation-State Identities in the New Europe" at the University of Essex (2000–2002), funded by the British Economic and Social Research Council. She has authored several articles on discourses and practices revolving around cultural diversity in Germany.

Robert Maier is Senior Research Fellow at the Georg Eckert Institute for International Textbook Research in Braunschweig. He received his degree from Marburg University. His expertise and special interests lie in the history of Stalinism, the history of the Soviet Union, and the Soviet women's movement. He is working on projects with Russia, Poland, the Czech Republic, and CIS (Commonwealth of Independent States). He has published widely on the history of the Soviet Union and on Poland. Among his publications are: *Die Stachanov-Bewegung 1935–1938. Der Stachanovismus als tragendes und verschärfendes Moment der Stalinisierung der sowjetischen Gesellschaft* (Stuttgart: Steiner, 1990); *Stalinismus. Die zwanziger Jahre* (Wiesbaden: Hessische Landeszentrale für politische Bildung, 1990); *Deutschland und Polen im zwanzigsten Jahrhundert. Analysen - Quellen - didaktische Hinweise*, edited with Ursula A.J. Becher and Włodzimierz Borodziej (Hannover: Hahn, 2001).

Rainer Ohliger is Research Associate at Humboldt University, Berlin. He is cofounder and board member of the *Network Migration in Europe e.V.,* a European association that deals with issues of migration, history, and political education. His main field of research is the history of migration, the public representation of migrants and minorities, and interethnic relations in Central and Eastern Europe. Among his publications are *Diasporas and Ethnic Migrants: Germany, Israel and Post-Soviet Space in Comparative Perspectives*, coedited with Rainer Münz (Oxford: Frank Cass, 2003), and *European Encounters, 1945–2000: Migrants, Migration and European Societies since 1945*, coedited with Karen Schönwälder and Triadafilos Triadafilopoulos (Aldershot: Ashgate, 2003). He has published numerous articles on questions of national identity, citizenship, and migration in Europe.

Miguel A. Pereyra is Professor of Theory and History of Education at the University of Granada, Spain. During the past decade he has been instrumental in the introduction of the debate about the reform of teaching history in Spain. He published the edited volume *La Historia en el aula* (Universidad de La Laguna, 1981). His research interests are in comparative education, curriculum history, and educational policy reforms. Among his publications is the edited volume (together with Thomas S. Popkewitz and Barry M. Franklin), *Cultural History and Education. Critical Essays on Knowledge and Schooling* (New York: Routledge, 2001).

Tim Pilbrow is Assistant Research Professor in the Department of Anthropology at The George Washington University (Washington, DC). He received his Ph.D. (2001) and M.A. (1993) in Socio-cultural Anthropology from New York University, and his B.A. (1987) in Slavic Languages and Social Anthropology from Monash University, Australia. His doctoral dissertation research was on changing conceptualizations of national identity in post-1989 Bulgaria, as seen from the vantage point of the secondary school history classroom. His book *The Historical Self: Nation and Identity in Contemporary Bulgaria* is forthcoming. His research interests include: social and cultural reproduction; formal education and the reproduction of social identity; history as a means to objectifying identity; and irony as a discursive and narrative strategy. He has taught at New York University, York College (City University of New York), Lafayette College (Pennsylvania), Central College (Iowa), and Georgetown University.

Hanna Schissler is Senior Research Fellow at the Georg Eckert Institute for International Textbook Research in Braunschweig and teaches history at the University of Hannover and at Central European University in Budapest. Among her publications are *The Miracle Years: West German Society from 1949 to 1968. A Cultural History* (Princeton University Press, 2001); *National Identity and Perceptions of the Past. International Textbook Research in Britain, the United States, and West Germany* (Berg, 1987), and a number of other books and numerous articles. Her research interests are textbook and curricular development, especially on questions of migration and world history. She has an on-going interest in questions of cultural history, in issues of gender and in German–American relations.

Yasemin Nuhoğlu Soysal teaches sociology at the University of Essex. She has researched and written extensively on the historical development and contemporary reconfigurations of the nation-state and citizenship in Europe, on cultural and political implications of international migrations, and on international discourses and regimes of human rights. She is the author of *Limits of Citizenship: Migrants and Postnational Membership in Europe* (University of Chicago Press, 1994), and has published in numerous journals including *American Sociological Review; Theory and Society; Sociology of Education; European Societies; and Ethnic and Racial Studies*. Her current research project "Rethinking Nation-State Identities in the New Europe: The Reconfigurations of Secondary School History and Civics Curricula and Textbooks" is funded by the Economic and Social Research Council (with additional funds from Leverhulme Trust and the British Academy). She is the past president of the European Sociological Association.

Kären Wigen is Associate Professor of History at Stanford University. A specialist on early modern Japan, she investigated the geography of early industrialization in her book, *The Making of a Japanese Periphery, 1750–1920* (University of California Press, 1995). With Martin Lewis, she co-directed the "Oceans Connect" project at Duke University, a Ford Foundation-funded initiative to reconceive area studies, and coauthored *The Myth of Continents: A Critique of Metageography* (California, 1997). Her current research focuses on the history of mountaineering and alpine landscape appreciation in the Japanese archipelago.

Index